BUILDINGS & LANDSCAPES

JOURNAL OF THE VERNACULAR ARCHITECTURE FORUM

VOLUME 23 | NUMBER 1 | SPRING 2016

BUILDINGS & LANDSCAPES

JOURNAL OF THE VERNACULAR ARCHITECTURE FORUM
VOLUME 23 | NUMBER 1 | SPRING 2016

A Reminder to Readers: Please remember to have a look at the digital supplement to *B&L,* which is hosted by JSTOR. A print and digital subscription to *B&L* is a courtesy of membership in the Vernacular Architecture Forum. If you've lost track of your user name or password, select "Forgot Your User Name or Password" on the JSTOR.com login screen and enter your e-mail address.

GRETCHEN TOWNSEND BUGGELN

Viewpoint: Teaching Buildings and Landscapes to Today's Undergraduates

Beyond the Classroom

Architectural historians, preservationists, and cultural resource managers accomplish great work every day for the sake of our built environment and communities. But let's face it: these are tough times. Out on the front lines of preservation and advocacy, practitioners struggle to do their important work with shrinking resources. Within the academy, scholars and teachers of architectural history face both economic and ideological challenges. Particularly in the sphere of undergraduate education, the humanities as a whole are waging a battle against the trending, widespread idea that higher education, now an unprecedented expense, should be almost exclusively for job preparation. The current intense focus on the STEM disciplines (Science, Technology, Engineering, and Mathematics) crowds out other academic pursuits. Called to accountability, administrators attend to cost–benefit analyses and measurable student learning objectives. Students, understandably concerned about a difficult job market, shrewdly pursue marketable skills as opposed to broad, humanistic—less quantifiable—aspects of their education. Enrollments in humanities courses, even at elite liberal arts colleges, have fallen noticeably.[1]

Our field of architecture and landscape history and preservation depends on good teaching to a broad audience. Not only do teachers train future professionals, but in an equally essential way, they introduce the next generation of citizens to the importance of the built environment. Teaching nonspecialist undergraduate students to look beyond their computer screens at buildings, landscapes, and objects with educated at-

tention is a special opportunity and a vital aspect of our calling as architectural historians.[2] Our students will become the audience for the future work of historians and preservationists; here is an opportunity to open their eyes and lead them to care about the built environment. Might the current criticism of higher education, especially at the undergraduate level, productively challenge us to be more creative and effective teachers of our subject? How can we take our subject's natural assets and teach in ways that engage even tentative and skeptical students while addressing the legitimate concerns of administrators and the wider culture? What, after all, are we hoping to accomplish with and for our students? We need not only to defend the importance of our particular corner of the humanities but also to think about *what* we teach undergraduates, *how* we teach it, and *for what end.*

My engagement with these questions began in earnest about a decade ago. In 2004 I left a position training graduate students in material culture and museum studies for a job at a small midwestern university. My new post required me to teach general interdisciplinary humanities to undergraduates in a comprehensive program grounded in the close reading of texts. When teaching graduate students, I had taken for granted that they were interested in material culture studies, perhaps even architectural history. My new students, however, were aspiring engineers, nurses, and teachers who took humanities courses because they enjoyed asking the "big" questions and, frankly, because they had general education requirements to fulfill. This was new territory for me. I began speaking to audiences I could not assume placed any value on the research and writing I so enjoy. The burden has since been on me to find ways to bring questions of the built environment into this setting.

One of the things I quickly learned was that these students needed conceptual ideas as much as—perhaps even more than—the delivery of information. They are inundated with information in their coursework and via the digital media they avidly consume. They come to the humanities classroom looking for a break from a certain type of data-centered instruction but also seeking frameworks for processing experience. They want to exercise their minds in different ways. My department's intensive type of seminar teaching requires careful listening. As a consequence, I have come to understand my students better—what they value, what motivates them, and what questions compel their attention. Here and there, I sneak in objects and spaces to remind students that the material conditions of life matter. My chance to remain a bona fide architectural historian in the classroom, however, has been in occasional upper-division seminars I offer in my field. With these courses, I have tried to bring a meaningful engagement with the material world into our text-heavy curriculum.

I would like to relate my experience with four iterations of a seminar I call the American Home and what it has taught me about the broad value of architectural history in the undergraduate curriculum. My schooling in how to take my knowledge of sash windows and Chinese export porcelain and make it useful for these students has been a meandering path with dead ends and backtracking. By now, however, the course has a rhyme and reason, albeit one as unpredictable as the dynamic between any collection of undergraduates in a classroom.

Round One

I first taught the American Home course in the spring of 2005, my first semester at Valparaiso University. Valparaiso, Indiana, an hour's drive from Chicago, is a city of about 32,000 people. Our school's 3,250 undergraduates largely come from rural and suburban communities in the upper Midwest. Many of their families make great sacrifices to send them to college, and parents and students alike are keenly aware of the tight job market they will face upon graduation. Most, although not all, of my students are enrolled in our honors program, meaning they have a greater than average interest in the humanities. Their majors, however, are all over the map. They are curious and diligent and want to do good work in their future communities. The majority of them have never looked seriously at a building.

I planned a seminar that would introduce students to the history of American housing and related social movements and problems. Toward this end, I attempted to model closely a transformative course I myself had at the University of California–Berkeley, Margaretta Lovell's American Domestic Architecture. Professor Lovell showed me, in her extremely articulate and persuasive way, what the built environment could reveal. She delivered compelling lectures to an audience of forty undergraduate and graduate students.

But my students (typically fifteen to twenty per seminar) did not want to hear lectures. They wanted to talk. I struggled (and still struggle) to find readings in architectural history that were accessible for nonspecialist undergraduates while suggesting fruitful discussion questions that did not require a mastery of the subject matter. Topics like the colonial revival or the arts and crafts movement generated discussion because students could grasp the identifiable cultural values that drove these aesthetic movements. Stories of architecture and social justice, such as the history of public housing, also engaged their attention and spurred lively debate. The publications of members of the Vernacular Architecture Forum, who use the built environment to interpret the lives of ordinary people, more effectively sparked interest than did histories that named and tracked styles or the achievement of famous architects. And primary sources, judiciously selected, drew the students in; in this context, reading Frank Lloyd Wright on the genius of Frank Lloyd Wright worked far better than a scholar's secondary assessment.[3]

Again following Professor Lovell's model, I

asked my students to choose a house in our small city and write a research paper about its fabric and social history. These papers were on the whole not very successful. Most students simply did not have the time or energy to pursue this on their own and were stymied by the demands of new vocabulary and method in which they had no long-term investment.

Another class assignment, however, went surprisingly well. In order to acquaint students with research methods, together we studied a house on campus, Linwood House (1960), the former home of the university president, fondly referred to by my colleagues as "Frank Lloyd Wright meets Howard Johnson's" (Figure 1). We investigated its architecture and informally interviewed past residents. After the semester it seemed a shame to keep that information to ourselves, so the students delivered a public presentation on their research. We were astonished by how many people attended and the depth of their interest. The audience appreciated the architectural history to a degree, but it was the stories of individual human lives that held their interest. Large crossbeams were far more intriguing once they imagined the president's teenage sons swatting a badminton birdie through the gap between beam and ceiling. The rigid geometries of the living room looked different when our imagination filled the space with postwar administrators loosening up over Friday cocktails and plotting the university's future. House history became an occasion for our community to remember its past.[4]

Lessons learned: I found that for this kind of

Figure 1. Linwood house, Valparaiso University, Valparaiso, Indiana, circa 1960. Courtesy of Valparaiso University Archives.

undergraduate class, promoting student engagement was more important than marching them through a comprehensive survey of American housing (although the survey portion of the class has remained important). I became convinced that a soup-to-nuts group project could anchor the class and result in deeper, more personalized learning. Much to my delight, I also discovered that the local community was eager to connect with the students and learn with and from them.

Round Two

Three years later, in the fall of 2008, I had another opportunity to teach the course. In the interim I had often driven down McIntyre Court, a one-block street on the edge of campus (Figure 2). This modest neighborhood with old-growth trees and 1930s, 1940s, and 1950s small homes is one of very few residential streets that intersect with our campus. I had noticed houses disappearing from the street from time to time, leveled by bulldozers overnight, a smooth brown field offering no hint of what was there the day before. Turning my students loose on this neighborhood made sense, for both proximity and preservation interests. By now having a sense of what could actually be accomplished in a semester of undergraduate teaching, I canvassed the street ahead of the students, discovered which houses were owned by the university and which were still in private hands, found a few dozen homeowners willing to open up their homes to student researchers, did preliminary work in local archives, and identified interviewees. The classroom component of the course remained a survey of American housing, but I also added workshops related to the course project (oral history, fieldwork, and research in government records).

McIntyre was the first of the American Home's neighborhood-based architectural and social history projects. Twenty students studied and wrote about twenty houses along the street, charting the development of the community, from the remaining early twentieth-century farmhouse to the small houses of the postwar era. They discovered the now invisible history of a once tight neighborhood, where block parties were frequent and lives were entwined. They also encountered a history of racial tension, when the first person of color, an engineering professor of Egyptian descent, moved to McIntyre. But the primary story that emerged from this research involved the relationship between the neighbors and the university, which has quietly been buying houses on the street, renting them until they are no longer good for that purpose, and then tearing them down. Homeowners resented the careless acts of a big institution that had designs on their property and little knowledge of or affection for their community.[5]

With a public presentation in view, I asked for three volunteer writers (subsequently, I have been able to pay these students a small stipend as departmental student assistants) to continue to work on the project after the semester ended. The writers (also the symposium speakers) read all the student papers, interviews, and other research materials and summarized the findings according to three themes selected by the class: architecture, community, and university relations. We then merged these papers into a coherent whole and produced a PowerPoint presentation. Some students left campus after the semester, and others lost interest, but most were still invested in the success of the project and looked forward to sharing their work. This component of the course, as you might gather, is a considerable amount of work for both instructor and students. But it has been worth the effort.

When the students shared their McIntyre neighborhood research with the public, a lecture and celebration advertised as a one hundredth anniversary for the neighborhood (a birthday party with cake!), over one hundred people turned out, including the university president. In the question-and-answer session, neighbors asked the university representatives some pointed questions about their future. There was some tension in the room but also a sense of relief as the neighbors aired grievances in a context that validated their existence. They enthusiastically thanked the students for their work, warmly greeted former neighbors, told more stories, and even solved architectural mysteries. One current faculty member, for instance, the daughter of a former government professor, explained that the

Figure 2. Houses on McIntyre Court, Valparaiso, Indiana. Photograph by Gretchen T. Buggeln, 2015.

large ceiling fan over the sunken living room in her 1960s house was to dissipate the cloud of smoke at frequent faculty cocktail parties.

This lecture and celebration provided a positive moment in a somewhat checkered town–gown relationship. The students learned the value of neighborhood and the beauty and practicality of small houses, and they internalized the importance of preservation. I encouraged them to try to understand the university's perspective and to work with it rather than demonize an institution that was, in fact, trying to do good in its own way. The future of the neighborhood remains uncertain, but at the very least a solid McIntyre Court history is now placed in the university archives.[6]

Lessons learned: The McIntyre project proved that neighborhood history could bring a group of disparate students together around a common problem and build coherence and momentum. Having one shared research project determined prior to the semester allowed us to jump right in, and I added class readings that would benefit the project directly. We read much more on the small houses of the mid-twentieth century, for instance, and to that end I built a small collection of reprinted pattern books. A fieldwork workshop was helpful, and I formalized the increasingly important oral history component of the research. Perhaps most important, I saw how delighted the students were to engage a neighborhood and see their humanities education matter beyond the classroom.

Round Three

Three years later, I chose a small neighborhood, called Linwood, on the south side of campus. Linwood's oldest home is a nineteenth-century farmhouse, but the majority of homes are 1950s postwar dwellings with large picture windows and open plans. Many university leaders built and resided in these homes for decades. In many ways Linwood was an idyllic postwar community: a rolling, wooded landscape with an enticing pond, no fences, and plenty of kids and things to do. The other kids in town, we heard, knew something interesting was always happening over in Linwood.

One of the most remarkable things that happened here was the process of racial integration during the 1960s. When selecting this neighborhood, I did not anticipate that integration would emerge as a central story line. In the late 1960s, a university professor, Walt Reiner, moved his family to Chicago to direct a semester-long urban studies program, and he and his family lived near the Cabrini-Green projects. As Walt was getting ready to return to small-town Indiana, Barbara Cotton, a black woman who worked in his office, a single mom with six kids, approached him about moving her family to the country. She dreamed of a "little red house" with a place for her kids to roam in the woods. If Walt could escape the projects and head home, she asked, why should she be stuck in the dangerous city, a place that offered her children no future? Walt accepted the challenge, took her question back to his university and community, and committed to finding a home for the Cotton family. After several false starts (one rental property mysteriously sold just as the Cottons were about to move in) and university administrators giving the "yes, but not yet" answer one too many times, Walt decided to offer the property adjacent to his own house. On this plot Walt, members of his Lutheran church, and a team of undergraduates built a four-bedroom Cape Cod house clad in red shingles (Figures 3 and 4). Some

in the community resisted; one older neighbor even sabotaged the water system. Yet the family found their way in an all-white Indiana community after weathering an especially difficult first year bullied by threats and abuse.[7] Barbara earned a university degree. The neighborhood modeled integration, centered on a little red house, for the larger Valparaiso community.

In the late 1960s, the Cotton house project had been the spark for forming the Valparaiso Community Builders (now Project Neighbors), an organization that further pursued integration and built low-income residences in town. Several decades later, after Barbara Cotton moved away, the university purchased the Cotton house. As a rental, it met the same fate as the McIntyre houses and was slated for demolition. The students found it shocking that a house with such an important history would be destroyed. Project Neighbors members, for their part, found it appalling that a "perfectly good" house would not be rehabbed into low-income housing. Although we managed to hold off demolition long enough to document the house, it is now gone. And despite their work recovering and documenting an

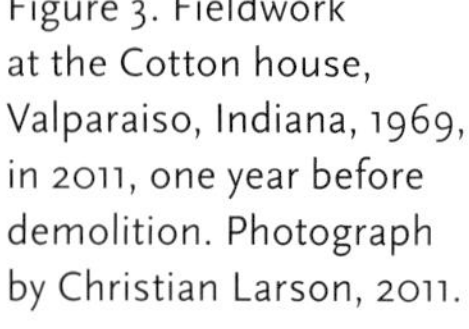

Figure 3. Fieldwork at the Cotton house, Valparaiso, Indiana, 1969, in 2011, one year before demolition. Photograph by Christian Larson, 2011.

important chapter in community history, the students all learned that without the building itself history is diminished.

The Cotton house was only one of the rich stories of space and place that emerged from the Linwood Project. One student, Ian Roseen, an English and creative writing major, wanted to write his paper on the intertwined history of the old farmhouse and its current owner, who had grown up in the house and came back to it after some years on the West Coast. This woman had experienced difficult struggles in her life, but as Ian showed her, the house had been an anchor throughout. I ran into the homeowner downtown some weeks after the project ended, and she told me, through tears, that Ian's story had "given me my life back." When I relayed her message to Ian, the significance of his gift visibly lifted his shoulders.

The students' public presentation felt like a family reunion, capped by the moment when Michael Cotton stood up and said, "I just want to take this opportunity to thank these people for my childhood." That felt "real world" to students in ways their classroom experience rarely could match. Their humanities work had value beyond the professor's desk and a grade on their transcript. They spoke and wrote effectively for the public with a sense of responsibility, and they began to see their community from other perspectives.

After the close of the Linwood Project, graduating seniors Emily Royer (theology major) and Jacob Just (art major) wanted to pursue the idea of architecture and community with a postgraduate project. They wrote a proposal to study another neighborhood in town and secured funding from the Indiana Humanities Council and AmeriCorps for their Central Stories project. This study, sponsored by our county historical museum, resulted in interviews, neighborhood conversations, a photo exhibition in a local coffee shop, and an innovative exhibition in the museum (Figures 5, 6, and 7).[8] The students' work also spun off into other programs, such as a revived home tour fund-raiser for the museum.[9] Needless to say, this kind of interaction between university, town, and museum has benefits all

Figure 4. Brittany Rosenau, engineering major, working inside Cotton house. Photograph by Gretchen T. Buggeln, 2011.

around. And, I am proud to relate, Emily and Jake won the Indiana Historical Society's Project of the Year Award in 2013.[10]

Lessons learned: To consistently integrate the project into the course, I needed to designate time for project catch-up in class, during which the students might interview a visitor, give research updates, or share ideas about where the project was headed. Diverse student interests prompted me to expand the range of potential research topics, allowing some students to move

Figure 5. University students interviewing local residents at Porter County Museum booth, Valparaiso Popcorn Festival. Photograph by Emily Royer, September 2012.

Figure 6. Central Stories exhibition, Porter County Museum, Valparaiso, Indiana. Photograph by Emily Royer, 2013.

Figure 7. Central Stories project photograph exhibition at Blackbird Café, Valparaiso, Indiana. Photograph by Emily Royer, 2013.

beyond the one student/one building model. A meteorology major, for example, wrote about the effect of the new and imposing Doppler radar tower placed in the neighborhood by the university. I also became more convinced that thinking beyond the semester is worthwhile. In addition to Emily's and Jake's project, one student, joined by Walt Reiner's widow, Lois, and childhood friends Robert Cotton and Elizabeth (Reiner) Gingrich, spoke about the Cotton house at a Martin Luther King Jr. Day event (Figure 8). And finally, embracing the chaos, I accepted that this course needs to adapt constantly to unexpected discoveries and research needs—this in fact models for students the unpredictable nature of actual research.

Round Four

The most recent iteration of the course in the fall of 2014 covered a nine-square-block section of one of the less-affluent sections of our town, the Hilltop neighborhood. Here, beautiful nineteenth-century homes mix with run-down apartment buildings and some newer Habitat for Humanity houses. Like the previous projects, the arc of the story developed as the students did their research. They learned about the last-

ing detrimental effects of the 1965 closure and demolition of the Columbia School, a beautiful but outdated 1893 neighborhood school. The history of a small 1940s church in the neighborhood revealed much about the changing composition of the neighborhood and its needs. Census records showed the primarily working-class nature of this side of town, and oral histories revealed the social cost of such an address for residents. One woman who grew up in Hilltop told the students that as a teenager she was "interviewed" by a group of popular girls at the local soda fountain, and when she answered their rather pointed question about where she lived, they did not respond. She never heard from them again.[11]

The age of the Hilltop neighborhood led many students to center their analysis on the choices made by homeowners who invested in historic buildings, choices dramatically illustrated when a storm roared through Valparaiso in October, sending a tree crashing through the roof of a brick Italianate gem. Would the owner find the money to restore her home or tear it down as unsafe? She chose to restore it, but it was a difficult and expensive decision, and finding able craftsmen was challenging. In this neighborhood a

Figure 8. Childhood Friends Robert Cotton and Elizabeth (Reiner) Gingerich sharing stories. Student presentation at Martin Luther King Jr. Day Symposium, Valparaiso University. Photograph by JoEllen Zromkoski, February 2012.

sense of community was harder to locate. Residents to a large degree were transient and somewhat wary of their neighbors. Yet one homeowner suggested the idea of a progressive meal at homes that were part of our project, and as a result friendships were formed. In the private spaces of living rooms and kitchens, neighbors and students found their way into each others' lives, and I believe the work of the students this semester made a small contribution to a common understanding of neighborhood among the homeowners.

Lessons learned: Working in an older and, in many ways, more complex neighborhood was difficult. Homeowners in a place like Hilltop are less willing to participate in the first place—I had to knock on many more doors to find houses to study. And with a less articulated sense of place among the owners and renters, a coherent storyline was elusive, and the students' findings seemed unfinished to a greater degree. Older homes also presented research problems. Sanborn maps, incomplete title records, and other forms of written documentation were harder to come by. These buildings were simply more complex than the small postwar houses of previous

projects, and many of my students, as a result, seemed overwhelmed with the fieldwork and documentary tasks.

The complexity of primary research has been a challenge for all of my students. I still stand by the value of introducing them to these sources, but I realize that process may be more important than product. Studying postwar housing is probably more effective in this kind of a course. Yet there is an undeniable magic to the older buildings. Students spent extensive time amid uneven wooden floors, crumbling brick, and quirky home improvements (one house's "extra bathroom" was a toilet installed at the top of the basement stair landing), and their affection for old buildings grew considerably. Finally, simply bringing this neighborhood to the attention of the university community might have been the most important thing the students accomplished (Figure 9).[12]

Reflections

Each new semester of the American Home brings a fresh adventure that taxes my ingenuity and patience as a teacher. That said, I think this is some of the best teaching I have ever done. I

Figure 9. Students presenting Hilltop Neighborhood Project to public audience. Photograph by David Purvis-Fenker, January 2015.

am relearning what I hope I have taught my students: the humanities matter—in real places, in real time, in real life. What our field has going for it, vis-à-vis many other types of humanistic study, is that we can take students and literally put them inside communities and multidimensional problems that have no easy answers. Is this building worth saving? Do the needs of the university outweigh those of the neighbors? How can people of different races and classes live together most equitably and effectively? I am sure questions such as these came up when I sat around a table with previous students, but I am also sure the enduring knowledge and the respect for the built environment generated by the two forms of teaching cannot compare. Furthermore, the collaborative nature of this kind of research, working with neighbors and fellow students, teaches humility and accountability. Hands-on architectural and social history is no classroom thought experiment.

Very rarely do veterans from my American Home course end up working in a related field. When I left my previous museum job, I expressed regret to the director that I would no longer be training museum professionals. "That's fine," she responded. "Train us some patrons." I do think studying architecture embedded in communities makes preservationists of many of my students. If I can believe what they tell me, they have learned to look beyond the obvious for meaning and to listen to the stories people and buildings tell. Their eyes are open to houses as they drive and walk; they feel connected to new places they encounter; and they look in fresh ways at the familiar architecture of their family homes. They themselves want to inhabit places of solidity, places where human lives have left an imprint, places with history and depth. My experience teaching the American Home course, as well as vernacular architecture in general, shows how, through the common experience of dwelling, we develop connections with others. Paradoxically, by studying these objects, we learn to see people as something other than objects, as autonomous beings who share our humanity in the ordinary activities of their lives.

I expect my experience will resonate with members of the Vernacular Architecture Forum and others who study, preserve and cherish common buildings. Since its origins over thirty-five years ago, the VAF has blended fieldwork, scholarship, preservation, and social justice. Scholars of vernacular architecture are by and large motivated not just by a love for buildings but by concern for people. Ours is a quintessentially humanistic study that aims to draw attention to what is important in our past and to use that knowledge to shape a better present.

The humanistic goals of our field line up with a broader defense of the humanities, a defense that generally takes one of three tacks. First, there is an argument that our lives will be richer and more meaningful if we take the time to explore human achievement in culture and the arts as well as to reflect on humanity's mistakes and tragedies. The humanities thus help us to be complete and wise human beings. Second, there is an appealing instrumental defense that claims instruction in the humanities teaches important critical thinking, writing, and speaking skills—useful in all types of employment. This line of reasoning seeks the real economic value of humanistic study but does run the risk of reducing it to an acquired skill set. Finally, since Cicero, there has been an argument that continues to make sense, one that has been especially influential in an American context: liberal education prepares us to flourish as democratic citizens within thriving political entities.[13]

These are all valid reasons for studying the humanities. The first, self-cultivation and the growth of wisdom, is ideally an outcome of all legitimate study. The second, the acquisition of practical skills—data analysis, crafting articulate and convincing arguments, public speaking—is a necessity. We should keep these skills in mind as we design courses. Writing instruction, in particular, is something our students need from us. This can be draining, time-consuming work for teachers, but it is hard to argue that any work we do with our students is more important, even (perhaps *especially*) as we move forward with new media. The third category, education for citizenship, is, I believe, an area where our discipline can outshine many others.

University of Chicago philosopher Martha Nussbaum, in her 2010 book *Not for Profit: Why Democracy Needs the Humanities,* confidently and passionately argues, "Thirsty for national profit, nations, and their systems of education, are heedlessly discarding skills that are needed to keep democracies alive. If this trend continues, nations all over the world will soon be producing generations of useful machines, rather than complete citizens who can *think for themselves, criticize tradition, and understand the significance of another person's sufferings and achievements.*"[14] That last sentence lays out, for Nussbaum, what the humanities can and should do for us. *Thinking for ourselves and criticizing tradition* lead to the formation of free, democratic individuals. These traits can be cultivated through the study of the built environment, particularly in a vernacular studies approach that is deeply rooted in historical context and criticism.

Nussbaum's third point, *"understanding the significance of another person's sufferings and achievements,"* is something we should consider even more carefully as applicable to our field. This kind of knowing is a personal understanding that activates the moral imagination, what Jane Addams of Hull House marvelously called "affectionate interpretation." There are times and circumstances when empathy functions better than cool scholarly detachment. In one of her many lyrical passages, Nussbaum worries that current methods of teaching undergraduates neglect "what it is for thought to open out of the soul and connect person to world in a rich, subtle, and complicated manner."[15] Something about studying architecture and community up close and personal resists the oversimplification of social problems and promotes just this sort of education. It is moving to witness students connecting deeply and individually with their diverse neighbors.

But how do we sell architectural history to our critics (including, for those of us in the academy, our deans and provosts)? Will experiences like these help our students get jobs, justify the high cost of tuition, figure in their subsequent lives? I suggest we utilize three concepts currently invoked in academic culture and peppered liberally throughout the promotional material our schools use to attract students: *empathy, hospitality,* and *service. Empathy* and *hospitality* are concepts appearing with vigor in a wide variety of conversations from politics to religion.[16] Particularly in complex, multicultural communities, the practice of these virtues seems necessary for mutual understanding and flourishing. There is something about walking a neighborhood, digging into its history, and getting to know residents in their homes that gives such concepts a unique grounding, without sacrificing any complexity. Furthermore, thinking of architectural history as *service* might actually be a ticket toward directing some resources our way. I had no idea that AmeriCorps would fund a neighborhood study. Another organization, Valparaiso University's Institute for Leadership and Service, has also been instrumental in promoting and expanding the work of my students, and many universities have similar offices eager to identify and further work that benefits the service mission of the university (and looks good on the service page of the website). Let's find our way to that table.

And, finally, why *undergraduates*, particularly those who will not take our courses to fulfill any sort of career ambition? Dianne Harris recently addressed the Society of Architectural Historians about the importance of making our work matter to a wider public.[17] She drew on a 2013 American Academy of Arts and Sciences report, *The Heart of the Matter: The Humanities and Social Sciences for a Vibrant, Competitive, and Secure Nation,* written by nationally prominent scholars and a few business leaders in response to a bipartisan request from national legislators.[18] Harris skillfully used this document to challenge architectural historians to reach out to the public more effectively so that they may engage the work we do. She cited the growth of online access to scholarship, the rise of public humanities festivals, NPR coverage, and websites such as publicbooks. org as encouraging signs and promising venues in which to place our work. This is good news and should motivate us to use our skills and energies to preserve and better understand the built environment and to communicate that knowledge to different publics.

In truth, however, we had this primed NPR audience at "humanities." Our undergraduate students, who are still deciding what matters to them, are a different matter. The built environ-ment has the power to captivate students, to help them inhabit many of the social problems of our time, to think about what makes community function. Why not find even more ways to hook a more diverse array of students at this formative time in their lives? How can we effectively bring questions of space and place to the surface of their undergraduate experience, perhaps beyond the confines of our own classrooms in collaboration with other faculty and departments? How do we think broadly enough to help students see that big and important human questions reside in the fabric of the buildings and landscapes they live in or walk by every day? How do we not just tell but *show* skeptical administrators, parents, and students that learning about and from buildings and landscapes is not just interesting but important? This is our challenge as teachers.

AUTHOR BIOGRAPHY

Gretchen Townsend Buggeln holds the Duesenberg Chair in Christianity and the Arts at Valparaiso University. She is author of *Temples of Grace: The Material Transformation of Connecticut's Churches* (2003) and *The Suburban Church: Modernism and Community in Postwar America* (Minnesota, 2016). Buggeln is the current president of the Vernacular Architecture Forum.

NOTES

Many thanks go to William Littman and Mark Schwehn for their insightful suggestions for this essay and to the students who have made teaching the American Home seminar such a rich and rewarding experience.

1. This is a complex situation with many causes, but the decrease in the relative number of students, certainly in the disciplines most closely connected to architectural history, such as history and art history, is clear. I have witnessed this marked decline in enrollment directly at my university, and colleagues at other institutions corroborate. Articles on the trend include Madeline Will, "For the Humanities, Some Good News Is Mixed with the Bad," *Chronicle of Higher Education,* April 13, 2015, http://chronicle.com/article/For-the-Humanities-Some-Good/229291/; and Colleen Flaherty, "Major Exodus," *Inside Higher Ed,* January 26, 2015, https://www.insidehighered.com/

news/2015/01/26/where-have-all-english-majors-gone. The reasons behind the decrease in enrollment and majors include changes in general education requirements that give students more freedom to plan a career-focused curriculum, a turn toward professional colleges, increasing numbers of women entering technical and scientific fields, and students arriving with more humanities dual-credit and AP courses under their belts. See Kellie Woodhouse, "Arts and Sciences Deficits," *Inside Higher Ed,* June 4, 2015, https://www.insidehighered.com/news/2015/06/04/colleges-arts-and-sciences-struggle-deficits-enrollment-declines. Woodhouse notes that the number of students enrolled in the humanities at the Ohio State University has "dropped by half in six years." Teachers of the humanities cannot simply hold the door to the classroom open and expect students to file in; they need to explain why their courses and disciplines are important.

2. In response to a decline in humanities enrollments, the dean of arts and humanities at Harvard College asked an interdisciplinary group of scholars to "examine the role and purpose of the humanities at Harvard." See "Addressing a Decline in the Humanities," *Harvard Magazine,* June 6, 2013, http://harvardmagazine.com/2013/06/reinvigorating-the-humanities. The committee's report, *The Teaching of the Arts and Humanities at Harvard College: Mapping the Future,* is a readable document worthy of study. It is available at http://artsandhumanities.fas.harvard.edu/files/humanities/files/mapping_the_future_31_may_2013.pdf. Especially interesting to me was the decision to focus a new curriculum on qualities of attention: The Art of Living, The Art of Reading, and The Art of Looking. Intensive study of texts and objects—think fieldwork—is Harvard's chosen path to reinvigorate the humanities.

3. I used Frank Lloyd Wright, *The Natural House* (New York: Horizon Press, 1954).

4. "Students Study History, Architecture of Linwood House," *Valpo: The Magazine of Valparaiso University* 22, no. 1 (Winter 2005): 6.

5. At the time of our study, the university master plan showed the area of McIntyre Court as athletic fields. The current master plan maintains the street as a neighborhood. See *Campus Master Plan: Executive Summary,* http://www.valpo.edu/masterplan/assets/docs/VU%20MP%20Exec%20Summary_final.pdf.

6. The student papers, maps, notes from interviews or MP3 files, and other research materials from the American Home have been deposited in the Valparaiso University Archives, unprocessed.

7. See Lois Reiner, "Shatz," unpublished typescript memoir, n.d.; Lois Reiner, "They Just Carted Away 857 So. Cedar Lane," April 12, 2012, unpublished paper; Brendan Morris, "Class Studies Trailblazer's Home," *The Torch,* September 30, 2011, A6.

8. Susan O'Leary, "Museum Exhibit Tells History of Downtown Valparaiso Neighborhood," *NW Indiana Times,* June 23, 2013, http://www.nwitimes.com/news/local/porter/valparaiso/museum-exhibit-tells-history-of-valparaiso-downtown-neighborhood/article_e1b0dcba-0231-5274-adbd-15537dbeaa22.html.

9. Following the completion of the Central Stories project, another veteran of the American Home seminar, Ian Roseen, spent a year as an AmeriCorps intern working with the lakeside community of Ogden Dunes. Roseen also produced exhibitions and related public programming. See Susan O'Leary, "Hour Glass Museum Hosts Ogden Dunes Stories Project," *NW Indiana Times,* April 31, 2014, http://www.nwitimes.com/news/local/porter/ogden-dunes/hour-glass-museum-hosts-ogden-dunes-stories-project/article_28d07630-0de6-54e9-9f75-a697c7f6013c.html. Another community, Beverly Shores, recently approached the museum about being the next "stories" project.

10. "Museum Wins Project of the Year," Porter County Museum of History website, 2013, http://pocomuse.org/storiesproject/csp/ihsaward/.

11. Jackie Watkins, class interview, December 1, 2014, Valparaiso, Ind.

12. Susan O'Leary, "VU Professor, Students Uncover Hilltop's Rich Architectural History," *NW Indiana Times,* April 19, 2015, http://www.nwitimes.com/news/local/porter/vu-professor-students-uncover-hilltop-s-rich-architectural-history/article_137a5f1a-ad24-52e4-9fd2-a18892108756.html.

13. There are many thoughtful books on this subject. Three I have found especially useful are Martha C. Nussbaum, *Not for Profit: Why Democracy Needs the Humanities* (Princeton, N.J.: Princeton University Press, 2010); Martha C. Nussbaum, *Cultivating Humanity: A Classical Defense of Reform in Liberal Education* (Cambridge, Mass.: Harvard University Press, 1997); and Michael S. Roth, *Beyond the University:*

Why Liberal Education Matters (New Haven, Conn.: Yale University Press, 2014).

14. Nussbaum, *Not for Profit,* 2; emphasis mine.

15. Nussbaum, *Not for Profit,* 6.

16. These conversations run the gamut from the scholarly to the popular, as some quick online searches will demonstrate. Recent critical texts include Anthony M. Clohesy, *Politics of Empathy: Ethics, Solidarity, Recognition* (London: Routledge, 2013); and Thomas Claviez, ed., *The Conditions of Hospitality: Ethics, Politics, and Aesthetics on the Threshold of the Possible* (New York: Fordham University Press, 2013).

The increasing presence of these terms in our common conversations emphasizes the concern for compassion and understanding across difference.

17. Dianne Harris, "Architectural History and Architectural Humanities," keynote plenary address to Society of Architectural Historians, April 2014, Austin, Tex., rev. version, http://www.sah.org/publications-and-research/sah-blog/sah-blog/2014/06/23/architectural-history-and-architectural-humanities.

18. The report is available at http://www.humanitiescommission.org/_pdf/hss_report.pdf.

MAURICIO F. CASTRO

Object Lesson: "All the Help I Needed, I Got Here"

Miami's Freedom Tower and the Freedom Tower's Miami

In the summer of 2005, South Florida's Terra Group was embroiled in a controversy over its plan to purchase and develop the iconic Miami property known as the Freedom Tower (Figure 1). The real estate development company, headed by Pedro Martin, had placed the winning bid with the family of the late Cuban American National Foundation chairman Jorge Mas Canosa for the eighty-year-old building. Mas Canosa and his family paid $4.1 million for the Freedom Tower in 1997 and, in conjunction with the foundation and other members of the Cuban American community, had invested $16 million into restoring and remodeling the structure. The foundation had been leading the effort to convert the former site of the federal Cuban Refugee Center (CRC) into a museum dedicated to the Cuban diaspora. Several bidders had sought to purchase the building from Mas Canosa's family, but the Terra Group offered a compromise by which the Freedom Tower would be preserved as a museum but a new condominium tower would be built behind it. The Terra Group had plans to construct a $500 million, sixty-two-story high-rise just thirty feet from the historic building, requiring the demolition of the back of the Freedom Tower complex.

The Terra Group's plan drew criticism from preservation activists and organizations including Florida's Bureau of Historic Preservation after news surfaced that in preparation for the sale the Mas family had withdrawn its nomination of the tower as a National Historic Landmark. Foundation chairman Jorge Mas Santos defended the decision by stating that the submission had been withdrawn to facilitate the sale and that it could be submitted again at any time. Pedro Martin, for his part, stated that the Terra Group might choose to enter a new application in the future. Others, however, stressed the importance of designating the tower as a National Historic Landmark. Barbara Mattick, of the Bureau of Historic Preservation, explained that such a designation meant the site had significance for the entire country; it was, after all, the "Cuban Ellis Island."[1]

There was a sense of irony to the efforts both to preserve the entirety of the Freedom Tower and to incorporate it into the creation of a new condominium complex. The creation of a new condominium tower almost four times as tall as the original building would continue a trend of intense new construction in Miami in the decades preceding the preservation controversy. The effort to preserve the tower was related to its time as the CRC, the Miami headquarters of the Cuban Refugee Program (CRP), a federal entity created in 1961 to aid the flow of exiles fleeing Fidel Castro's revolution. The CRP disbursed nearly $2 billion in aid to some seven hundred thousand exiles arriving in the United States.[2] In over a decade of operation, the CRC saw thousands of Cuban exiles seek governmental assistance and was the local source for the distribution of hundreds of millions of dollars. The presence of the Cuban refugees and the access to an unprecedented level of federal benefits fundamentally altered the political, social, and economic landscape in Miami.

The effect of these processes on the built environment around the Freedom Tower was significant. Where the tower was once a prominent part of the Miami skyline, it came to be dwarfed by urban development driven by both federal expenditures and investment from Latin America spurred on by the Cuban presence in the city. The very processes that made the Freedom Tower notable as the Cuban Ellis Island helped bring about the real estate explosion in South Florida that threatened its continued existence as a historical landmark. The history of the Freedom Tower and the different roles it played in Miami serve to illustrate the changes to the city in the wake of the Cuban Revolution. The Freedom Tower represented the point from which the physical, economic, social, and political changes to the city of Miami radiated. As a physical location, the Freedom Tower embodied a particular government policy, and its meaning would become a point of contention between different ethnic and social groups in the city.

The Home of the News

The building now known as the Freedom Tower was completed in 1925 by the firm of Schultze & Weaver to serve as the home of the *Miami News.* The seventeen-story Mediterranean revival–style building was modeled after the Giralda Tower in Seville, Spain.[3] It cost $2 million to build and featured a front door made of solid mahogany weighing 1,500 pounds, Italian light fixtures, and bronze-colored tiles from Valencia.[4] Architects Leonard Schultze and Major Spencer Fullerton Weaver had a history of designing and completing projects in both Miami and Havana. They had previously overseen the construction of Coral Gables' Biltmore Hotel, the Roney Plaza on Miami Beach's Collins Avenue, and the Ingraham Building in downtown Miami. They had also constructed an addition to the Sevilla Hotel in Paseo del Prado, designed the Havana American Jockey Club and the Casino Nacional, and by 1928 were working on the La Concha Swimming Club, all located in the greater Havana area.[5] Schultze & Weaver worked on both sides of the Florida Straits with ease.

Miami's proximity to the island of Cuba made it a logical gateway to the Caribbean and Latin America for the United States. The city's boosters

Figure 1. The Freedom Tower; Schultze & Weaver, architects; Miami, Florida, 1925. Courtesy of the Library of Congress. Photographs in the Carol M. Highsmith Archive, Library of Congress, Prints and Photographs Division.

actively sought to establish ties with Latin American countries and set Miami as a tourist destination for their affluent citizens. Likewise, the city was meant to present a Latin American flavor to American tourists and investors. In attempting to establish a connection between the city and the Americas, city boosters wanted to make parts of Miami's physical environment reflect a "Spanish" sensibility. In doing so, developers sought design ideas from Havana, going so far as to purchase weathered roofing tiles and fixtures from buildings about to be demolished in that city for use in new South Florida developments.[6]

The tower was commissioned by James Cox, former governor of Ohio and owner of the *Miami Daily News.*[7] The newspaper's name initially had been the *Miami Metropolis,* but its second name, adopted in 1924, gave the tower its original identity as the Miami Daily News Tower. The building's opening in July 1925 was a major event, and it drew some twenty thousand guests.[8] The *Miami Daily News* would serve as one of the city's major news outlets for decades. It was headquartered at the tower, now a prominent feature in the Miami skyline, for much of its history (Figure 2). By the late 1950s, however, the building was simply too small to hold the newspaper's operations. For decades the structure had served not only as the newspaper's office but also as its printing

Figure 2. Miami skyline as seen from the County Causeway, Miami, Florida, 1947. The Freedom Tower, then one of the most imposing buildings in the skyline, can be seen to the far right of the image. Courtesy of the HistoryMiami Archives & Research Center. *Miami Herald* Collection, HistoryMiami, 1983-26-229. Photograph by Richard B. Hoit.

facility. The building's central location became a problem for the distribution of the paper, as delivery trucks ran into significant delays in the heavy traffic on Biscayne Boulevard.[9] Beyond the problems of production, the tower structure of the building had simply become too small in relation to modern office buildings. In 1957 the newspaper, now known simply as the *Miami News,* moved to a new facility, and the building was sold to a real estate speculator named Irving Maidmore for $1.25 million.[10]

A Changing City and a New Purpose

The building stood vacant for five years after the *Miami News* moved out in 1957. Those five years, however, were very momentous ones for Miami and for the neighboring island of Cuba. The year before the building was vacated, Fidel Castro and other revolutionaries landed in Cuba and began guerilla operations against the regime of Fulgencio Batista. The conflict of the Cuban Revolution spilled over into the streets of Miami. The city was a refuge for many Cubans who opposed Batista's dictatorship. The conflict continued, sometimes devolving into brawls on the streets of Miami, after Batista fled Cuba and a new revolutionary regime established itself on the island in 1959.

Much of the conflict in the city stemmed from a stream of exiles that began leaving Cuba and seeking refuge in the United States, many of them arriving through Miami International

Airport. As the new Cuban government solidified its hold on the island and many of Castro's former allies began to part with him, the stream of exiles began to gain strength and soon became a flood. The exodus overwhelmed the small, established Cuban community in the city, as well as local civic and governmental organizations. By January 1961 officials estimated 33,000 Cuban exiles were living in the Miami area, often in dire economic conditions.[11] The federal government answered the call of local government and community leaders for assistance as the refugee crisis had completely overwhelmed local resources. In February 1961 the Kennedy administration took the lead in the management of the exile influx and established the CRP as an entity within the framework of the Social Security Administration in the Department of Health, Education, and Welfare.

Commissioner of Social Security William L. Mitchell appointed Marshall Wise as the director of the CRP. Wise was to be the program's point man in Miami, working out of a facility called the Cuban Emergency Refugee Center (CERC).[12] As the program grew and its operations in Miami expanded, the CERC would move from one temporary location to the next. In 1962 the former Miami News Building was leased by the U.S. General Services Administration and became, for the next twelve years, the home of the CRC (Figure 3). During that period the CRC served as the processing center for more than 450,000 Cuban exiles seeking assistance in the United States.[13] The center was a location from which the CRP provided services to the refugees, including financial assistance, hospitalization and medical care, surplus food, adult education, and professional training. As the flood of refugees continued and their presence in the city grew, the expenditures of the CRP kept pace. By the end of March 1964, the CRP's expenditures totaled an estimated $138,618,000, the majority of which was used to provide welfare assistance and services for refugees in need in Miami.[14]

It was in the early years of the CRC's operations that the building was dubbed the Freedom Tower. This was part of a larger branding effort by the CRP. Officials named the arrival gate at

Figure 3. Cuban refugees line up for assistance outside the Cuban Refugee Center, Miami, Florida, 1962. Courtesy of the Cuban Heritage Collection, University of Miami.

Miami International Airport the Freedom Gate and operated a facility at the airport, which they dubbed Freedom House. Once in the city, all program activity revolved, in one way or another, around the CRC. Registration with the center was not a requirement for Cuban exiles who wanted to remain in the United States, but it was mandatory if they sought assistance from the CRP in Miami or elsewhere (Figure 4).

The federal government had a keen interest in relocating as many of the refugees as were willing.[15] The original problem with the Cuban influx was the sheer concentration of refugees in South Florida. It was clear to many in the federal government that dispersing the Cubans would allow them greater work opportunities than could be found in a single city. In its attempt to disperse as many of the exiles as possible, the center provided office space for volunteer agencies cooperating with the federal government to ease the process of resettlement. Refugees could seek resettlement aid from religious and secular volunteer agencies.[16] By the end of 1970, the volunteer agencies, with the support of the federal government, had resettled 267,251 Cubans from the Miami area and dispersed them to every single state in the union.[17] While many of the resettled refugees would return to the Miami area, the

Figure 4. Cuban refugee family registers for assistance at the Cuban Refugee Center, Miami, Florida, 1962. Courtesy of the Cuban Heritage Collection, University of Miami.

Freedom Tower served as the point from which hundreds of thousands of Cubans would move out to other areas of the United States. In this manner, the federal government and the volunteer agencies established the tower's reputation as the Cuban Ellis Island.

A significant portion of the Cuban exiles who registered with the CRC chose to remain in Miami. The level and duration of the help these refugees received at the center varied based on their specific cases. Many of those who sought aid at the Freedom Tower would not soon forget the support they received from the refugee program (Figure 5). While this experience was not universal among Cuban exiles, it was sufficiently widespread that the tower gained yet another moniker. Within the community it came to be known simply as *el refugio* ("the refuge" or "the shelter"). The building that had been built to house one of Miami's main sources of information took on a new significance, and it became the physical symbol of the United States' welcome of the exile community.

While both the Cuban refugees and federal government officials had hoped for a prompt collapse of the Castro regime, this development did not come to pass. In time, more and more Cuban exiles embraced the immigration and citizenship opportunities provided by the federal government. The growing Cuban American community became a vibrant and integral part of the city. The Cuban community in South Florida grew in size, power, and wealth in the decades that followed the revolution, thanks, in part, to the federal government's investment.

The Changing Miami Landscape and the Many Afterlives of the Freedom Tower

By the mid-1970s, the federal government's aid became less and less necessary, as the influx of refugees had nearly ground to a halt. From 1965 to 1973, an agreement between the United States and Cuba allowed for direct flights from Havana to carry those Cuban citizens who wished to leave the island to settle in the United States. These so-called Freedom Flights were the main avenue of entry for Cuban refugees into the United States for the better part of a decade. On April 6, 1973, the Freedom Flights came to an end when the Cuban government decided to stop the flow of its citizens toward the United States.[18]

Cuban refugees who had first taken asylum in third countries constituted the majority of the exiles who came to the United States between 1973 and 1980. While the number of refugees arriving in the United States during these years was not insignificant, it was merely a fraction of the mass arrivals of the Freedom Flights. This diminished flow was met by a larger, wealthier, and more powerful Cuban community in Miami, one better able to meet the needs of arriving compatriots. Throughout the 1970s, the CRP would shrink and wind down and, by the end of the decade, simply cease to exist.

For the CRC, the end came earlier. In 1974, with the need for a large facility from which to dispense aid to large groups of incoming refugees gone, the federal government closed the CRC. Following the exit of the CRP, the Freedom Tower was once again put up for sale by its owner. The tower stood vacant for two years. In 1976 the new owner, Sam Polur, offered the Cuban community an exclusive option for the purchase of the property. He proposed the tower be bought and presented by Cuban Americans as a gift to the United States as part of the celebrations for the bicentennial of their host nation. The idea failed, and by 1978 the mortgage holder, Citibank, had purchased the building for $700,000 after foreclosure proceedings.

Despite standing vacant since the end of the refugee center's occupancy, the building retained significance for the Cuban community in Miami and for the city at large. In the years that followed, several attempts were made to preserve the structure. In 1979 the building was placed on the National Register of Historic Places. Four years later, in 1983, the Miami City Commission declared the building a historic site, and two years later, the state legislature allocated $15,000 to study the preservation of the tower as a landmark.[19]

As the tower stood empty, the city around it continued to evolve. The month that the Freedom Flights ended, the Dade County Board of County Commissioners voted to recognize the contributions of the Hispanic community, still overwhelmingly Cuban, in the greater Miami area by passing an ordinance declaring the county officially bilingual.[20] Cuban Americans had integrated themselves into every facet of professional life in South Florida and had started thousands of new businesses in the area. The Cuban presence helped drive an influx of capital into South Florida from Latin America. Businesses in Miami had made the best of the large, available Spanish-speaking workforce, many of whom served as clerks in department stores that catered to the ever-increasing number of tourists from Latin America. An estimated five hundred thousand Latin American tourists visited Miami in 1978 and spent an average of one thousand dollars each during their visits, with some spending as much as "$20,000 in one spree."[21]

While some worried about the provenance of funds from Latin America being tied to the increasing narcotics trade, the effects on the city were undeniable. Groups of international and national banks began to move into the area and gave Miami the second-largest concentration of banks in the United States after New York City. The city also saw a booming real estate market in a period in which sales had dropped 9 percent nationwide. Contracts for new housing units increased

Figure 5. Waiting room inside the Cuban Refugee Center, Miami, Florida, undated. Courtesy of the Cuban Heritage Collection, University of Miami.

33 percent in this same period. This boom was driven, in part, by wealthy Latin Americans seeking a relatively familiar environment in which to safeguard their money. More than one-third of Miami property sales were to foreigners, with one realtor indicating that Latin American buyers had increased by 1,000 percent since Anastasio Somoza was deposed in Nicaragua.[22]

The years after the closing of the CRC were not without their challenges for Miami's Cuban Americans. Internal political strife had strained the community throughout the 1970s, and the Mariel boatlift of 1980 saw an influx of approximately 124,000 refugees in the span of a few months.[23] Unlike those who had come before them, these refugees had a more negative public image, arrived with far greater intensity, and were not met with the same level of federal largesse. This proved a significant problem for the established Cuban American population, particularly in the area of public relations.

Despite these challenges, Cuban Americans remained a vital part of South Florida's social, political, and economic landscape. The 1980s saw a significant number of Cuban American firsts, including the election of the first Cuban American mayor of the city of Miami and the first Cuban American member of the U.S. House of Representatives. And as the Cold War began to wind down, many of those who had come from Cuba decades before began to hope they might soon see the end of Castro's government and be able to return to the island.

Through it all, the Freedom Tower remained vacant or the site of failed ventures. For a time in 1985, the county commissioners considered moving city hall into the building and transforming the tower into city offices. Around the same time, the president of Miami-Dade Community College (now Miami Dade College), Robert McCabe, unsuccessfully lobbied the state to purchase the property for the college and convert it into a complex of offices, museums, and art studios. The building's fate appeared to be changing when the Saudi firm Zaminco International purchased the property for $8.7 million and spent $12 million to partially refurbish the building, with the intent to transform it into an office tower. This work included the replacement of all of the steel beams on the top six floors of the structure (Figure 6).[24] The space that had served as the newsroom for the Miami News was transformed into a luxurious banquet hall.[25] In November 1988 some four hundred people gathered to celebrate the proposed future of the tower as a small conference center and office building. By the following year, however, construction companies and suppliers began filing claims against Zaminco for lack of payment. Without a full-time paying tenant, the Freedom Tower was placed in foreclosure once again in 1992.[26]

By 1997 the tower had become a place in which the area's homeless sought shelter. Thieves seeking to salvage copper tubing had torn up significant sections of the interior walls.[27] The previous year, the executive director of the Dade Heritage Trust, Becky Matkov, began the processes of convincing the state to purchase the property. By mid-1997 the trust obtained a unanimous vote from Florida's Conservation and Recreational Lands acquisition program declaring the Freedom Tower a priority purchase. Before the trust was able to buy the property, Miami businessman and chairman of the Cuban American National Foundation Jorge Mas Canosa purchased the building and announced plans for the creation of a permanent museum at the site. The Dade Heritage Trust made inquiries with the Mas family about its continued interest in acquiring the property, only to be told the building was not for sale.[28]

Unsteady Ground

The acquisition of the building by Jorge Mas Canosa and his family came at a time when the Cuban community at large felt as though it was under siege. The purchase was completed two years after a significant reversal of Cuban refugee policy by the federal government. In the summer of 1994, a new crisis arose as conditions in Cuba caused a new wave of refugees to take to the sea in makeshift rafts in an attempt to reach the United States. President Bill Clinton and Attorney General Janet Reno sought to avoid a repeat of the Mariel crisis fourteen years earlier and issued orders to move any rafter intercepted at sea to Guantanamo Naval Base in Cuba. Over the course of ten months, the population of rafters in Guantanamo reached nearly thirty thousand.[29]

Despite lobbying by the Cuban American community and the Cuban American National Foundation (CANF), the Clinton administration made an announcement in May 1995 that fundamentally changed previous policy related to refugees from the island. The refugees already in Guantanamo would be accepted into the United States, but rafters rescued at sea by American authorities from that point forward would be returned to Cuba. Cuban Americans were glad for the entry of the Guantanamo refugees, but many were shocked and outraged at the policy reversal. The CANF was so enraged that it pulled its offer to spend millions of dollars to help resettle the Guantanamo refugees. "They made this policy alone," said Mas Canosa of the administration's decision, "let them now solve the problems of Guantanamo alone."[30]

More problematic, perhaps, for Mas Canosa and for the Cuban community was the way in which many other Americans, particularly non-Cuban Floridians, greeted the new policy as necessary. Some were heartened by the prevention of an increased Cuban presence in Miami, and others, like *Miami Herald* editor Jim Hampton, simply thought the policy change was difficult but sensible. "No community should be asked to live with the indefinite tension of worrying about being inundated with refugees," Hampton wrote days after the policy announcement.[31]

Mas Canosa felt as besieged as his community. His position and reputation as a political power broker was damaged by the perception that he had been left powerless in the determination of Cuba policy by the Clinton administration. The previous year, an article in the *New Republic* had portrayed Mas Canosa as a powerful figure with sufficient clout to slap and thump on the table when speaking to the president, who had taken time away from his own birthday party to meet with a Florida delegation. Mas Canosa had allegedly demanded that the president punish Castro for the rafter crisis and had "bellowed" at Clinton that he should show the Cuban leader no mercy. The story had also described Mas Canosa as a "mobster and megalomaniac."[32] Mas Canosa, unsurprisingly, sued the author of the piece, Ann Louise Bardach, and the *New Republic*. While the lawsuit was ultimately settled out of court, the depositions taken from Mas Canosa left him more exposed to public scrutiny than ever before. The CANF chairman's testimony proved him to be "tough and combative, but certainly not a 'mobster,'" noted the *Miami Herald*. The depositions brought to light some of Mas Canosa's less savory practices and clearly showed the businessman and lobbyist to be "a study in contradictions."[33] Despite Mas Canosa's fearsome reputation and coercive tactics, the power of the Cuban community and of one of its most influential members had not been sufficient to prevent significant changes to American policy or to turn public opinion toward their cause.

A Rallying Beacon

Mas Canosa died a few months after purchasing the tower, but the feeling that those outside their community had turned against them would only grow among Cuban Americans. On Thanksgiving Day 1999, a boy named Elián González was rescued at sea and placed with family members in Miami who were adamant they did not want the boy sent back to Cuba.[34] The boy's mother had died during the crossing, and his father wished Elián returned to him. Elián soon found himself at the center of an international controversy as the Cuban government and the Cuban American community engaged in a battle of words across the Florida Straits. After months of legal maneuvering by the different parties involved in the conflict, the Clinton administration mounted an armed raid on the home of Elián's great-uncle Lázaro González in late April 2000. Within hours the boy had been returned to his father and was headed back to Cuba.[35]

Figure 6. The Freedom Tower in the midst of the partial restoration by Zaminco International, Miami, Florida, 1989. Courtesy of the HistoryMiami Archives & Research Center. *Miami Herald* Collection, HistoryMiami, 1983-26-229.

Figure 7. Freedom Tower draped with the Cuban Flag in the wake of the Elián González affair, Miami, Florida, 2000. Courtesy of the Cuban Heritage Collection, University of Miami.

There was a feeling of outrage among many in the Cuban American community over the decision to forcibly remove Elián González from his relatives' home in Miami and return him to Cuba. Others, often those outside the Cuban community, went so far as to call Attorney General Reno a hero and to state their belief that Cuban Americans were used to operating outside the laws of the United States.[36] In the aftermath of the Elián González affair, there was urgency to restore the Freedom Tower and use it as a tool to influence the opinion of the surrounding community and the nation about Cuban Americans (Figure 7). A year after the raid on the González home, the Cuban American National Foundation made a renewed push for the restoration of the Freedom Tower. CANF spokesman Joe García noted that when visitors came to town and wanted to experience Cuban culture, "you take them to Versailles restaurant to have a *medianoche* and a *cafecito*," but this was simply not sufficient. "We have to do a better job of telling our story," García went on, "and the Elián González case showed we haven't been able to do that."[37]

The foundation had started restoration work on the Freedom Tower in January 2000 and spent $4.5 million in structural repairs alone. One of CANF's directors, engineer Jose G. Puig, served as project director and made an assessment of the renovation work done in the 1980s. He qualified it as a simple facelift, noting all that had been done was to "cover up the bad and make it look pretty." Nothing had been done to actually preserve the tower's integrity.[38] As restoration costs continued to mount on the project, the CANF decided to involve the larger Cuban American community in covering these expenses. Part of this effort involved a media blitz regarding the tower and its importance. In May 2001 the CANF, through the subsidiary Freedom Tower Foundation, published a multiple-page insert in the *Miami Herald* entitled "The Freedom Tower . . . A Dream Come True." The insert included sections in which Mas Canosa's son and new CANF chairman Jorge Mas Santos outlined his father's vision and CANF president Francisco Hernandez outlined the foundation's "commitment to Cuba's freedom," as well as providing details about the renovations the building needed.[39]

The insert also included a full-page advertisement for the "Grand Opening Celebration" of the Freedom Tower to take place in and around the building on May 19, 2001. This event was intended to help raise millions of dollars to continue the renovations. The celebrations were to include an inaugural mass, exhibits, booths, the illumination of the tower, fireworks, and musical entertainment from the Florida Chamber Orchestra and entertainers like Celia Cruz, Jon Secada, and Willy Chirino. The event drew over ten thousand people who heard Jorge Mas Santos call the tower the Cuban community's gift to South Florida and renew his pledge and that of the foundation: "I will not rest until one day these doors are opened again to shout to the world that Cuba is free."[40]

Many among Mas Santos's audience had personal history with the building. "All the help I needed, I got here," said a man holding a large Cuban flag. One woman recounted how she was ten years old when she came to the United States in 1962 and that she was brought to the tower directly from the airport. There, she was given a brooch of the Virgin Mary that she still treasured. She was overjoyed by the idea of renovating the tower. "This is something beautiful," M. Mayra Najara said. "The museum means a lot to us. It was our first home. It gave us security."[41]

The Cuban American National Foundation hoped the new museum would be ready by May 20, 2002, for the hundredth anniversary of Cuban independence. The tower was also meant to house the offices of the CANF. In order to prepare this new facility, the restoration of the building would require another $40 million. The Mas family had committed $20 million to the project, and it was hoped through events like the inauguration gala and with the help of other private donors the rest of the funds could be raised.[42]

The Mas family and the Cuban American National Foundation were ultimately unable to materialize the promise of a museum in the Freedom Tower. In February 2005 the Mas family sold the building to the Terra Group, and the controversy over its preservation and the construction of the condominium tower began to rage. In time the Terra Group was threatened with the possibility

Figure 8. Downtown Miami photographed from the north, 2008. The Freedom Tower can be seen center right, close to the American Airlines Arena. Photograph by Marc Averette.

Figure 9. Preserved Freedom Tower in the midst of a constantly changing environment, Miami, Florida, 2007. Photograph by Marc Averette.

the promise of the Freedom Tower becoming a museum of the Cuban diaspora by opening the Cuban Diaspora Cultural Legacy Gallery, a "permanent space dedicated to the impact of Cuban culture on South Florida and throughout the world," and by hosting exhibits like the Miami Herald Media's pictorial exhibit *The Exile Experience: Journey to Freedom*.[46] The Freedom Tower has also served as an educational space and been used for private events that take advantage of the tower's history and beauty.

One such event occurred in April 2015 when Cuban American senator Marco Rubio announced he would be seeking the Republican presidential nomination in 2016. At the announcement Rubio made allusion to the opportunities afforded his parents once they left Cuba for the United States, leading one supporter to declare he loved the senator's "immigrant story."[47] One member of the Miami press remarked on the location of the announcement, explaining to readers its status as "Miami's Ellis Island." He also noted the fact it would not hurt Rubio's cause that the tower was a photogenic setting "with a GOP-friendly name like the 'Freedom Tower.'"[48] The author of the piece did not note the irony, however, of Rubio, an ardent small-government conservative, announcing his bid for the presidency at a location best known as the site from which massive government expenditures were disbursed as part of a vast federal assistance program.

A Future Preserved

The Freedom Tower is now a quaint and distinctive part of the Miami skyline, but one that is often dwarfed by surrounding structures, including the American Airlines Arena (Figure 8). *El refugio* remains a significant part of Miami's shared history. For the Cuban American community, the Freedom Tower is a symbol of the welcome a group of exiles received in a strange country. For the city of Miami, the Freedom Tower is the physical representation of the rapid changes that came to South Florida in the decades following the Cuban Revolution. Ultimately, the battle to preserve the Freedom Tower mirrored the struggles in the city between a powerful new social

of a lawsuit against it by Cuban American attorney and activist Rafael Peñalver. Peñalver sat on the board of directors of the Dade Heritage Trust, and he insisted the building was a symbol of freedom and hope and as such was "something that we should pass on to our children and the future generations."[43]

The Terra Group ultimately relented. The group's chief executive, Pedro Martin, held a news conference on a terrace overlooking the tower and noted the building was the first place he went after arriving in Miami as a Cuban refugee. Speaking in Spanish, he recalled the history of the building as a haven for the refugees: "We hear the voices of the children that went there for medical attention. We hear the voices of our mothers who gave us hope," Martin stated. "Here we don't forget the tears of the Cuban families . . . the voices of the greatest patriots who have fought for Cuba's freedom." Martin and the Terra Group presented the building, including the printing facility in the back, as a donation to Miami Dade College. The Terra Group's condominium tower might still be built on land adjacent to the property, but the donation ensured the structural integrity of the building and that it would be maintained as a cultural space.[44]

In August 2012, Miami Dade College formally opened their Museum of Art + Design, dedicating seventeen thousand square feet as art exhibit space.[45] Miami Dade College also fulfilled and ethnic group attempting to secure the gains it had made, other groups fearing displacement because of those gains, and the forces of transnational capitalism that had converged upon South Florida's Gateway to the Americas.

The tower's size had been insufficient for an office building fifty years before the preservation battles (Figure 9). Functionally, the building was not worth preserving. The tower was simply too small to serve as a modern commercial property. The former production space was extremely limited, and the traffic concerns that had plagued the *Miami News* distribution trucks in the late 1950s were now far worse. Multiple efforts to make the building commercially viable had failed. Incorporating the front of the tower into a modern housing complex would have required sacrificing the building's historical integrity. The building primarily served as a symbol for an ethnic group that had gained a significant amount of political and economic power in the five decades since the *Miami News* vacated the structure.

The drive to preserve the building came at a time when the Cuban American community's gains appeared to be endangered or diminished. By preserving the Freedom Tower as the embodiment of the struggles and successes of the Cuban community in Miami and in the United States, the building could serve as a message to the city and to the country of the community's broader aspirations and reach. Beyond being the launch pad for the ambitions of a bright, young Cuban politician, the structure served as the point of origin for a powerful ethnic group that fundamentally changed its host city and would have a significant say in the foreign policy of its host country. Preserving the Freedom Tower ensured that the first decades of the postrevolutionary Cuban American community's journey would be memorialized, whatever future decades might bring. The Freedom Tower's persistence ensures that it will continue to serve as a spiritual beacon for the Cuban community in times of need.

AUTHOR BIOGRAPHY

Mauricio F. Castro earned a PhD in American history from Purdue University in 2015.

NOTES

1. Joaquim Utset, "Polémica decision con la Torre de la Libertad," *El nuevo herald,* July 31, 2005.

2. Miguel A. De La Torre, *La Lucha for Cuba: Religion and Politics on the Streets of Miami* (Berkeley: University of California Press, 2003), 37.

3. Nina Korman, "Free at Last," *Miami New Times,* May 17–23, 2001.

4. Gail Meadows, "¿Se salvará la Torre de la Libertad? Voto será decisivo," *El nuevo herald,* August 9, 1997.

5. Freedom Tower Foundation, "An Inspiring Beacon," *Miami Herald,* May 17, 2001, special section.

6. Louis A. Pérez Jr., *On Becoming Cuban: Identity, Nationality, and Culture* (Chapel Hill: University of North Carolina Press, 1999), 432–33.

7. Korman, "Free at Last."

8. Stephen Smith, "Freedom Tower Part of Past, Future for Architect," *Miami Herald,* May 13, 2001.

9. Fabiola Santiago, "Freedom Tower to Get New Life, Mark Exiles' History," *Miami Herald,* May 13, 2001.

10. Smith, "Freedom Tower Part of Past."

11. Tracy S. Voorhees, "Report to the President of the United States on the Cuban Refugee Problem," 1961, Folder T. S. Voorhees President's Representative for Cuban Refugees—Documents—Reports—TSV Final of Jan 18 1961, Box P, Tracy S. Voorhees Papers, Special Collections and University Archives, Rutgers University, New Brunswick, N.J.

12. Mauricio Castro, "Casablanca of the Caribbean: Cuban Refugees, Local Power, and Cold War Policy in Miami, 1959–1995" (PhD diss., Purdue University, 2015), 78.

13. Smith, "Freedom Tower Part of Past."

14. Cuban Refugee Program, "The Cuban Refugee Center, Freedom Tower, Miami, Florida: How It Operates," 1964, Folder 10, Box 1, Series I, Cuban Refugee Center Records, Cuban Heritage Collection, Coral Gables, Florida (Hereafter CHC).

15. In February 1961, while setting up the aims and structures of the CRP, Health, Education, and Welfare Secretary Abraham Ribicoff wrote that the federal government needed to ensure that "appropriate resettlement of Cuban refugees outside the Miami area be encouraged and supported" and that it should "provide supplemental support including such items as transportation and adjustment costs." See Abraham A. Ribicoff, "Report of Secretary Abraham A. Ribicoff on the Cuban Refugee Program," February 2,

1961, Folder 2, Box 1, Series I, Cuban Refugee Center Records, CHC.

16. The CRC provided office space for Catholic Relief Services, the Protestant Church World Service, the United Hebrew Immigrant Aid Society, and the nonsectarian International Rescue Committee. See Cuban Refugee Program, "The Cuban Refugee Center, Freedom Tower, Miami, Florida."

17. Cuban Refugee Program, "Fact Sheet," December 31, 1970, Folder 14, Box 1, Series I, Cuban Refugee Center Records, CHC.

18. María Cristina García, *Havana USA: Cuban Exiles and Cuban Americans in South Florida, 1959–1994* (Berkeley: University of California Press, 1996), 43.

19. Smith, "Freedom Tower Part of Past."

20. Sam Jacobs, "Bilingual Bill Passed by Dade," *Miami Herald,* April 17, 1973. The passage of the ordinance also helped resolve problems of governance created by a growing population of Spanish speakers. This was, however, largely the result of sustained activism by the increasingly empowered Cuban community. Even those members of Dade County's government who supported the ordinance were unsure how it would affect the day-to-day operations of government service agencies. Ultimately, the passage of the ordinance spoke to the growing power of the Cuban American community. See Mauricio Castro, "Casablanca of the Caribbean," 169–70.

21. Susan Harrigan, "Blemished Bloom," *Wall Street Journal,* November 28, 1979.

22. Harrigan, "Blemished Bloom."

23. García, *Havana USA,* 68.

24. Smith, "Freedom Tower Part of Past."

25. Meadows, "¿Se salvará la Torre de la Libertad?"

26. Smith, "Freedom Tower Part of Past."

27. Meadows, "¿Se salvará la Torre de la Libertad?"

28. Smith, "Freedom Tower Part of Past."

29. Tom Fiedler and Alfonso Chardy, "Goal of 'No More Mariels' Led to Clinton's Painful Choice," *Miami Herald,* May 3, 1995.

30. Christopher Marquis, Rachel L. Swarns, and Andres Viglucci, "Joy, Outrage Greet Cuba Policy Shift," *Miami Herald,* May 3, 1995.

31. Jim Hampton, "Why We're for New Cuba Policy," editorial, *Miami Herald,* May 7, 1995.

32. Ann Louise Bardach, "Our Man in Miami," *New Republic,* October 3, 1994, 20.

33. Lisa Getter and Jeff Leen, "Suit Prompts Tough Look at Mas Canosa in Depositions," *Miami Herald,* August 2, 1996.

34. "The Future of Elian Gonzalez," *New York Times,* November 30, 1999.

35. "Lightning Move Took Agents Just 154 Seconds," *Miami Herald,* April 23, 2000.

36. Fabiola Santiago, Daniel de Vise, and Martin Merzer, "Raid Stuns, Enthralls Fractured Public," *Miami Herald,* April 23, 2000.

37. Fabiola Santiago, "Freedom Tower to Get New Life."

38. Santiago, "Freedom Tower to Get New Life."

39. See Freedom Tower Foundation, "The Freedom Tower . . . A Dream Come True," *Miami Herald,* May 17, 2001, special section.

40. Elaine De Valle, "Freedom Tower Gala Lures Thousands," *Miami Herald,* May 20. 2001.

41. De Valle, "Freedom Tower Gala Lures Thousands."

42. De Valle, "Freedom Tower Gala Lures Thousands."

43. Oscar Pedro Musibay, "Fighting for the 'Grandeur' of the Freedom Tower," *Miami Daily Business Review,* November 11, 2005.

44. Oscar Pedro Musibay, "Freedom Tower Developer Gives Miami Landmark to College," *Miami Daily Business Review,* December 1, 2005.

45. "MDC Museum of Art + Design History," Miami Dade College website, http://mdcmoad.org/about/history.aspx.

46. *The Legacy of the Cuban Cultural Diaspora* exhibit focused on the contributions of the Cuban exile community in areas including business, literature, and the visual arts, among others. *The Exile Experience: A Journey to Freedom* exhibit included news photographs of the experiences of the refugees arriving in the United States. See "Exhibitions" under "Freedom Tower," Miami Dade College website, http://www.mdcmoad.org/freedom-tower/exhibitions.aspx.

47. Patrick O'Connor, "Marco Rubio Kicks Off 2016 Campaign with Miami Speech," *Wall Street Journal,* April 13, 2015.

48. Tim Elfrink, "Marco Rubio's Freedom Tower Presidential Announcement: What You Need to Know," *Miami New Times,* April 13, 2015.

DANA E. BYRD

Motive Power

Fans, Punkahs, and Fly Brushes in the Antebellum South

ABSTRACT

In many elite Southern homes, punkahs, ceiling-mounted fans manipulated by enslaved workers, were an integral part of the architecture of the dining room in the antebellum United States. Paralleling their relationship to American slavery was their use in British India, where the fans had a long history of being powered by low-caste workers. Pushing past the fans' decorative and utilitarian qualities, this essay examines the devices' shifting relationship to slavery and freedom through an examination of their operation within the spaces of elite homes. Both planters and their workers benefited, albeit differently, from their interactions with the fans. Elite planters enjoyed the fans' cooling breezes, insect-free mealtimes, and the opportunity to display their wealth and refinement. Even though they were consigned to labor at the fans, enslaved workers likely used their proximity to elite whites to learn "genteel" codes of behavior, while gleaning information about the plantation world and beyond. The end of slavery did not mark the end of punkahs; rather, the fans were used to celebrate the "noble" history of the Old South while eliding any reference of slavery.

In the dining rooms of antebellum Southern homes, slaves manually powered large fans—variously known as punkahs, shoo-flies, or great fans—to cool diners and keep insects away from the dining table. These fans were an integral part of the architecture of many Southern dining rooms and more than decorative and utilitarian elements. They represented opportunity: elite planters demonstrated their wealth, while the enslaved youth who operated the punkahs were privy to elite conversations and able to engage with local and national current events for their own and their communities' benefit. Today, the fans remain fixed in historic house museums and private homes across the South. Although they are no longer operated by enslaved workers, their presence testifies to the enduring relationship between slavery and the region's material culture (Figure 1). More than thirty examples survive across the United States, with extant objects clustered in Virginia, Mississippi, and Louisiana.

In the antebellum period, flies and other insects were rightly understood to be conveyers of disease. Domestic manuals, including Mary Randolph's *The Virginia Housewife* and the more popular *Southern Gardener* and journals such as *DeBow's Review,* contained instructional texts advising readers how to best deter the flying creatures. These journals counseled audiences (especially Southerners) to envelop their bedsteads in mosquito netting to avoid disease. Some authors advocated the use throughout the house of flycatchers filled with sweet syrupy solution to trap the pests, while author Phineas Thornton suggested leaving a mix of brown sugar, cream, and pepper on the sideboard to "destroy flies" (Figure 2).[1] All these texts encouraged repelling flies from the dining room at mealtime. The punkah, designed to move air to prevent insects from

settling on the table, was an ornamental health measure.

William Marshall Merrick's drawing of a fly-plagued teatime in Alexandria, Virginia, dramatizes the experience of being persecuted by insects during one's meal (Figure 3).[2] The punkah's design aimed to ameliorate these conditions. In theory, when the rope attached to the fan was pulled, most punkahs circulated enough air to prevent flies and other insects from settling on food or diners.

Although such fans were used in dining rooms throughout the antebellum South, their appearance varied according to local traditions. The construction of these fans also varied widely: some were improvised from local materials such as pine, cypress, or walnut, whereas others were carefully crafted on a grand scale, making use of precious and expensive woods such as highly figured mahogany. The single commonality among these American fans was that they were inextricably intertwined with the institution of chattel slavery.

American fans and their South Asian precedents as well as more ephemeral related objects such as fly brushes—smaller, portable handheld devices—were kept in motion by slaves and servants to ensure the comfort of the ruling class.[3] Curiously, the American fans were rarely recorded in estate inventories, advertised for sale by craftsmen, photographed, or depicted in antebellum illustrations. *The Party at Supper & Breakfast, Chapman's Springs*, a watercolor by traveling artist Lewis Miller (1796–1882) is believed to be

Figure 3. William Marshall Merrick, *Tea*, Alexandria, Virginia, July 14, 1860. Pencil drawing in sketchbook. Print Division, New York Public Library.

the only extant image of an antebellum punkah in use (Figure 4).[4] Now preserved at Colonial Williamsburg, it depicts a three-leaved punkah fluttering above a lively dinner party. The table is anchored at one end by the party's host, who carves meat, and at the other end by the hostess, who pours a hot beverage. Enslaved servants attend to them at the table: one delivers a beverage; another carries a loaf of bread; a third one is tasked with managing the fan. The fringed and patterned fan extends the length of the table. Although Miller's image does not depict any insects and the medium of watercolor cannot capture the sense of the heat plaguing the diners, we must imagine the conditions that such fans were intended to counteract.

Miller's watercolor is a rare document testifying to the punkah's presence in Southern dining rooms. However, the device's placement and use appear to differ from those of the Indian punkah and suggest American fans, unlike those in India, were not used just for cooling. One would expect that if the device were solely to cool, it would be found in every area of the house, including parlors, halls, and bedrooms. The American punkah's

placement in the dining room distinguished it from its likely British Indian precedent, which was used in a variety of spaces.

The Indian Punkah

The origin of the word *punkah* dates to the seventeenth century and is given in the Oxford English Dictionary as a Hindi modification of the Sanskrit word *paksa* (wing), a term used to describe the large wing-like fans hung from the ceiling in British Indian homes; the worker tasked with operating these fans was dubbed a *punkah-wallah*.[5] One East India Company historian claimed the punkah was a late eighteenth-century invention by a British clerk who, in a desperate attempt to circulate air, suspended a table leaf from the ceiling of his room. Other evidence shows the design had existed for centuries in South Asia.[6] These large fabric-covered wooden frames were found in British Indian residences and churches, and they were ubiquitous in upper-class British Indian homes from the eighteenth century until Indian independence in 1947 (Figure 5).

The use of punkahs was so deeply ingrained in colonial British culture that nineteenth-century school children at home in England read about the fans in India as part of their education. Notably, a passage from the pages of *Children of India Written for the Children of England* (1884), a Sunday school chapbook, offered churchgoing children a detailed description of the punkah and its use:

Another thing the English people have in their rooms in the hot weather is a very large fan, called a punkah. It is a light frame of wood covered with calico, with a short curtain fastened to it; the frame is hung from the ceiling by ropes, another rope is a passed through the wall to a servant outside, who pulls it backwards and forwards, and so makes a little air in the room. They keep on doing this all day and all night. I believe some of the men are so clever, that they can go to sleep and yet not stop pulling; but sometimes they do stop, and then, even if the English people are asleep, they feel the heat directly, and wake up.[7]

This passage reinforces the fact that English polite society, even in India, was ordered through hierarchies of race and class. Young Indian boys labored to provide comfort to English people. Since these young Indian children were subject peoples of the imperial British state, the Sunday school children in England were in effect being socialized by the text to understand themselves as colonizers. Children were taught to view the Indian body as a literal extension of a machine designed to increase their own comfort. Britons in India, as Mark Harrison argues, feared that without these protective measures the foreign climate would degenerate their minds and bod-

Figure 4. Lewis Miller, *The Party at Supper and Breakfast*, in *Sketchbook of Landscapes in the State of Virginia*, 1853–67. Watercolor on paper. Abby Aldrich Rockefeller Folk Art Museum, Colonial Williamsburg Foundation, gift of Dr. and Mrs. Richard M. Kain in memory of George Hay Kain.

Figure 5. Punkah, Church of St. Francis at Fort Kochi, Kerala, India, building 1503, punkah circa 1795. Photograph by Anna Lise Seastrand, 2008.

ies.[8] Environment was a potent metaphor for differences between rulers and ruled, and the punkah mediated that difference.

The average Indian punkah consisted of a light wooden frame about fifteen feet long and four feet wide, over which was stretched a single piece of cloth or canvas, with a loose fringe or border on the lower edge. Indian punkahs were placed high on the ceiling and often hung along the walls of a room. This placement ensured the wallah was in a separate space, but not so far removed that he might lose control of the fan. From the veranda the punkah-wallah sat pulling the rope up and down with his hands, or occasionally, he lay on his back and pulled it with his feet. Punkahs could be found in all sorts of spaces and buildings in India. One observer noted, "There is a punkah over the sleeper in bed; over the preacher . . . in the pulpit; over the party at dinner, whether on land or sea; over every man, woman or child who wishes to breathe with any degree of ease."[9] The ubiquity of the punkah, powered by Indian subjects, contributed to the British conquest of the Indian subcontinent and made living conditions more tolerable for British rulers and residents.

By the late eighteenth century, the British Crown controlled a global empire of territories. In 1858 the Crown gained dominion over the Indian subcontinent by nationalizing the East India Company, which had ruled India since 1757. Britons who were appointed to govern the Indian colony or who went there to seek their fortune were likely to suffer the wretchedness of seasickness on the voyage out and were punished by the unforgiving climate and the agony of prickly heat after they arrived. One British traveler, Ellen Drummond, describing the painful affliction, wrote that it felt as though "a-hundred needles were running into her" until the dry heat of northern India "developed finally into an obsessive torture dominating thought and talk and action."[10] Company officials noted that the steamy heat of Bengal "takes all the strength and succour out of you like a vapour bath." India proved a torment to the British physique, and new arrivals found themselves in need of unfamiliar devices, such as the punkah, to ease their adjustment to an unfamiliar land.[11]

Illustrations of Indian punkahs circulated in the form of drawings, postcards, and photographs as a means of communicating the exotic circumstances of Britons adapting to India. A watercolor from 1863 is one such example; the double punkah fluttering overhead enables the seated woman to read comfortably in her Berhampore, West Bengal, parlor despite the torrid climate (Figure 6). At the same time, the punkah is one of the few exotic details in the fashionable parlor, which is well appointed with Victorian scroll-foot furniture and a Persian carpet. In this watercolor, moreover, the punkah-wallah's labor is invisible. Scenes like this one recurred in images of Britons in India produced for those at home and abroad and served to disseminate information about the punkah's role in ameliorating the oppressive heat.

To cope with the forbidding climate, Britons in India also adopted other aspects of local architecture by building thatched bungalows or flat-roofed houses made from plastered brick, called *pucka,* or renting them from wealthy Indians. The typical mat-built, thatched country house followed Indian models, with a single story, a veranda, and a gently sloped gabled or hipped roof.[12] Over time solid masonry structures built in India also came to be known as bungalows. Bungalows stood alone on large plots, separating their owners from Indians who lived in the surrounding villages. Britons and Indians alike associated such structures specifically with British authority over local lands and, more generally, with British control over the subcontinent.[13] In urban centers middle- and upper-class Britons and Indians lived in one- or two-story pucka homes with flat roofs attached to classical façades and with plaster walls all around each lot to create a compound.[14] A fusion of Indian forms and techniques with classical architectural features made these homes symbols of foreign rule. A legion of Indian servants constantly circulated through the homes of Britons who possessed even moderate wealth.[15]

Britons also adopted other local Indian traditions of furnishing and room use to obtain relief from the heat.[16] Cots consisting of thin mattresses over interlaced rattan strips were lighter, cheaper, and cooler than European-style bedsteads.[17] Windows were covered with wetted woven grass mats called *tatties.* Roofed verandas constructed of wood or bamboo gave Britons access to the outdoors without subjecting them to full exposure to the elements. The ground floor of houses was reserved for storage and service rooms, unlike in Britain or America, where the rooms on that level were typically the parlor, dining room, and kitchen. Middle- and upper-class homes in London, Philadelphia, and Natchez had sharply delineated spaces separated by solid locking doors, and discrete servant quarters. The upstairs living spaces of similar homes in Indian cities flowed together, as the rooms often lacked doors (and most of the doors that did exist had no locks), and there were no dedicated living quarters for servants.

The British in India used the punkah and other architectural means in a variety of spaces to ameliorate the harsh climactic conditions of subtropical India and to signal their dominance over the indigenous population. Paralleling the relationship of colonizer to the colonized, the deployment of these fans required low-caste Indian workers to labor for their British masters. In a related fashion, punkah use in the United States was similarly marked by political conditions; in the American case chattel slavery required enslaved laborers to work for the benefit of their masters. Although punkah use in the United States was limited to the dining rooms of antebellum Southern homes, the object was no less significant.

The Punkah in Antebellum America

Just as Britons in India were securing conditions of maximum comfort for themselves between the seventeenth and nineteenth centuries, exported Indian goods were becoming fashionable in Britain and the United States. Turbans, banyans, and textiles that could be fashioned into "Indianesque" muslin dresses were especially the rage in Anglo-America at the turn of the nineteenth century. Philadelphia merchants, such as E. M. Dougal, imported large shipments

of turbans from London, which had in turn come from India. Dougal advertised "Rich India Turbans," gold and muslin turbans, as well as "Silver spangled turbans, with silver thistles" and "white crap'd turbans with argus plumes."[18] According to an 1819 American reprint of London's *La Belle Assemblée,* "madras turbans still continue in vogue; those made of real Madras handkerchiefs, royal blue and orange in color, are most in estimation."[19] One Southerner, John Steele, wrote from Philadelphia to his wife at home in Rowan County, North Carolina, in 1797 that "the turban is the fashionable head dress," particularly to accompany "a new dress for ladies . . . made of muslin [that] hangs loose all round."[20] Historian Jonathan Eacott has outlined the popularity of "India goods," which in the United States extended beyond turbans to shawls, sun umbrellas, and even fragrances, and he noted the importance of ports along the eastern seaboard in the dissemination of India-related goods and fashions.[21] Although there are no known accounts of punkahs im-

ported from India to the West, their popularity in the United States may be linked to the antebellum craze for all things Indian.

A punkah in a 1932 photograph from Tallwood Plantation in Albemarle County, Virginia, suggests the relationship between Indian models and American examples. According to family history, Fulwar Skipwith, an American diplomat and politician, procured the punkah from India for his aunt, Helen Skipwith Coles.[22] Known only through visual documentation, this punkah was probably not made or acquired in India. Unlike Indian forms, it was constructed of a triangular wood-framed panel covered with wallpaper and embellished with classical motifs (Figure 7). However, it does resemble Indian punkahs in one important respect: it was hung from a wooden pole that passed through an aperture in the wall between the dining room and the tearoom. According to family lore, the young enslaved boy who operated the fan was separated from the room being fanned. The first-floor plan of Tallwood made in

Figure 6. *A Woman Reading under a Punkah in a Comfortably Furnished Room,* circa 1863. Inscribed on reverse: "Mrs Gladstone Lingham's drawing room at her residence in Berhampore, 1863." Watercolor on paper. Courtesy British Library, London, U.K. Copyright the British Library Board, WD 2904.

1932 illustrates this arrangement (Figure 8). The young boy would have demonstrated considerable dexterity as he manipulated the fan at a remove in the Indian style. He would have kept the swinging fan in constant motion to ensure it created a sufficient breeze to keep flies from settling on the food without creating a current so strong it would extinguish the candles on the table.

At Tallwood the removal of the slave from the room would have also insulated diners and their conversations from the slave. This form of the punkah isolated the servant from the master and his peers and had the effect of creating separate zones of labor and leisure. In other words, the slave would have operated the punkah from a workroom while the master, his family, and his guests enjoyed a meal in a space of their own dedicated to leisure.[23] In this case, maintaining the original form of punkah operation, derived from India, kept slaves out of privileged spaces for extended periods of time. The Tallwood punkah is the only known fan actually installed in the United States to have removed the actual labor of the punkah operator to a different space, although other manually operated fans, some known through designs and others through extant examples, have been documented in antebellum Virginia.[24]

The most intriguing of the Virginia examples is a design created by Thomas Jefferson for use at Monticello, the home and estate that he began to build in 1770 when he was twenty-six years old (Figure 9).[25] Although the fan he designed was never installed, its intended arrangement was similar to that of the Tallwood punkah in its isolation of labor from leisure. Jefferson's fan, however, did not need to be powered by a slave; it was automatic, relying on a clock jack for its operation. It excluded the slave from the dining room and any sensitive conversations held within, thus giving paramount importance to privacy rather than to the extravagant display of labor. Jefferson's design for this automated fan, which cleverly eliminated slaves' exposure to the conversation and behavior of the elite, also fit neatly with Jefferson's program of isolating the gentry from enslaved labor.[26]

Jefferson's strategies for limiting the visibility of enslaved servants at meals were in contrast to the dining practices at most Southern plantations, where noontime and evening meals formed part of an elaborate pageant designed to ensure maximum pleasure for the planter class while demonstrating to visitors the wealth and taste of the homeowners. Mealtimes were elegant and included luxurious surroundings, flavorful food, and sumptuous service, all of which promised contented consumption. On large plantations enslaved servants prepared and served these elaborate meals in a manner that celebrated the complexity of the dining service.[27] For example, in some regions of the South, to enhance the dining experience, the owners of plantations with large staffs of house servants often obliged them to dress in livery at mealtimes—a practice that continued through the first half of the nineteenth century.[28] In South Carolina, Jacob Read dressed his slaves, including the eventual runaway Mungo, in "brown Yorkshire cloth lined with white, with a scarlet cape [collar]."[29]

A planter's wealth could be divined by the number of slaves he owned, and the allocation of a single slave to the task of pulling a punkah's cord made the master's wealth visible. Regardless of which particular device was used to repel flying insects—a punkah or a more portable fly

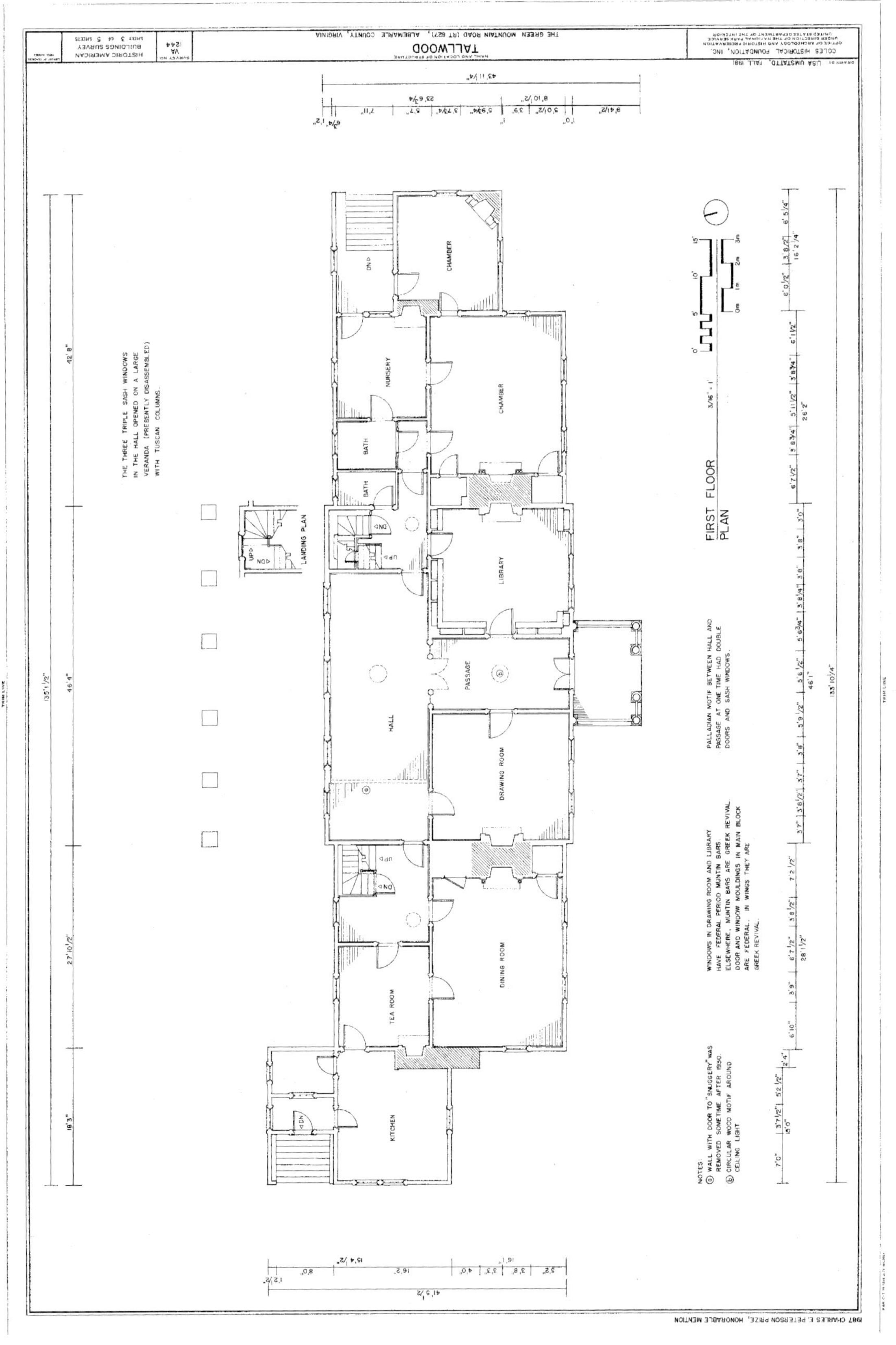

Figure 8. First-floor plan, Tallwood Plantation, Green Mountain, Virginia, 1981. Lisa Umstattd, Historic American Buildings Survey VA 12–44, Library of Congress, Washington, D.C.

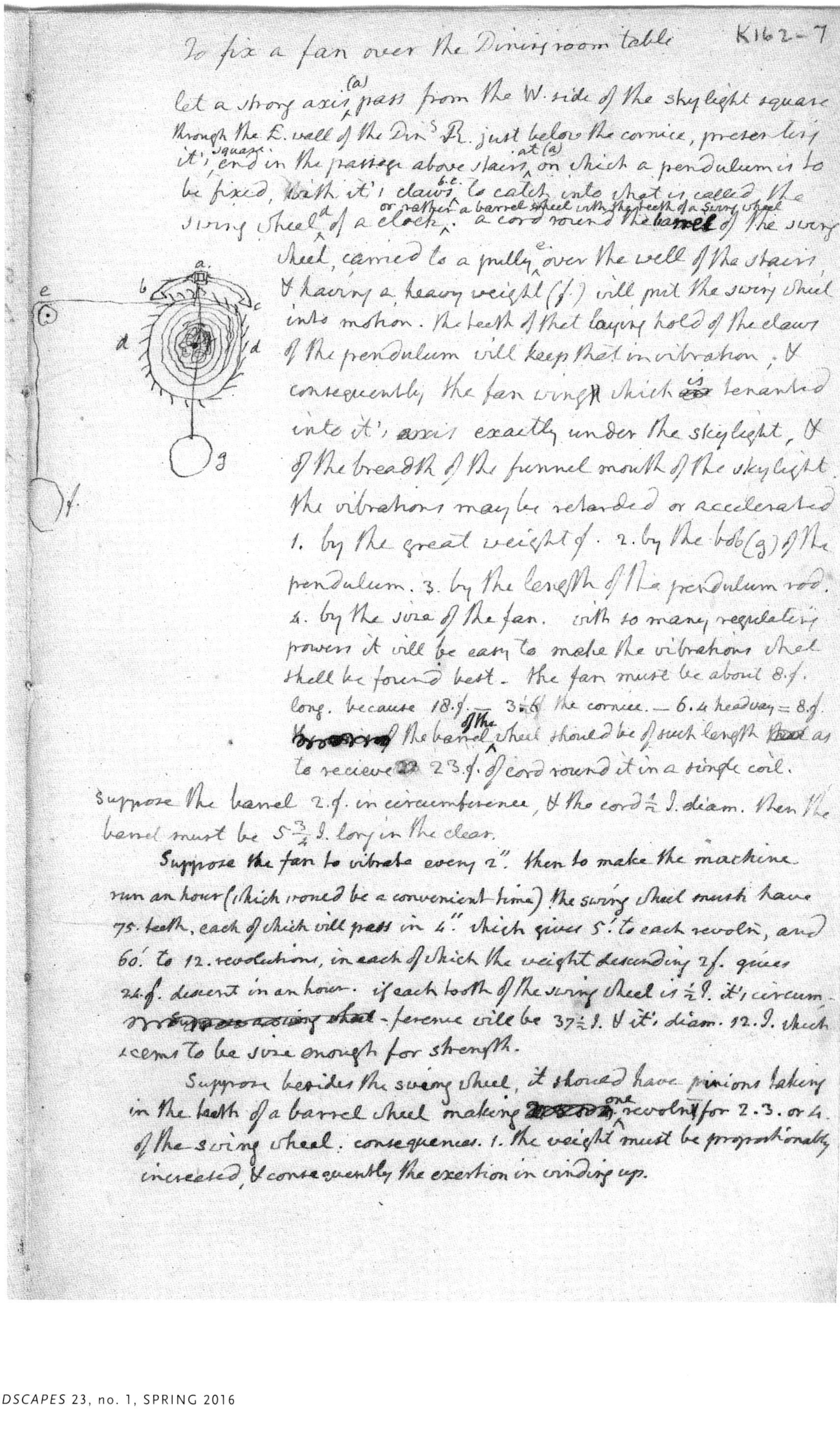

Figure 9. "To Fix a Fan," in Thomas Jefferson, *Notebook of Improvements, Monticello* (Virginia, 1804–7), pl. 162. The Coolidge Collection of Thomas Jefferson Manuscripts at the Massachusetts Historical Society.

To fix a fan over the Dining room table   K162–7

let a strong axis (a) pass from the W. side of the skylight square
through the E. wall of the Din.s R. just below the cornice, presenting
it's squar'd end in the passage above stairs, on which a pendulum is to
be fixed, with it's claws b.c. to catch into what is called the
swing wheel.d of a clock. or rather a barrel wheel with the teeth of a swing wheel. a cord round the barrel of the swing
wheel, carried to a pulley e over the well of the stairs,
& having a heavy weight (f.) will put the swing wheel
into motion. the teeth of that laying hold of the claws
of the pendulum will keep that in vibration, &
consequently the fan wings which is tenanted
into it's axis exactly under the skylight, &
of the breadth of the funnel mouth of the skylight.
the vibrations may be retarded or accelerated
1. by the great weight f. 2. by the bob (g) of the
pendulum. 3. by the length of the pendulum rod.
4. by the size of the fan.   with so many regulating
powers it will be easy to make the vibrations which
shall be found best. the fan must be about 8.f.
long. because 18.f. — 3.f. the cornice. — 6.4 headway = 8.f.
the barrel of the wheel should be of such length as
to recieve 23.f. of cord round it in a single coil.
suppose the barrel 2.f. in circumference, & the cord ½ I. diam. then the
barrel must be 5¾ I. long in the clear.
    Suppose the fan to vibrate every 2″. then to make the machine
run an hour (which would be a convenient time) the swing wheel must have
75. teeth, each of which will pass in 4″ which gives 5.′ to each revoln, and
60.′ to 12. revolutions, in each of which the weight descending 2.f. gives
24.f. descent in an hour. if each tooth of the swing wheel is ½ I. it's circumference will be 37½ I. & it's diam. 12. I. which
seems to be size enough for strength.
    Suppose besides the swing wheel, it should have pinions taking
in the teeth of a barrel wheel making one revoln for 2.3. or 4.
of the swing wheel. consequences. 1. the weight must be proportionally
increased, & consequently the exertion in winding up.

brush—the decision to have it powered by an enslaved worker for the comfort of diners would have undoubtedly been regarded as an extravagant use of labor. Just as food that required a great deal of time, labor, and elaborate utensils to prepare conferred the prestige of elevated purchasing power on the host, so did assigning a slave to operating the punkah signify wealth.

Consider the example of the punkah at Prestwould Plantation, in Clarksville, Mecklenburg County, Virginia (Figure 10). Leila and Humberston Skipwith, cousins of the owners of Tallwood Plantation, commissioned a fan from Petersburg cabinetmaker Samuel White.[30] It relied on wallpaper for most of its ornamentation, and its construction was an improvised adaptation of a familiar form—a bed rail modified into the hanging apparatus for a fan. This construction choice suggests that the Prestwould fan was an anomaly in White's oeuvre and, perhaps, in that of other cabinetmakers in that region of Virginia as well. The unwieldy construction was cumbersome to operate, as the slave was required to stand beneath the window and power the fan by using both hands to move a pair of chains attached to it. Although elements of the Prestwould and Tallwood punkahs, such as the triangular shape and the use of wallpaper as ornament, are similar, they afforded different experiences at the two plantations: at Tallwood the slave was insulated from the diners, whereas at Prestwould the slave was required to perform an action that put him and his labor in full view as part of the spectacle of mealtime service. In fact, the very system of bondage that enabled planters to extract labor from black slaves depended on the master maintaining the appearance of constant surveillance.

Henry Coleman, a former slave who worked the Fairfield Plantation in McClellanville, Charleston County, South Carolina, gave the following account of his fly brush preparation, use, and misuse when he was a boy, as recorded during the late 1930s by a Works Progress Administration interviewer, Caldwell Sims, when Coleman was eighty-two:

> In dem days de dining room wuz big and had de windos open all de summer long. . . . Quick as de mess of victuals began to come on de table, a little nigger boy was put up in de swing, I calls it, over de table to fan de flies and gnats off'en de Missus' victuals. Dis swing wus just off'n de end of de long table. Some of de white fokes had steps a leadin' up to it. . . . Well, when I got my pants, my maw fetched me in and I clumb up de steps dat Marse Johnson had, to git up in his swing wid. At fus dey had to show me jus how to hole de brush, kaise dem peacock feathers wuz so long, iffen you didn't mind your bizness, de ends of dem feathers would splash in de gravy er sumpin nother, and den de Missus table be all spattered up. Some o' de Marsters would whorp de chilluns fer dat carelessness, but Marse Johnson, he always good to his niggers. . . . It twad'nt long for I got used to it and I nebber did splash de feathers in no rations. But iffen I got used to it, I took to again to sleep up thar. Marse Johnson, he would just git up and wake me up. All de white fokes at the table joke me so bout bein' so lazy, I soon stop dat foolishness. My maw, she roll her eyes at me when I come down atter de marster had to wake me up. Dat change like ever thing else.[31]

Sims's transcripts of the Coleman interview and others feature an exaggerated approximation of former slaves' dialect that is difficult to parse. In the quoted passage, Coleman describes his role in creating and operating a fly brush (peacock-feather fan). His mention that "some of de white fokes had steps a leadin' up to it" suggests that in the Santee River region, at least, it was fashionable to have a slave boy seated in a swing above the dining room table to shoo away the flies. Such labor required the slave's constant attention: any lapse, "iffen you didn't mind your bizness," could result in the peacock feathers making contact with the food. Coleman's reference to "when I got my pants" indicates that manipulating the brush was a task given only to slave children, often boys, who had matured enough to wear pants rather than the skirted dresses of younger years.[32] His invocation of "rations" belies his status as a slave and the fact that he was used to having his food distributions limited.[33]

Coleman's account prompts consideration of the experience of the servant while he operated the fan. For an enslaved worker this proximity was

dual-edged: slaves labored to ensure the comfort of their masters while ignoring their own discomfort. At the same time, they were able to capitalize on being able to see and hear their owners at the dinner table. If the fan placed the slave and his labor in full view of diners, the diners were placed in full view (and hearing) of the slave. A slave in this position was thus privy to the conversations of his master, with access to information traditionally reserved for white elites, which could be advantageous for him. He might learn vital information about the plantation and about local, national, or global events, as well as glean clues to understanding refined behaviors and practices.[34] Architectural historian Bernard L. Herman has argued that enslaved workers in Charleston, South Carolina, involved in the foiled Denmark Vesey conspiracy were able to outwit the planter's surveillance by "exploit[ing] the false confidence engendered in their perceived personas as animated furnishings."[35] Workers consigned to the punkah may have similarly exploited their position.

Booker T. Washington's 1901 autobiography contains a vivid narrative of his boyhood as a slave on Burroughs Plantation, near Hardy, in Franklin County, Virginia, during the early years of the Civil War, when his duties included manning a punkah: "When I had grown to sufficient size, I was required to go to the 'big house' at meal-times to fan the flies from the table by means of a large set of paper fans operated by a pulley. Naturally much of the conversation of the white people turned upon the subject of freedom and the war, and I observed a good deal of it."[36] In Washington's account, he appeared to be submissive to the master while he was in fact gathering information about the war and his status as a slave. We can imagine the punkah-pulling slave girl in Miller's watercolor, while at her mistress's beck and call, was also privy to vital information exchanged at the table, including habits of genteel behavior. This arrangement is called out visually in Miller's rendering; the servant stands and pulls the punkah directly behind her mistress (see Figure 4). Miller portrays the slave as her mistress's double, in dress and posture.

Similarly, Coleman's recollection of his operating the punkah includes a reference to his master and the verbal punishment he received when he failed to "mind his bizness." Coleman's master monitored him enough to ensure that he was doing his job, and he was able to observe his master and guests enough to glean information about their manners and mannerisms as well as the foremost concerns of the day. The ability to mimic genteel habits was a vital tool for enslaved workers planning to escape the bonds of slavery. Paul Gilroy has noted that "survival in slave regimes . . . promoted the acquisition of what we might now understand to be performance skills, and refined the appreciation of mimesis by both dominant and dominated . . . apart from the work involved in enacting their servitude and inferiority while guarding their autonomy, people found significant everyday triumphs."[37] Access to the codes of refined behavior occurred through a willful blindness of masters whose overriding concern was holding on to their slaves and preserving the system of slavery.

During the Civil War more than a few slaves who overheard information discussed at masters' dinner tables reported it to Northern army officers in hopes of gaining their freedom. Here is a report of one such instance recorded in the diary of Catherine Ann Devereux Edmondston, wife of a planter in Halifax County, North Carolina:

> August 18, 1863. . . . All of our negroes have left together with two of Sister Mats and seventeen of Williams, indeed negro property is worse than useless for they do no work unless they choose & the owners dare not correct them else off they go and report at Moscow & then he (the master) may look out the next raid that is made. I wish sometimes that there was not a negro left in the country, for they keep the Federals informed of everything & they (the Federals) are always ready to believe & act on what the negroes tell. And as to the idea of a *faithful servant, it is all a fiction*. I have seen the favourite & most petted negroes the first to leave in every instance. So disgusted have I become with the whole race that I often wish I had never seen *one* & tho the learning to do our own work would be hard, I believe we would all be happier & healthier.[38]

Enslaved workers' attempts to gather information were not limited to self-promotion. Slaves' desire for knowledge constituted a deep engagement with the currents of modern events, and their understanding and strategic deployment of ideas with power in the "white" public sphere. As an example, the slaves who ran to the federal fortress in Pensacola, Florida, in the spring of 1861 placed their actions very much in light of the secession crisis, just as those who ran to Benjamin Butler at Fortress Monroe knew their actions had broad implications.[39] These small individual instances illustrate a broad and important phenomenon whereby the enslaved did more than just gain individual advantage from overheard conversations. Thus slaves' knowledge extracted from exposure to whites could lead to freedom or, in the case of Booker T. Washington, could spark the hope that freedom was within his or his community's grasp.

Afterlives of the Punkahs

Despite its close association with slavery, the punkah endured beyond emancipation. The formation of Southern historic house museums, heritage celebrations, a thriving market for antique and reproduction punkahs, and even popular films disseminated knowledge of the fan. Without slave labor to operate it, the punkah functioned as a prism, refracting different postbellum aims: early object historians used it to recall the noble grandeur of the Old South; reenactors used it to stoke nostalgia for the antebellum era; collectors of regional decorative arts acquired examples of the form; and museum curators seized upon the fan as a necessary element for accurately furnishing historic house museums. These circumstances extended the utility of the punkah beyond emancipation.

In January 1862, less than a year after the Battle of Fort Sumter, two inventors, R. P. Moore and N. Thompson of Box Springs, Georgia, registered a patent for a mosquito and fly brush machine with the Confederate Patent Office in Richmond, Virginia.[40] They invented the device because they could see that slavery was bound to end sooner or later in the United States. Their intention was to replace the comfort produced

Figure 11. Fly fan, circa 1893. Wood, brass, and cotton, height 24 inches, width 50 inches. Private collection. Photograph by Dana E. Byrd, 2006. For a detailed image, see the online version of this article at JSTOR.

through the system of chattel slavery, in this case by substituting a machine for the punkah puller. In that respect their invention was related to Jefferson's design for an automatic fan. Unfortunately, during the fall of Richmond in April 1865, most of the models and documents pertaining to Confederate patents were lost; if any examples of Moore and Thompson's invention did survive, they have not yet come to light. One invention that has survived is an automatic fly fan patented by H. S. Brewington in 1885 (Figures 11 and 12).[41] The fan's two arms resemble fly swatters, and they can be adjusted to increase the range of the circulating air that they generate. This pair of inventions, the automatic tabletop fly fan and Moore and Thompson's mechanized fan, were in the vanguard of devices designed to automate tasks that had been performed by slaves.

Slavery certainly heralded the end of the punkah's everyday use, but changing tastes also contributed to its decline. In the United States before the Civil War, the punkah had been deployed

Figure 12. Fly fan label, circa 1893. Paper. Private collection. Photograph by Dana E. Byrd, 2006.

only in dining rooms, where it was a device and a design choice, serving as the room's visual focal point and harmonizing with its existing décor of moldings or wallpaper. The use of a punkah also eliminated the ability to employ elaborate candlelit chandeliers. However, the innovation of gas fixtures was irresistible to some, and gasoliers (chandeliers fitted with gaslights) resulted in the punkah's disappearance from some dining rooms and its ever more frequent consignment to porches and attics.[42] As seen in a Historic American Buildings Survey photograph from the early twentieth century, members of the Koontz-Beltzhoover family, who owned Green Leaves in Natchez, Adams County, Mississippi, removed the punkah to the front porch and installed a fashionable Bohemian crystal chandelier in the place of honor in their dining room (Figure 13).[43]

As punkahs were physically relegated to attics and porches, these objects came alive in ex-slave testimonies collected as part of the WPA's Federal Writers' Project in the 1930s. Coleman's description of operating a fly brush is perhaps the most extensive account of that device, but numerous

other freed slaves remembered their time in service in the creation and manipulation of punkahs or fly brushes. In popular culture such films as *Jezebel* (1938) and *Gone with the Wind* (1939) included scenes showing Southerners being cooled and kept free of flies by such fans. In *Jezebel,* after Bette Davis's character, Julie Marsden, and her family learn that there is an outbreak of yellow fever in New Orleans, they seek refuge at their country estate, Halcyon Plantation. The punkah appears as part of the backdrop of elegant furnishings that evoke the antebellum plantation, circa 1852, as a physical and spiritual haven for whites.[44] *Gone with the Wind,* one of the most popular films of all time, established a flawed but powerful visual grammar for antebellum plantation life.[45] The "heroine" of that film, Scarlett O'Hara (played by Vivien Leigh), is depicted as a headstrong, vivacious Southern belle who is tested by the tribulations of lost love and the destruction of her beloved plantation, Tara, and the Southern way of life during the Civil War and Reconstruction. In a scene early in the film, Scarlett demonstrates her independence from the conventional mores of Southern white women by eschewing a belles-only postdinner slumber during an all-day party at a neighboring plantation. While a young slave attends to the slumbering women by waving a peacock-feather fly brush over them, Scarlett sneaks away to seek out her would-be beau, Ashley Wilkes (Figure 14). During her covert hunt for Wilkes, she overhears that the Civil War has begun, acquiring news of the war by violating genteel behavior, much in the same way that Booker T. Washington did. Unlike the WPA, which recorded and disseminated ex-slaves' memories of real experiences laboring on plantations for their white masters, Hollywood films presented the public with a sanitized version of slavery. However, the WPA's accounts and popular films both revived tales and images of the punkah and related devices in an era when these fans were no longer in use.

Efforts by historians of the decorative arts have also been crucial in perpetuating the memory of the punkah. One of them, Mrs. Arthur F. Shuey of Natchez, endeavoring to promote the furnishings of the Old South and preserve them in collections, crafted the following brief missive on the importance of the punkah for *The Magazine Antiques* in 1935:

Even if you are from the South, you will hardly remember the punkah, that, in olden days, hung

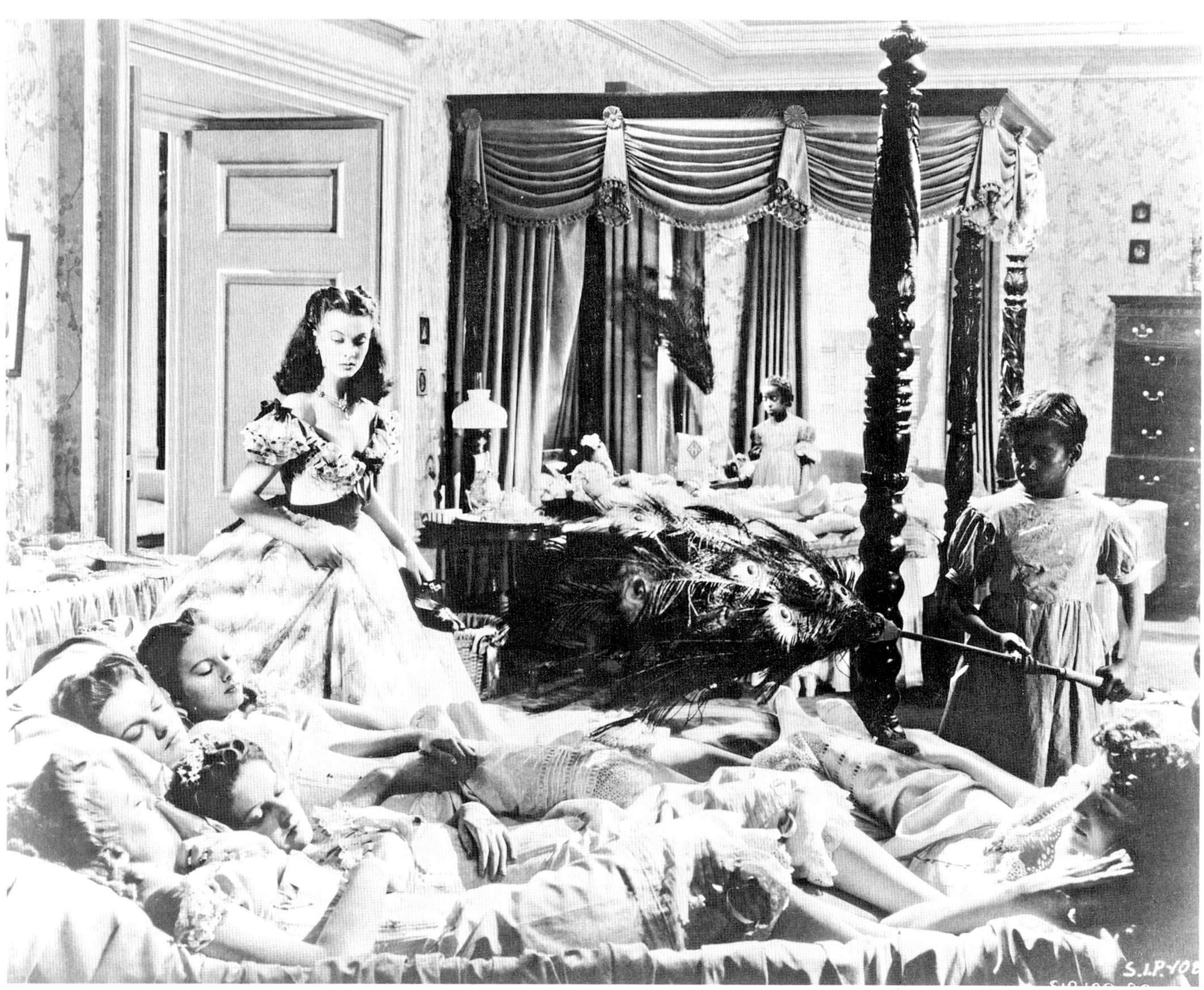

above the dining-room table. That was long before your time; but your grandmother probably remembers; and those fortunate enough to visit the old plantation houses may have seen these contrivances, even recently. But I doubt that any new punkahs have been installed within the past seventy-five years: few in many more. Most of the surviving examples date back to the days when Creole planters wanted breezes in their dining rooms even more than they wanted the crystal chandeliers which they had brought from France. . . . The punkah was the forerunner of the electric fan, an ingenious arrangement by which the air was kept in motion and the impertinent advances of flies and mosquitoes were discouraged. It was suspended from a large hook in the ceiling, and was usually of fabric stretched tight on a frame. There were plain, utilitarian punkahs of coarse linen, others elaborately embroidered with roses, daisies, and violets of shaded silk. Some, again, were of undecorated metal, or of metal adorned by the artistic daughters of the family with landscapes cooling to the eyes— mountains, and seashores, and even snow scenes.[46]

Mrs. Shuey's description of the punkah credits "Creole planter ingenuity" both for crafting the "contrivance" and for showing restraint by eschewing the luxury of chandeliers in favor of comfort. The "artistic daughters" who ornamented the form get credit for creating "landscapes cooling to the eyes," a suitable display of their artistic talent and wit. Absent in Shuey's notice is any account of the labor that powered the fan: the slave. No one is identified as carrying out the labor that was required; the punkah just moved itself. By masking the work of slaves, slavery itself is masked, putting the focus instead on the beauty and ingenuity of Creole life. Shuey's history of the punkah set the tone for the interpretation of objects related to slaves' life on Southern plantations.

Special events such as the Natchez Pilgrimage Tours of antebellum mansions gave new visitors access to the fans.[47] During Pilgrimage, as it is informally called, descendants of Old South families have celebrated and shared their heritage with other family members and visitors since the 1930s. That is when members of the

Natchez Garden Club, an organization founded to promote and preserve the city's historic landscape, began such heritage tours, offering the middle class an opportunity to glimpse the genteel homes and furnishings of the "Natchez Nabobs." A celebratory article in a 1949 issue of *National Geographic* breathlessly reported on the events organized by this elite group.[48] The whirlwind of Pilgrimage culminated in a ball at which attendees were required to dress in period attire. The *National Geographic* article was illustrated with photographs, one of which pictured descendants of Nabobs at a dinner at Melrose Plantation (Figure 15). In this color photograph, the descendants appear to be dining there in worship of their ancestors. The centerpiece of the photograph is the large, elaborately ornamented punkah suspended over the table, which a young African American at the extreme left is conscientiously pulling. The residents of Tallwood similarly documented their fan in use during the twentieth century (Figure 16). Of particular note is the way the photographer framed the image so that the boy pulling the punkah is included within the frame. His labor is visible, when the very architecture of that fan was designed to make his labor invisible. Together, these two images place the punkah in a modern service context where nostalgia for antebellum Southern life is on display.

Most guidebooks, articles, and souvenirs produced during the first half of the twentieth century obscured the relationship between the decorative arts and slavery, as in this description of the Melrose Plantation punkah in a 1940s guidebook: "A handsome mahogany punkah swings over the dining table. This bespeaks undeniable antiquity. Until quite recently the owners of Melrose cared for several old slaves who pulled the punka [*sic*] to create breezes for the comfort of the family during meals."[49] Here, the labor of the slave was understated while the charity of the homeowners and the beauty of the object were emphasized. Such an emphasis on materials and aesthetics is a familiar but unfortunate trope of some material culture scholarship, which has all too often minimized issues of use and given prominence to elegant artistry, fine craftsmanship, and the

circumstances of production. A century after the form was supplanted by advances in the technology of cooling interiors and repelling insects, it became a site from which to erase black labor while glorifying the object's aesthetic value and elite white Southern lifestyles. Thus, in the antebellum era, the punkah was a furniture and architectural form wedged between the issues of white control over the black body and black subversion of that power.

Twentieth-century revivals of the punkah, predominantly in the period rooms of historical societies and plantation mansions open to tourists, often displayed the device without its slave

operators, simply as a beautiful ornament evocative of a genteel past. Consequently, the power of observation inherent in the position assumed by young slaves who operated the punkahs a century and a half earlier has been all but lost to history. Coleman's narrative offers concrete details about the ephemeral fly brush, but more intriguing, it offers an opportunity to read his experience more poetically. In lieu of pulling a rope, as with a punkah, his body and the feathers that extended from it become the vehicle for providing physical comfort to the diners below. Ensconced in the swing, Coleman assumed a vantage point unusual for someone of his young and enslaved condition. Though still at his owner's beck and call, he was positioned above the fray, given license to observe and apprehend the entire scene below him with all his senses—that is, omniscient and empowered and, for just a brief moment, achieving something close to flight and a fleeting feeling of freedom.

AUTHOR BIOGRAPHY

Dana E. Byrd is assistant professor of art history at Bowdoin College.

NOTES

The author wishes to thank Mimi Miller and the late, great Robert "Bobby" DeBlieux for introducing her to many of the extant punkah sites, as well as Timothy Barringer and Kellie Jones, who encouraged this project. Presentations at the Museum of Early Southern Decorative Arts, the New Orleans Antiques Forum, and the Southern Historical Association's annual meeting allowed me to showcase this project and solicit valuable feedback from learned audiences. Ben Colman, Edward S. Cooke Jr., Bernard L. Herman, and Anna Seastrand read earlier versions of this essay and provided critical feedback. Coeditors Anna Andrzejewski and Cynthia Falk gave close attention to earlier drafts of this essay and were encouraging of this project. Links to Punkahville, the fan-mapping project created with the assistance of Tyler DeAngelis, is available at https://www.bowdoin.edu/faculty/d/dbyrd/.

1. Phineas Thornton, *The Southern Gardener and Receipt Book,* ed. Mrs. Mary L. Edgeworth (Philadelphia: J. B. Lippincott & Co., 1860), 10.

2. Patti Carr Black, *Art in Mississippi, 1790–1980* (Jackson: University Press of Mississippi, 1998), 89. In 1853, William Marshall Merrick, a twenty-year-old civil engineer and draftsman from Boston, was sent

to the South by the Mobile and Ohio Railroad. The New York Public Library holds two sketchbooks filled with pencil drawings made by Merrick in the South; David Guynes, "Managing Household Pests the Old-Fashioned Way: Defenses against Pest Damage in the Eighteenth and Nineteenth Centuries," *Material Culture Review/Revue de la culture matérielle* 44, no. 1 (Fall/Automne 1996), http://journals.hil.unb.ca/index.php/MCR/article/view/17709/22270.

3. "Jimmy Crack Corn," the American folk song from the 1840s written from the perspective of a slave who publicly laments (and secretly celebrates) his master's death in a riding accident, makes reference to a fly brush. One of the versions goes as follows: "When I was young, I used to wait / On Massa's table an hand de plate; I'de pass de bottle when he dry, An brush away de blue tail fly. An scratch 'im &c." Virginia Minstrels, *De Blue Tail Fly: A Negro Song* (Boston: Oliver Ditson, 1846). For more on the variation in the song's lyrics, see Dorothy Scarborough, *On the Trail of Negro Folk-Songs* (Cambridge, Mass.: Harvard University Press, 1925), 201–2. Eric Lott details the song's appearance in minstrel shows of the antebellum era in *Love and Theft: Blackface Minstrelsy and the American Working Class* (New York: Oxford University Press, 1993), 199–200. Dana E. Byrd, "Punkah," *World of a Slave: Encyclopedia of the Material Life of Slaves in the United States,* ed. Martha B. Katz-Hyman and Kym S. Rice (Santa Barbara, Calif.: ABC-CLIO, 2011), 381–85.

4. Therese O'Malley and Kathryn R. Barush, with Emily Pugh, Jessica Ruse, and Courtney Tompkins, "'In the Park': Lewis Miller's Chronicle of American Landscape at Mid-century," *Nineteenth-Century Art Worldwide* 12, no. 1 (Spring 2013), http://www.19thc-artworldwide.org/index.php/spring13/in-the-park-lewis-miller-chronicle-of-american-landscape-midcentury. This particular watercolor is from Miller's *Sketchbook of Landscapes in the State of Virginia,* which is in the Abby Aldrich Rockefeller Folk Art Museum at Colonial Williamsburg. Note that "this 'book' may never have been organized as such. . . . None of Miller's numerous sketchbooks was ever published or, probably, intended for publication. Instead, the sketchbooks served as personal diaries crammed with often disparate, disconnected, and run-on texts, poems, marginal notes, and drawings;" Barbara Luck, "Lewis Miller's Virginia Slavery Draw-

ings," *Encyclopedia Virginia,* last modified November 15, 2012, http://www.encyclopediavirginia.org/Lewis_Miller_s_Virginia_Slavery_Drawings.

5. *Oxford English Dictionary Online,* s.v., "Punkah," 2012. The Hindi word *punkah* was appropriated from the word *pankhā,* which originates from the Sanskrit term *paksaka* (fan), which derives from *pakṣa* (wing). *Punkah* appears in the English language during the first quarter of the seventeenth century as a result of Great Britain's incursion into India.

6. W. H. Carey, *Good Old Days of the Honourable John Company* (Calcutta, India: R. Cambray, 1906–7), 1:81; and Henry Yule and A. C. Burnell, *Hobson-Jobson: The Anglo-Indian Dictionary* (1886; repr., Hertfordshire, U.K.: Wordsworth, 1996), 742–43.

7. Annie Wright Marston, *Children of India Written for the Children of England* (London: Religious Tract Society, 1884), 15.

8. Mark Harrison, *Climates and Constitutions: Health, Race, Environment, and British Imperialism in India, 1600–1850* (New York: Oxford University Press, 1999), 215.

9. Norman MacLeod, *Peeps at the Far East: A Familiar Account of a Visit to India* (London: Strahan and Co., 1871), 122.

10. As cited in E. M. Collingham, *Imperial Bodies: The Physical Experience of the Raj, c. 1800–1947* (Malden, Mass.: Polity Press, 2001), 1.

11. Hugh Murray, *Historical and Descriptive Account of British India: From the Most Remote Period to the Conclusion of the Afghan War,* vol. 3 (London: Oliver and Boyd, 1944), 203–5; Edward Wakefield, *Past Imperative: My Life in India, 1927–1947* (London: Chatto and Windos, 1966), 8–9.

12. Anthony King, *The Bungalow: Production of a Global Culture* (New York: Oxford University Press, 1995), 18–35; and Philip Davies, *Splendours of the Raj: British Architecture in India, 1660–1947* (London: J. Murray, 1985), 103–5.

13. King, *The Bungalow,* 35–38.

14. The Muslim Indian custom of walling-in urban property fit easily with the English tradition of fencing deployed throughout the empire. For more, see Patricia Seed, *Ceremonies of Possession in Europe's Conquest of the New World, 1492–1640* (New York: Cambridge University Press, 1995), 20–31.

15. Swati Chattopadhyay, "Blurring of Boundar-

ies: The Limits of 'White Town' in Colonial Calcutta," *Journal of South Asian History* 59, no. 2 (June 2000): 158–63, 166–77.

16. Jonathan Eacott, "Owning Empire: The Matter of India in the English-speaking World, 1730–1780" (PhD diss., University of Michigan, 2008), 162. Thomas McTennet's 1762 Calcutta inventory contained a punkah, but not until the second half of the 1790s did punkahs appear in inventories as standard household items, a position they retained until the 1820s.

17. In the 1760s only 1 percent of inventories contained European-style bedsteads, rising slightly over time to 2 percent in the 1790s and about 25 percent in the 1820s. Thomas McTennet inventory P/154/62, Bengal Inventories, Asia, Pacific, and Africa Collections, British Library, London, as cited in Eacott, "Owning Empire," 145.

18. *Poulson's American Daily Advertiser,* October 17, 1805, 1.

19. *La Belle Assemblée or, Bell's Court and Fashionable Magazine Addressed Particularly to the Ladies* (March 1819): 39. Published in London from 1806 to 1832, *La Belle Assemblée* was a British women's magazine popular with women on both sides of the Atlantic.

20. John Steele to Mary Steele, January 5, 1797, John Steele Papers, "Records of Ante-Bellum Southern Plantations from the Revolution through the Civil War," ser. J, Selections from the Southern History Collection, Manuscripts Department, Library of the University of North Carolina at Chapel Hill, pt. 13, Piedmont, North Carolina (Frederick, Md.: University Publications of America, 1989–1993), microfilm.

21. Eacott, "Owning Empire," 145.

22. Elizabeth Coles Langhorne, K. Edward Lay, and William D. Rieley, *A Virginia Family and Its Plantation Houses* (Charlottesville: University Press of Virginia, 1987), 74. The punkah at Prestwould Plantation, Clarksville County, Virginia, resembles the Tallwood punkah in its triangular shape and wallpaper ornament, but it was operated by an enslaved worker in the same room. Distant relatives of the Coles family owned this punkah, which will be discussed later in this article.

23. The literature on the zonal organization of architectural space is extensive. Excellent examples

include Dell Upton, *Architecture in the United States* (New York: Oxford University Press, 1998), 28–32; Anna Andrzejewski, *Building Power: Architecture and Surveillance in Victorian America* (Knoxville: University of Tennessee Press, 2008), 98–116; Gwendolyn Wright, *Building the Dream: A Social History of Housing in America* (New York: Pantheon Books, 1981); Clifford Clark, *The American Family Home, 1800–1960* (Chapel Hill: University of North Carolina Press, 1986).

24. See Dana E. Byrd and Tyler DeAngelis, "Punkahville," https://www.bowdoin.edu/faculty/d/dbyrd/, for more information on these fans.

25. Jefferson's Monticello was a working plantation that required the labor of two hundred slaves in a typical year. See K. Edward Lay, *The Architecture of Jefferson Country: Charlottesville and Albemarle County* (Charlottesville: University of Virginia Press, 2000), 94–98; Annette Gordon-Reed, *The Hemingses of Monticello: An American Family* (New York: W. W. Norton, 2009), 91–130; William M. Kelso, "The Archaeology of Slave Life at Thomas Jefferson's Monticello: 'A Wolf by the Ears,'" *Journal of New World Archaeology* 6, no. 4 (June 1986): 5–20; and William M. Kelso, "Mulberry Row: Slave Life at Thomas Jefferson's Monticello," *Archaeology* 39, no. 5 (September–October 1986): 28–35.

26. Barbara J. Heath, *Hidden Lives: The Archaeology of Slave Life at Thomas Jefferson's Polar Forest* (Charlottesville: University of Virginia Press, 1999). In keeping with the idea behind his automatic fan, Jefferson developed an elaborate program for serving guests that restricted access to the dining room to a single trusted slave butler, Burwell Colbert. Colbert's work was facilitated by a system of dumbwaiters, which kept all of the other slaves out of Monticello's cloistered spaces. This system was also implemented at the White House during Jefferson's tenure as president.

27. The Southern cooking tradition, with its high seasonings and emphasis on frying and simmering, was an amalgam of African, English, French, Spanish, and Indian foodways. See David A. Davis and Tara Powell, eds., *Writing in the Kitchen: Essays on Southern Literature and Foodways* (Jackson: University of Mississippi Press, 2014); Marcie Cohen Ferris, *The Edible South: The Power of Food and the Making of an American Region* (Chapel Hill: University of North Carolina Press, 2014); Jessica B. Harris, *High on the*

Hog: A Culinary Journey from Africa to America (New York: Bloomsbury Press, 2011); Sam Bowers Hilliard, *Hog Meat and Hoecake: Food Supply in the Old South, 1840–1860* (Carbondale: Southern Illinois University Press, 1971); Sarah Rutledge, *The Carolina Housewife* (Columbia: University of South Carolina Press, 1979); and David S. Shields, *Southern Provisions: The Creation and Revival of a Cuisine* (Chicago: University of Chicago Press, 2015).

28. Barbara Carson, "Livery," *World of a Slave: Encyclopedia of the Material Life of Slaves in the United States,* ed. Martha B. Katz-Hyman and Kym S. Rice (Santa Barbara, Calif.: ABC-CLIO, 2011), 320–22; Barbara Carson, Ellen Kirven Donald, and Kym S. Rice, "Household Encounters: Servants, Slaves, and Mistresses in Early Washington," in *The American Home: Material Culture, Domestic Space, and Family Life,* ed. Eleanor McD. Thompson (Winterthur, Del.: Henry Francis du Pont Winterthur Museum, 1998), 71–93.

29. Linda Baumgarten, *What Clothes Reveal: The Language of Clothing in Colonial and Federal America* (Williamsburg, Va.: Colonial Williamsburg Foundation in association with Yale University Press, 2000), 130.

30. Museum of Early Southern Decorative Arts, Salem, North Carolina, research files S-5843X and S-5823.

31. Caldwell Sims, interview by Henry Coleman, "Born in Slavery: Slave Narratives from the Federal Writers' Project, 1936–1938," WPA Slave Narrative Project, South Carolina Narratives, vol. 14, part 1, Library of Congress archive, http://www.gutenberg.org/files/18912/18912-h/18912-h.htm#Page_210; see also the Library of Congress's online archives of these slave narratives at https://memory.loc.gov/ammem/snhtml/snhome.html. The narratives are rife with mentions of punkahs and fly brushes and constitute the broadest descriptions of the use of these objects. The WPA-generated ex-slave narratives are a wonderful source, yet they should be read with a critical eye. The interviews were conducted nearly seventy years after the constitutionally mandated end of slavery, calling into question the accuracy of the recollections of people who were enslaved during childhood and adolescence. The rarity of black interviewers introduced an important source of bias while the de facto code governing race relations frequently distorted the nature of the interviews. For more on the challenges and benefits of ex-slave narratives see Paul D. Escott, *Slavery Remembered: A Record of Twentieth-Century Slave Narratives* (Chapel Hill: University of North Carolina Press, 1979); Norman Yetman, "The Background of the Slave Narrative Collection," *American Quarterly* 19, no. 3 (Fall 1967): 534–53, and "Ex-Slave Interviews and the Historiography of Slavery," *American Quarterly* 36, no. 2 (Summer 1984): 181–210.

32. Katie Knowles, "Fashioning Slavery: Slaves and Clothing in the United States South, 1830–1865" (PhD diss., Rice University, 2014). For more on slave clothing, see Linda Baumgarten, " 'Clothes for the People': Slave Clothing in Early Virginia," *Journal of Early Southern Decorative Arts* 14 (1988): 26–70; Helen Bradley Foster, *New Raiments of Self: African-American Clothing in the South* (Oxford: Berg Publishers, 1997); and Madelyn Shaw, "Slave Cloth and Clothing Slaves: Craftsmanship, Commerce, and Industry," *Journal of the Museum of Early Southern Decorative Arts* 33 (2012), http://www.mesdajournal.org/2012/slave-cloth-clothing-slaves-craftsmanship-commerce-industry.

33. Herbert C. Covey and Dwight Eisenach, *What the Slaves Ate: Recollections of African American Foods and Foodways from the Slave Narratives* (Santa Barbara, Calif.: ABC-CLIO, 2009), 20–21.

34. Richard Bushman, for instance, describes a growing American gentility that was "concentrated among the wealthy and was nearly absent among the more abjectly poor." His refinement is one wrapped up in the consumption of objects. Here, I wish to illuminate through the punkah the ways in which objects could be used to facilitate the acquisition of skills related to refined behavior. See Richard L. Bushman, *The Refinement of America: Persons, Houses, Cities* (New York: Vintage Books, 1992), xv.

35. Bernard L. Herman, *Town House: Architecture and Material Life in the Early American City, 1780–1830* (Chapel Hill: University of North Carolina Press, 2005), 119–54.

36. Booker T. Washington, *Up from Slavery,* ed. William Andrews (New York: Oxford University Press, 2000), 6.

37. Paul Gilroy, " . . . to be real: The Dissident Forms of Black Expressive Culture," in *Let's Get It On: The Politics of Black Performance,* ed. Catherine Ugwu (London: Institute of Contemporary Arts, 1995), 12–33.

38. Beth Crabtree and James W. Patton, eds., *Journal of a Secesh Lady: The Diary of Catherine Ann De-*

vereux Edmondston, 1860–1866 (Raleigh, N.C.: Division of Archives and History, Department of Cultural Resources, 1979), 463–64.

39. G. D. Brasher, *Peninsula Campaign and the Necessity of Emancipation: African Americans and the Flight for Freedom* (Chapel Hill: University of North Carolina Press, 2012); Joseph T. Glatthaar, "The African American Role in Union Victory," in *Major Problems in the Civil War and Reconstruction: Documents and Essays,* ed. Michael Perman and Amy Murrell (Belmont, Calif.: Wadsworth Publishing, 2010), 308–22; Kate Masur, "'A Rare Phenomenon of Philological Vegetation': The Word 'Contraband' and the Meanings of Emancipation in the United States," *Journal of American History* 93, no. 4 (March 2007): 1050–84.

40. January 9, 1862, patent number 62 was issued to R. P. Moore and N. Thompson of Box Springs, Georgia, for a mosquito and fly brush machine. The Confederate Patent Office was established in Richmond. During the fall of Richmond, all (or almost all) documents were lost. Therefore, it is impossible to find drawings or prototypes of this or other patents registered with the Confederate States of America. If other patents were granted from November 1864 until the fall of the Confederacy, they are lost. Kenneth W. Dobyns, *The Patent Office Pony: A History of the Early Patent Office* (Frederick, Va.: Sergeant Kirkland's Museum, 1994), 18.

41. This fly fan has long been associated with a Natchez plantation. It is thought to have been acquired in the last quarter of the nineteenth century. More antebellum punkahs survive in situ in Natchez than in any other place in the United States. Anonymous, interview by author, Natchez, Adams County, Mississippi, July 2006.

42. Natchez, Mississippi, likely had a gasworks supplying gas to town and plantation homes by 1857. "Natchez Historic District Information," Mississippi Department of Archives and History, 2015. For more on the popularity of lighting in the South, see James R. Marsh, *Early American Chandeliers* (Pittstown, N.J.: J. R. Marsh, 1961); and William Paul Gerhard, *The American Practice of Gas Piping and Gas Lighting in Buildings* (New York: McGraw Publishing, 1908).

43. James Butters, "Rear View (East Elevation)—Green Leaves, 303 Rankin Street, Natchez, Adams County, MS," photograph, Historic American Building Survey, National Park Service, U.S. Department of the Interior, 1936, Prints and Photographs Division, Library of Congress (HABS MISS,1-NATCH,9–4).

44. Charlotte Chandler, *The Girl Who Walked Home Alone: Bette Davis, a Personal Biography* (New York: Simon and Schuster, 2006), 120–22.

45. See Molly Haskell, *Frankly My Dear: "Gone with the Wind" Revisited* (New Haven: Yale University Press, 2010).

46. Mrs. Arthur F. Shuey, "An Ante-Bellum Fan," *The Magazine Antiques* 27, no. 1 (January 1935): 8–9.

47. For more on the industry of Old South heritage tourism, see Stephen Hoelscher, "The White-Pillared Past: Landscape of Memory and Race in the American South," in *Landscape and Race in the United States,* ed. Richard H. Schein (New York: Routledge, 2006), 39–72.

48. William H. Nicholas, "History Repeats in Old Natchez," *National Geographic Magazine* 95, no. 2 (February 1949): 181–208.

49. A quintessential celebration of Natchez and the Old South is Nola Nance Oliver, *Natchez: Symbol of the Old South* (New York: Hastings House, 1940), 75.

ALLISON S. FINKELSTEIN

A Female Sanctuary on the Former Western Front

The Gold Star Pilgrimage Rest Houses in France, 1930–33

ABSTRACT

The U.S. Army's Quartermaster Corps erected temporary rest houses for the Gold Star Mothers and Widows Pilgrimages at the military cemeteries of the American Battle Monuments Commission (ABMC) in France between 1930 and 1933. The army intended the architecture of the rest houses to be familiar to the pilgrims and to provide them with a female place of comfort and respite. The decision to create the rest houses demonstrated the government's desire to include women in the commemoration of World War I, yet its choice to demolish them at the end of the pilgrimage program indicates the constrained role of women in that process.

By virtue of their appearance and short life, the rest houses' style, form, and temporary nature reveal the limitations on women's participation in commemoration and military culture during the interwar period. The rest houses separated the pilgrims into their own female space, carefully crafted and controlled by male military leaders. Their destruction erased the story of the female pilgrims from the visible commemorative narrative at the cemeteries. Unearthing the history of these structures restores the rest houses and the agency of American women to the larger narrative of interwar American commemorative culture.

On August 19, 1931, members of Party O of the Gold Star Mothers and Widows Pilgrimage posed for a group photograph during their visit to the Meuse-Argonne American Cemetery in France (Figure 1). During the depths of the Great Depression, these women journeyed to Europe at the expense of the U.S. government to visit the graves of their children and husbands who died in World War I. The cemetery visit constituted the climactic moment of their trip as they encountered these graves. Significantly, the pilgrims did not pose in front of the cemetery's pristine rows of headstones, its high-style chapel, or even its formal circular fountain.[1] Rather, with their military escorts and the cemetery's superintendent, they stood in front of the simple rest house built specifically to accommodate their needs. A one-story, craftsman-style building with a long front porch, this rest house looked as though it could have been located anywhere in the United States in the early 1930s. Nothing in the photograph indicated its actual location on the former Western Front rather than in the United States.

The army intended the architecture of the Gold Star Pilgrimage rest houses to be familiar to the pilgrims who traveled to France as part of the program, which lasted from 1930 to 1933. By building the rest houses, the army intended to provide these women with a place of sanctuary, comfort, and respite at the cemeteries. Through these simple structures, the government demonstrated the importance of the Gold Star Pilgrimage program and attempted to officially include women in World War I commemorations.

Yet after the program ended, the government demolished or otherwise removed the rest

houses from the cemeteries. This action erased the physical traces of the pilgrimage program and its memory from the monumental landscape being created by the American Battle Monuments Commission (ABMC) to honor American participation in World War I.[2] It demonstrated the often partial and temporary nature of American women's inclusion in official government World War I commemorative programs.

Even though the rest houses included women in government commemorations during the pilgrimages, these structures also relegated them to separate, protective female spaces within the male-dominated military landscapes of the cemeteries and surrounding battle sites. The eventual demolition of the rest houses erased the memory of women's participation in memorialization at the cemeteries and diminished the visible evidence of women's significant roles in postwar commemorative culture. The demolition also eliminated the tangible reminders of personal loss and mourning and allowed the cemetery landscapes to more strongly communicate ideas of communal, patriotic losses and sacrifices.[3]

As they had after the Civil War and the Spanish–American War, American women made significant contributions to the memorialization of World War I. They formed organizations of female veterans and veterans' family members, built monuments, constructed living memorial buildings, and engaged in community service and veterans advocacy as forms of commemoration.[4] Widows and mothers of deceased service members organized, and they lobbied Congress to be sent on pilgrimages because they believed they had a special right and duty as mothers and wives to honor and commemorate their children and husbands buried overseas. The passage of the Gold Star Pilgrimage legislation by Congress and the army's dedicated efforts to execute the program revealed women's ability to gain a unique, government-sanctioned role in commemoration rooted in their personal, familial, and domestic sacrifices.

By successfully convincing the U.S. government to sponsor and pay for the entire pilgrimage program, women also demonstrated their growing power at the national level and their

Figure 1. Rest house with Party O, Meuse-Argonne American Cemetery, Romagne-sous-Montfaucon, France, August 19, 1931. The original caption noted that this photo included "Captain [Boyette], Lieutenant Wiley, Cemetery Superintendent Shields, Major Campbell." Courtesy of the National Archives, College Park.

increasingly important place in shaping postwar commemorative discourse. Even after the ratification of the Nineteenth Amendment in 1920, women continued to frame their civic identities in terms of uniquely female issues such as motherhood, marriage, and volunteerism.[5] Women eligible for the Gold Star Pilgrimage, many of them newly able to vote, used their growing power in civic and political life to influence military commemoration and government policy while still adhering to the uniquely female roles they played before and during the war.

Tasked with leading the pilgrimages, the U.S. Army's Quartermaster Corps went to great lengths to ensure the success of the trips and the women's safety and well-being. Military officers attempted to create a sense of what they perceived to be familiar female domestic areas by constructing the rest houses. In doing so, they carved out gendered spaces to accommodate the women's needs at the cemeteries.[6] Despite the stereotypes of domesticity that may have informed the officers' choices, these structures gave women a place in the male commemorative landscape and provided physical evidence of women's key roles in World War I commemorations.

The rest houses also illuminate the limitations on women's participation in commemoration and military culture during the interwar period. These structures separated the pilgrims into their own architecturally familiar female spaces created by male military leaders. These officers may have also intended the rest houses to shield the pilgrims from temptations such as alcohol, legal in France but illegal in Prohibition-era America. The rest houses relegated women to gender-specific commemorative activities that restricted their full and equal entrance into American military culture.

The American Battle Monuments Commission
Even before the end of World War I, the United States grappled with the question of what to do with the remains of U.S. service members who died in Europe. In September 1918, Secretary of War Newton D. Baker publicly pledged the government would repatriate the war dead to the United States for burial at home, as had been the case during the Spanish–American War.[7] This promise ignited controversy as no task of this size had been attempted overseas. Over 116,000 American service members died in World War I, and America's Allies did not immediately support the repatriation plan.[8] In response, the War Department sent a questionnaire to the next of kin that asked whether they wanted the remains returned home or buried in a permanent overseas American military cemetery (Figure 2).[9]

Many next of kin struggled with the emotional decision of selecting a final resting place for their loved ones as they grieved and negotiated the government's bureaucratization and collectivization of their mourning process. Americans remained deeply concerned with the treatment and burial of the dead in the aftermath of battle, what they described during the Civil War as the "work" of death.[10] In dealing with the immense death toll of the Civil War and the military's struggle, and often failure, to properly bury the dead during that conflict, the War Department initiated a system of burial that accorded honor to the fallen.[11] The War Department directed the army to create a standardized process for military burials and to establish a national cemetery system, which began to operate in 1862.[12] From these beginnings during the Civil War, the government's treatment of and responsibility for fatalities continued to evolve, especially after the Spanish–American War when the military repatriated soldiers' remains to the United States.[13]

During World War I, Americans contemplated these earlier struggles with military burials as they considered plans for those recently lost overseas. The issue of World War I burials became politicized when former president Theodore Roosevelt, who lost his son Quentin in 1918, publicly declared he intended to leave his son's body in France because he believed in the biblical idea that "where the tree falls, there let it lie."[14] Even after this emotional public statement from Roosevelt, many families struggled with the decision of what to do with their loved ones' remains.

Elizabeth Conley of Philadelphia, for example, lost her sons William and Francis in World

War I. The army buried Francis in a temporary grave in France, but it never found nor identified William's remains. As she contemplated what to do with Francis's body, Conley changed her mind at least five times. In 1921 she wrote to tell the Quartermaster Corps that after "seeing so many others being brought back to the United States, I want mine back too."[15] But on learning that William's remains could not be identified and repatriated, she wrote again to say she wanted Francis to be buried in France. She explained, "If I can't get both back, I will let them stay there."[16] Conley's final request came too late to be canceled, since the army had already shipped Francis's remains to the United States. In 1931, with her friend and fellow Gold Star mother Katherine M. Gallagher, Conley traveled to the Meuse-Argonne American Cemetery as part of the Gold Star pilgrimage to view William's name on the Walls of the Missing.[17] Conley's tortured decision-making process reveals the difficult choices faced by Gold Star women.

Although many next of kin decided to repatriate their loved ones' remains to the United States, the families of 30,922 deceased service members chose an overseas burial.[18] Their decisions justified the creation of permanent American military cemeteries in France, Belgium, and England. In 1917 the army established the American Graves Registration Service (GRS) under the Quartermaster Corps to identify and bury American fatalities in temporary cemeteries in Europe.[19] After the war these scattered graves needed to be consolidated into permanent American cemeteries, and the creation of haphazard makeshift battlefield memorials, controlled.[20] Congress enacted legislation on March 4, 1923, that established the American Battle Monuments Commission to fulfill these missions. An independent federal agency of the executive branch, Congress tasked the ABMC to act as the "guardian of America's overseas commemorative cemeteries and memorials."[21] First led by General John J. Pershing, the commander of the American Expeditionary Forces (AEF) in World War I, the ABMC established eight permanent cemeteries for the war dead and built fourteen monuments to honor the AEF.[22] The cemeteries include Walls of the Miss-

ing that memorialize those service members determined missing in action or lost at sea. Today, the ABMC administers twenty-five permanent overseas military cemeteries and twenty-seven memorials and continues to carry out its worldwide mission.[23]

The decision to establish permanent overseas military cemeteries for those who died during World War I originated in military cemeteries created during and after the Civil War, which contained standardized rows of identical headstones. These cemeteries created a collective landscape of mourning and provided a powerful formal language of military memorialization that shaped aspects of American society and culture for the next century.[24] This same landscape of sacrifice would be repeated in the meticulous rows of identical crosses and Stars of David used at the ABMC cemeteries. After the Civil War a systematic accounting of the dead

Figure 2. Grave of Harry Ernest Adams in Suresnes American Cemetery, Suresnes, France. Each grave in the permanent overseas cemeteries received a standard headstone shaped like a cross, pictured here, or a Star of David. Photograph by Allison S. Finkelstein, July 2012.

and subsequent burials constituted obligations of the government, which led to the later creation of the GRS and ABMC.[25]

The design, architecture, and landscape features of the ABMC cemeteries reflected the influence of Civil War cemeteries, private cemeteries established in the United States during the late nineteenth and early twentieth centuries, and the hundreds of World War I cemeteries constructed by the different combatant nations.[26] The United States needed overseas cemeteries to position the nation equally alongside these other countries and therefore took some inspiration from the cemeteries constructed by the Allies.

The ABMC hired eleven architects, all of whom practiced in the United States, to design the cemeteries and the planned memorials to the AEF.[27] They included supervising architect Paul Cret, John Russell Pope, and Egerton Swartwout, among others. The resulting cemeteries and monuments included elements of neoclassicism and the medieval, Egyptian, and French Romanesque revival styles, as well as the occasional influence of art deco.[28] Although each cemetery was individually designed, they all included highly controlled, mostly symmetrical spaces with precisely landscaped grounds, formal entrances, long walkways, stone memorials, and chapels as well as offices and buildings for visitors (Figures 3 and 4).[29] The sprawling landscapes at the ceme-

teries resembled parks, a similarity that linked them to the pastoral burial grounds popular in nineteenth-century America and to the new memorial parks that emerged after 1917.[30]

The process of designing the cemeteries involved intense discussions and exchanges between the architects and the ABMC commissioners. Like other civic design projects, the overseas cemeteries reflected the tastes and values of both the designers and their client, in this case the U.S. government. The cemeteries were more than just American commemorative landscapes. They also served diplomatic purposes and represented the United States overseas. The cemeteries subsumed the individuality of the graves into the larger missions of these national shrines.[31]

Dominated by monumental civic architecture that served as a diplomatic tool, the cemeteries seem unlikely locations for the unpretentious Gold Star Pilgrimage rest houses.[32] In fact, the original plans for the ABMC cemeteries did not include the Gold Star rest houses at all. The army's Quartermaster Corps constructed them specifically for the pilgrimages after the ABMC designed the cemeteries. As temporary structures meant only to fulfill the specific needs of the government's official Gold Star Pilgrimages, the army intended to demolish the rest houses after the pilgrimages.

The Gold Star Mothers and Widows Pilgrimages

The Gold Star Mothers and Widows Pilgrimages formed an important part of the national mourning process after World War I.[33] Americans adopted the Gold Star as an emblem for relatives of the war dead during World War I; the Gold Star replaced traditional black mourning clothes (Figure 5).[34] After the war, Gold Star women organized and joined associations such as the Gold Star Association; the Gold Star Mothers, Inc.; and the American War Mothers to create communities for collective mourning and support.[35] In the 1920s these groups lobbied Congress for official government-sponsored and government-funded pilgrimages to the overseas cemeteries. They justified the program and convinced the government of its necessity through an appeal to their sacrifices as mothers, the goodwill it would foster

Figure 3. View of the Meuse-Argonne American Cemetery looking toward the chapel, Romagne-sous-Montfaucon, France. Note the park-like setting; the square, symmetrical grave plots separated by rows of trees; and the expertly manicured landscape. Photograph by Allison S. Finkelstein, July 2012.

with the former Allies, and the endorsement of the politically powerful American Legion. The idea for the pilgrimages emerged because of the expense required to visit the overseas cemeteries and the difficult journey required to visit most of them, especially those located in remote, rural regions of France.[36]

Women lobbied so passionately for government-sponsored pilgrimages because they believed Gold Star mothers and widows had served the nation through their losses and could gain some closure and comfort by visiting the cemeteries. Gold Star mother Ethel Stratton Nock, an active advocate for the pilgrimages who served as the Gold Star liaison officer for the American War Mothers, experienced the healing power of a cemetery visit during her independent trip to her son's grave in the Meuse-Argonne American Cemetery in 1927.[37] After her visit she wrote to General Pershing to thank him for his assistance with her trip and for his work with the ABMC. She told Pershing that she felt "uplifted mentally and physically because of this pilgrimage and will be able, I am sure, to bring peace to many troubled hearts of Gold Star Mothers."[38] Nock's trip affected her so profoundly that she made it her mission to help other Gold Star mothers visit the cemeteries through a government pilgrimage. She told the 1929 American War Mothers Convention that her "greatest object in life was to bring the comfort I had received to all other mothers of our glorious sons whose bodies are guarded by the Stars and Stripes in the beautiful fields of honor overseas."[39] Nock's experience helped her justify the pilgrimages to the government. After debate in Congress and the endorsement of President Calvin Coolidge, in 1929 Congress passed a bill that authorized the pilgrimages and committed the government to fully funding and organizing them.[40]

Although the Gold Star could be worn by any parent or spouse of a wartime fatality, fathers and husbands did not receive the same special status and recognition as mothers and widows. While earlier versions of the pilgrimage bill included fathers, the final legislation did not include male relatives in the program. The exclusion of men resulted from more than just a lack of strong ad-

Figure 4. View of St. Mihiel American Cemetery taken from within the cemetery's memorial, Thiaucourt, France. Photograph by Allison S. Finkelstein, July 2012.

vocacy. It had to do with the historical connections between women and the mourning process, especially in the context of motherhood.[41]

Beginning in the early republic, the ideology of republican motherhood obliged American women to support the nation by raising their children to become patriotic and politically virtuous citizens. While women were expected to have limited civic roles and to occupy the domestic sphere, motherhood ultimately became a civic duty. Over time this role evolved to include the raising of sons to serve in the military.[42] During the Progressive Era, some Americans asserted that a mother's domestic responsibilities could be coupled with other

Figure 5. Gold Star pin worn by Julia C. Underwood as a pilgrim on the 1932 Gold Star Pilgrimage. Courtesy of the Julia C. Underwood Pilgrimage Collection, National World War I Museum Archives, Kansas City, Missouri.

societal roles. Progressive women in particular argued that women's special qualities made them well suited to shaping certain aspects of public policy involving reform work, social services, and the needs of mothers and children.[43]

During and after World War I, Americans frequently interpreted motherhood as a national service. World War I propaganda and popular music portrayed women as heroic maternal figures and idealized the mothers of service members, called "war mothers."[44] Most famously, an American Red Cross poster described the Red Cross nurse as "the world's greatest mother" (Figure 6).

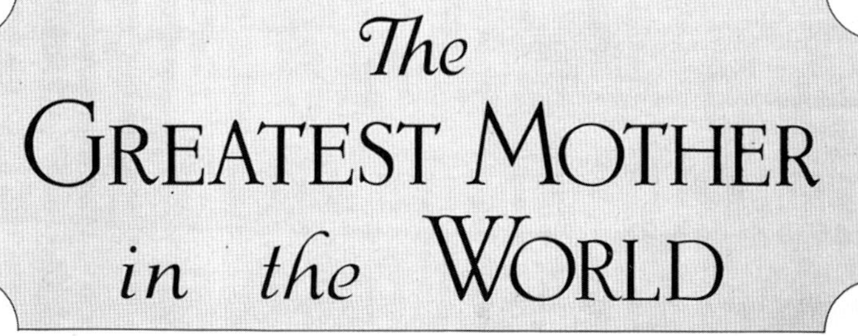

Figure 6. American Red Cross poster, "The Greatest Mother in the World," circa 1918. Courtesy of the Library of Congress, Prints & Photographs Division, LC-USZC4-3161.

Mothers gained a special place in the war effort and the postwar commemorative process. Some Gold Star mothers even believed they were more deserving of the pilgrimages than widows.[45] Although the final pilgrimage legislation included widows who had not remarried, widows did not lobby as persistently for the legislation as mothers, who outnumbered widows on the trips.[46]

Whether mothers or widows, the pilgrims represented a cross-section of American society—up to a point. They came from urban and rural locations, varying economic and social classes, and different religious, ethnic, and racial backgrounds. Even though the government invited all eligible women to participate in the pilgrimages and brought a diverse group of pilgrims overseas, in keeping with the practices of Jim Crow segregation, the government racially segregated the pilgrimages. Just as their children and husbands served in segregated units of the AEF during the war, African American pilgrims traveled in separate groups apart from the white pilgrims (Figure 7).[47]

The decision to racially segregate the pilgrimages resulted in criticism of the program from the African American community and its supporters and tainted it with the scars of Jim Crow America. The 168 African American mothers and widows who accepted their pilgrimage invitations traveled in separate, segregated parties during the summers of 1930 and 1931.[48] This obviated the need for separate rest houses at the cemeteries, since the pilgrims were segregated temporally rather than through the creation of distinct spaces.[49] Despite making the same sacrifices as white women, African American Gold Star pilgrims received unequal treatment on the trips. The government insisted their trips would be practically identical to those of the white pilgrims, but the African American pilgrims sailed on different transatlantic ocean liners and often stayed in less expensive hotels than their white counterparts.[50] The segregation of the pilgrimages epitomized the even more restricted inclusion of African American women in American commemorative culture.

This racial segregation of the Gold Star pilgrimages harkened back to the years after the Civil War when white women, especially in the South, led the movement to create military cemeteries and institute mourning traditions.[51] As the daughters or granddaughters of the generation of women who commemorated the Civil War, the women of the World War I era were inspired by their predecessors. Like the women of the Civil War era, they wanted to make pilgrimages to the graves of those they lost.

The decision to name the Gold Star mothers and widows' trips "pilgrimages" purposefully endowed the program with religious significance. The terms "pilgrimage" and "pilgrim" offered ways to connect the trips to religious rituals of grief and infused the program with a sense of the sacred.[52] The ABMC cemeteries themselves contained overtly religious symbolism and spaces. Each cemetery included a chapel specifically for prayer. Unlike the rectangular slab headstones at Arlington National Cemetery and other national cemeteries in the United States, which often included small engraved emblems of belief, the headstones chosen by the ABMC were carved in the shape of crosses or Stars of David.[53]

At the heart of the meaning of a pilgrimage is the sense that pilgrims can capture part of the past and experience an event even if they did not participate themselves. Pilgrims try to set themselves apart from regular tourists through the connections that bring them on their journeys. They want their pilgrimages to be viewed as public rituals linked to ideas of either national or religious identity.[54]

In this way, the Gold Star Pilgrimage rest houses helped to differentiate the Gold Star pilgrims from other cemetery visitors. The pilgrims used the rest houses to privately prepare for their visits to the cemeteries where they performed their acts of collective mourning. The rest houses can also be seen as a type of spiritual structure, like a sanctuary or a chapel, which sheltered the pilgrims from the prying eyes of the public and provided a sequestered place of respite and contemplation.

The army's Quartermaster Corps organized, planned, and paid for the entirety of every Gold Star pilgrim's trip. The army accounted for all details of each pilgrim's journey, from her transportation from her home to the point of embarkation at New York City, to her identification badge and medical and dietary needs.[55] The Quartermaster Corps split the pilgrims who accepted its invitations into groups that traveled in parties identified by a letter, such as Party O. The sizes of the parties varied—for example, the first 1930 pilgrimage group, Party A, included 234 women, whereas Party E in 1932 included just 79 women. In total, 6,654 women took part in the program between 1930 and 1933.[56] Each party's overseas itinerary varied based on the location of the main cemetery to be visited, but most trips to France included visits to the major sights such as the Arc de Triomphe and the Eiffel Tower.[57]

The pilgrims received special treatment and respect from their military officer escorts, the trip's nurses, and the European officials whom they met on their journeys.[58] The cemetery visit received careful consideration, since the Quartermaster Corps realized it could be an upsetting moment for a pilgrim as she finally knelt by her relative's grave. The army forbade formal ceremonies at the cemeteries or other activities that could agitate the pilgrims. Officers wanted to "keep the emotional reaction at a minimum."[59] This effort to maintain the composure and dignity of the pilgrims at the cemeteries helps to

Figure 7. An African American pilgrim traveling in her segregated group as part of Party L kneels at the grave of her loved one at Suresnes American Cemetery, Suresnes, France, July 26, 1930. Courtesy of the National Archives, College Park.

explain the main purpose of the rest houses. Created specifically to care for women's needs and comfort as perceived by men, the rest houses gave the pilgrims some privacy at the cemeteries and shielded them from the public or potentially upsetting encounters.

While the pilgrimages honored Gold Star women and the war dead, they also generated publicity that advertised the work of the ABMC and the military during a period of increasing isolationism and pacifism.[60] Colonel Richard T. Ellis, the main officer in charge of the pilgrimages, created a scrapbook in which he saved both positive and negative newspaper articles and publicity materials about the pilgrimages. Over one hundred pages long, it documents the high level of public interest in the program.[61] The pilgrimages also gained national exposure through John Ford's motion picture *Pilgrimage* (1933). Based on a 1932 fictional short story, the film depicted the story of a Gold Star mother from Arkansas who struggled with regrets about her relationship with her son during the trip.[62] With so much public interest in the program, the army carefully molded the official image of the pilgrimages. It attempted to use the pilgrimage program to improve public opinion about the military and to showcase efforts to include women, many of whom could now vote, in commemoration.[63] By building the rest houses, the army visually demonstrated its commitment to

the pilgrims and the lengths to which it went to care for them during the trips.

The Gold Star Rest Houses: An Architectural Analysis

When it planned the pilgrimages, the Quartermaster Corps decided to erect what it interchangeably called "rest houses" or "hostess houses" at the major permanent cemeteries: Meuse-Argonne, Aisne-Marne, Oise-Aisne, St. Mihiel, and the Somme. On October 18, 1930, Colonel Ellis reported that the army had already built three temporary rest houses and expected to erect "one more such Hostess House for the coming year at the cost of approximately $5,500.00."[64] At least three rest houses built expressly for the pilgrimages operated during the first pilgrimages in 1930 (Figure 8).

As part of its extensive planning for the pilgrimages, the Quartermaster Corps examined the cemeteries and surrounding areas to ascertain whether they met the pilgrims' needs. The cemeteries already contained buildings designated for use by visitors, often referred to as visitors' buildings (Figure 9). The small, formal rooms inside these visitors' buildings could not accommodate the large number of women who often traveled in each party (Figure 10).

In his report on the 1930 pilgrimages, Colonel Ellis explained that he had visited the cemeteries and noted that "accommodations already existed at these cemeteries for ordinary casual visitors but such accommodations were entirely inadequate for the large groups of pilgrims who were to visit these places."[65] This posed a problem, since most of the cemeteries and adjacent villages, located in isolated parts of the countryside, did not furnish the amenities needed by a sizable group of mostly older women. The Quartermaster Corps conducted a study of the cemeteries to be visited by the pilgrims to determine the suitability of their facilities. Ellis reported that at the Meuse-Argonne, Oise-Aisne, and St. Mihiel cemeteries

the nearby towns furnished no suitable refreshment, rest or toilet facilities. The visits to the cemeteries required a more or less lengthy automobile trip from the hotels in which the pilgrims were

Figure 8. Rest house, St. Mihiel American Cemetery, Thiaucourt, France, circa 1930, undated photograph. Positioned close to a grave plot, this rest house would have been easily visible to the cemetery's visitors. The nearby graves provided a stark reminder of the purpose of the pilgrimage. Courtesy of the National Archives, College Park.

lodged. Therefor[e] the problem of caring for these pilgrims during the half or the whole of a day at each cemetery presented itself and it was necessary to provide a place where the pilgrims could rest, relax, be furnished with refreshments, and find suitable toilet facilities.[66]

Ellis saw the need for buildings to accommodate the pilgrims, at least at the cemeteries to receive the most traffic; others would not need new buildings. With the nation in the grips of the Great Depression, the Quartermaster Corps tried to make do with existing amenities. Ellis noted that at the Aisne-Marne and Somme cemeteries additions could be made to current buildings to furnish a rest room and extra toilet facilities for the pilgrims, although each later received a rest house. At Flanders Field American Cemetery in Belgium, which would receive smaller groups of pilgrims, only the toilet facilities needed to be increased. Brookwood American Cemetery, located just beyond London, England, required no alterations at all (Figure 11). Suresnes American Cemetery, located near the more substantial town of Suresnes outside Paris, relied on a local restaurant to accommodate the pilgrims' rest and toilet needs.[67]

The officers in charge of the pilgrimages frequently repeated the importance of providing ample toilet facilities and a place for rest and refreshment at the cemeteries. Although most of the widows were middle-aged or slightly younger, the mothers were often more elderly and in poorer health.[68] Throughout the journey the health and safety of the pilgrims remained the utmost concern, as demonstrated by the reports the Quartermaster Corps gathered on each pilgrim prior to departure and the detailed records it kept about each pilgrim's state of health and medical problems.[69] The officers ensured the rest houses were "tastefully furnished with all the necessities for rest and comfort, with certain minor hospital supplies and equipment, and for the preparation of tea, coffee, and refreshments."[70] Since the trip could prove physically and emotionally demanding, the officers wanted the appropriate facilities to be available.

The pilgrims utilized the rest houses to relax,

Figure 9. Visitors' building, Aisne-Marne American Cemetery, Belleau, France, 1932. This structure's stonework and arches evoked the sensibilities of the French Romanesque revival style. Courtesy of the National Archives, College Park.

Figure 10. Aisne-Marne American Cemetery, interior of the reception room, Belleau, France, 1925. Note the formal leather furniture and fireplace. Courtesy of the National Archives, College Park.

Figure 11. Party H being addressed by Major General Sir Fabian Ware (founder of the Commonwealth War Graves Commission) at Brookwood American Cemetery, Brookwood, England, July 1930. Major General Ware stood at the entrance to the reception room so that the pilgrims inside and outside the building could hear him. Located close to London, Brookwood did not require a rest house to meet pilgrims' needs. Courtesy of the National Archives, College Park.

the nurses and the hostess, as well as a kitchen equipped with electric stove, water heater and coffee perculator [sic] were installed. Each house had a comfortable, shady porch and a large open fire-place.[72]

Judging from photographs, the rest houses at the Meuse-Argonne, St. Mihiel, Aisne-Marne, and Oise-Aisne cemeteries all looked similar to one another if not exactly alike. It is likely that builders used a standardized plan for all of the rest houses, possibly because the army wanted to save money or time (Figures 12 and 13; see also Figures 1 and 8). The choice to construct identical rest houses contrasted with the widely differing designs of each of the ABMC cemeteries. By duplicating the rest houses at the different cemeteries, the army created a common architectural language for the pilgrimages, one that differentiated and separated the pilgrims from the other visitors and parts of the cemeteries.

The rest houses displayed many characteristic features of the craftsman style and, more specifically, of the bungalow. These included a hipped roof with a central projecting cross gable on the front façade, a Palladian window centered in this gable, decorative faux posts articulated on the exterior, exposed rafters under the eaves, and a roof with diamond-shaped shingles. According to photos and Ellis's description, the houses had wooden horizontal exterior siding, and the large double front doors contained six lights in the upper two-thirds to match the windows. On the front and sides, the houses included what appear to be paired casement windows with two tall sashes that opened out from the center.

Each rest house included a central front porch with narrow grouped porch supports (three) and a pergola-like flat roof with exposed beams. This asymmetrically positioned porch ran across approximately two-thirds of the front façade. Many photographs show furniture on the porches and plants climbing up the porch supports, demonstrating that the pilgrims used this outdoor space to sit and relax, as Ellis indicated. At the Meuse-Argonne rest house what appears to be a blind or sunshade could be lowered from the porch roof to provide shade and privacy from the other

enjoy refreshments, and use the toilet while they spent time at the cemeteries. The pilgrims always stayed overnight in local hotels and never at the rest houses, since these structures did not have any bedrooms, apartments, or spaces for them to sleep. Rather, the rest houses contained ample tables and chairs for the pilgrims to eat the box lunches provided to them in a relaxed setting similar to that of their own homes. Kitchens and dining spaces further enhanced the domestic atmosphere of the buildings.[71] Inside the rest houses, spacious, open rooms incorporated some craftsman features like exposed beams and horizontal wood siding on the walls. Large brick fireplaces topped with vases of flowers enhanced the familial atmosphere, as did the abundant wicker furniture.

Although no Gold Star rest houses survive, photographs and documentary evidence enable architectural analysis. In his 1930 report, Colonel Ellis described the rest houses as

> attractive wooden one-story houses laid out and furnished something along the lines which one would expect to find in an attractive country-club. The house at the Meuse-Argonne Cemetery had a surface area of 2853 sq. feet while the other two each had a surface area of 2133 sq. feet. Tables, comfortable chairs and a rest room for the use of

visitors at the cemetery (Figure 14). Photographs from multiple cemeteries show the rest houses surrounded by plants and landscaping much more casually designed than the highly formalized horticulture of the cemetery grounds.

Eleanor Barnes visited the rest house at the St. Mihiel American Cemetery during the 1930 pilgrimage season. A member of the Women's Overseas Service League (WOSL), an organization of American women who served overseas during World War I, Barnes traveled to the cemetery after attending the WOSL's convention in Paris. She wrote about her interactions with the Gold Star pilgrims in an article published in the WOSL's organizational magazine, *Carry On,* in February 1931. Barnes described the St. Mihiel rest house as "gay with red-and-white checked gingham curtains, reed furniture with red interwoven, and an ample brick fireplace with a log fire. Here a charming little French widow served 'very good café Americain' and 'no good tea.' It did much toward bracing up the mothers after their difficult visit."[73] Barnes's description provides a female assessment of the effectiveness of the rest houses in creating a positive environment for the pilgrims. The homey interior she reported indicated her belief that the pilgrims seemed comfortable in the rest houses.

While Barnes's recollection of this interior matches the views shown in period photographs, she emphasized certain aspects of the space over others. An image of the interior of the St. Mihiel rest house showed a lieutenant presenting an illustrated talk, probably an account of the Battle of St. Mihiel, to the pilgrims using a large military map over the fireplace (Figure 15). This battle map stands out in contrast to the home-like environment of the rest house. While intended to be female-oriented areas of relaxation, at least on this one occasion, if not others, rest houses also served more educational purposes for the military officers leading the trips. Yet this use and the wall map did not warrant mention in Barnes's published description.

The exact location of the rest houses is unknown except for that of the rest house at the St. Mihiel American Cemetery.[74] A 1931 photograph of the construction of the chapel at St. Mihiel

Figure 12. Rest house, Aisne-Marne American Cemetery, Belleau, France, circa 1930–32, undated photograph. The "private" sign indicated regular cemetery visitors could not use the rest house. Courtesy of the National Archives, College Park.

Figure 13. Postcard showing the rest house at Oise-Aisne American Cemetery, also known during the 1930s as Fère-en-Tardenois, located in Seringes-et-Nesles, France, circa 1930–33. The landscaping around the building and its porch are much more casual than the formal landscaping elements at the ABMC cemeteries. Courtesy of the American Battle Monuments Commission.

shows the Gold Star rest house in the far-left background of the image (Figure 16). This unpretentious rest house contrasted with the surrounding architecture of the formal and fairly symmetrical cemetery and created an opposition between the rest house and the overall cemetery

Figure 14. Rest house with pilgrims from Party T, Meuse-Argonne American Cemetery, Romagne-sous-Montfaucon, France, circa 1930, undated photograph. Note the sunshade that covered the exposed beams of the porch roof. Courtesy of the National Archives, College Park.

Figure 15. Lieutenant Lucas giving an illustrated talk to pilgrims inside the rest house at St. Mihiel American Cemetery, Thiaucourt, France, circa 1930–33. While the military map provided a reminder of the reason for the pilgrims' visit, it contrasted with the home-like atmosphere of the rest house's interior. The exposed beams in the ceiling were a common feature in craftsman-style architecture, and the wicker furniture created a domestic feeling in the room. Courtesy of the National Archives, College Park.

landscape (Figure 17). Furthermore, the style of the rest houses represented a direct import from the suburban American landscape of the period. The architectural design, form, and function of the rest houses would have been visually familiar to the pilgrims and their military escorts and understood as a distinctly female space that stood in stark contrast to the monumental civic architecture of the rest of the cemeteries.

The Architectural Origins of the Gold Star Rest Houses

The pilgrimage rest houses drew from several similar types of buildings found in the United States in the early twentieth century: country clubs, ladies rest rooms, and military base hostess houses. The most explicit comparison came from Colonel Ellis, who likened the rest houses to country clubs.[75] The country club movement grew during the 1920s as country clubs became a recognizable feature of the American landscape. Country club architecture varied in the 1920s and 1930s, but many clubhouses included verandas or porches like the rest houses, and they occupied locations in open, park-like settings not so different from the cemeteries. Clubhouse interiors provided members with spaces intended to provide the comforts of home with fireplaces, comfortable furniture, and cozy decor. Many country clubs included separate spaces designated for male or female use.[76] When a male military officer like Ellis wanted to convey his impressions of the Gold Star Pilgrimage rest houses, the country club with its domestic interiors, gendered spaces, and close relationship to the surrounding landscape seemed an apt comparison.

Other building types specifically intended for use by women would have been less familiar to male military officers like Ellis, although they likely influenced planning for the rest houses. Found throughout America, especially in country towns, ladies rest rooms provided women with a safe, clean, and private place to rest, use a proper bathroom, and feed, change, and care for babies and children. Ladies rest rooms could encompass an entire stand-alone building or just one room within a larger structure. These rest rooms frequently served as relaxation spaces for women who visited country towns or cities. They often contained sitting rooms, bedrooms, toilet facilities, and kitchens for women's needs while visiting the otherwise male-dominated, public landscape of the town. Many rest rooms were architecturally simple, freestanding, single-use buildings such as the colonial revival ladies rest room in Lewisburg, Tennessee (Figure 18).[77] They typically contained furnishings such as chairs, couches, tables, and desks and were comfortable and home-like, much like the Gold Star rest houses.[78]

Ladies rest rooms became widespread features of the American landscape at the turn of the twentieth century as women spent more time outside the home and participated more fully in public life. They enabled middle-class women, still considered delicate and vulnerable in public,

Figure 16. The memorial and chapel at St. Mihiel American Cemetery while under construction, Thiaucourt, France, 1931. The rest house can be seen in the far-left background of this photograph. It stands out in contrast to the formal architectural elements being constructed. Courtesy of the National Archives, College Park.

Figure 17. Aerial view of the Somme American Cemetery, Bony, France, circa 1925–35. Note the formal, geometric, and somewhat symmetrical layout of the cemetery. Courtesy of the National Archives, College Park.

Figure 18. Ladies rest room in Lewisburg, Tennessee, 1924. Photograph by Carroll Van West, 1995.

to travel by providing them with private, female spaces.[79] In 1918 Anne M. Evans, a contributor to the *Yearbook of the United States Department of Agriculture,* described how a rest room run by a hired matron met "the daily needs of a large number of country women."[80] While not as popular in the 1930s as they had been earlier, ladies rest rooms remained a common part of American communities during the time of the pilgrimages, and they continued to be closely associated with women's travel needs.[81]

Even if the male army officers in charge of the pilgrimages were not intimately familiar with ladies rest rooms, they likely knew of the Young Women's Christian Association (YWCA) hostess houses erected on army bases in the United States during World War I. The large numbers of men who entered the military required the expansion of existing bases and the creation of new sites for the stateside training of draftees.[82] These bases needed buildings to accommodate female family members who came to visit the soldiers. This prompted the YWCA, in conjunction with the War Department's Commission on Training Camp Facilities (CTCA), to build hostess houses on bases. The YWCA hostess houses provided a place for soldiers to interact with their families and enjoy the comforts of home while the military controlled their social interactions. Similar to the pilgrimage rest houses, these host-

ess houses represented a separate female space within the military landscape and were often demolished when no longer needed.[83] In keeping with the racial policy of the AEF, the YWCA created separate, segregated facilities for the use of African American service members and their families.

Photographs of the YWCA hostess houses show them as larger yet architecturally similar in style and form to the Gold Star rest houses. Many resembled elongated craftsman-style dwellings or bungalows, and they often included large porches (Figure 19). Like the Gold Star rest houses, their interiors contained exposed beams, large fireplaces, and wicker furniture that created an informal, home-like environment (Figure 20).[84] The YWCA's wartime hostess houses allowed women to negotiate portions of male-oriented military bases but relegated them to separate, restricted female spaces.

The success of these YWCA hostess houses led to the creation of other similar buildings during and after the war. In Europe the YWCA constructed buildings specifically for the use of the American women who served overseas. These buildings evolved into hybrid canteens, rest rooms, hostels, and recreational facilities used by Allied female war workers. The YWCA also established twelve Signal Corps Houses to accommodate the Hello Girls, who served as telephone operators with the U.S. Army Signal Corps.[85] After the war the YWCA built more temporary rest houses at some of the American cemeteries created by the GRS before the establishment of the ABMC. The YWCA's houses at the Meuse-Argonne, Somme, Belleau-Wood, and Oise-Aisne cemeteries provided much-needed facilities to aid the relatives of the dead and other visitors to these developing cemeteries.[86] During the interwar period, the War Department also set up Citizens Military Training Camps (CMTC) each summer and erected hostess houses modeled on the ones used during the war.[87]

The resemblance of rest houses architecturally and functionally to country clubs, ladies rest rooms, wartime hostess houses, and similar postwar YWCA and military facilities identified them as familiar and comforting structures for the pilgrims. These precedents demonstrate that although women's inclusion in military commemoration remained limited, the government tried to accommodate the pilgrims at the cemeteries by drawing on common architectural traditions of the day. While the Western Front may have been a traumatic place for the pilgrims to visit, the rest houses tempered the experience by providing the pilgrims with a safe sanctuary for respite and relaxation that evoked the familiar comforts of home.

The Gold Star Rest Houses: Their Necessity and Success

The national press coverage of the pilgrimages and their depiction in popular culture through John Ford's film *Pilgrimage* increased the pressure to safeguard the pilgrims and prevent any potential mishaps.[88] The army needed to ensure the safety, well-being, and propriety of the pilgrims to avoid controversy or criticism. It may have used the rest houses as ways to protect the reputations of the pilgrims, the program, and the army. The Quartermaster Corps faced a potential public relations disaster if the trips compromised the pilgrims' health or morality, and, if successful, the rest houses could provide evidence of the army's dedication to caring for the pilgrims and honoring their wartime sacrifices.

The army might have used the pilgrimages and the rest houses as a type of propaganda to positively promote the armed services. Such publicity would have been helpful during the Great Depression, a time of public disdain for the military, disillusionment with World War I, and increasingly angry veterans' protests such as the 1932 Bonus March.[89] The pilgrimages, like the cemeteries, also supported diplomatic purposes and helped strengthen American ties with Europe during the tumultuous 1930s when isolationism thrived in the United States.[90] Stories of pilgrims behaving inappropriately in Europe or experiencing medical problems could have compromised these missions.

Many of the pilgrims had probably never traveled far from home, and as John Ford's *Pilgrimage* suggested, the trip likely introduced them to modern European customs much different from

Figure 19. Hostess house at Plattsburgh Barracks, Plattsburgh, New York. From "Report of Hostess House Committee," War Work Council, National Board of the Young Women's Christian Associations, 1920.

Figure 20. Interior of the YWCA hostess house for African American soldiers and their families at Camp Dix, New Jersey. Like the AEF and the Gold Star pilgrimages, these wartime facilities were also segregated. African Americans visited their own military base hostess houses and could not use the facilities designated for whites. Note the wicker furniture, large brick fireplaces, and exposed architectural elements, all features seen in the Gold Star rest houses. From "Report of Hostess House Committee," War Work Council, National Board of the Young Women's Christian Associations, 1920.

their own.[91] In the film the pilgrims on board the ship to France experienced the luxuries of ocean voyages and witnessed elegantly dressed young ladies smoking cigarettes. Once in Paris, the American women, many of them portrayed as country bumpkins or poor immigrants, visited a modern French clothing boutique and watched glamorous women model evening gowns and negligée while "How're You Gonna Keep 'Em Down on the Farm," a wartime song that depicted the Doughboy's modernization overseas, played in the background.[92]

Although fictional, the film provided a contemporary depiction of how the experience could have been eye-opening for women who found themselves in a country quite unlike their own. In fact, pilgrim Katherine M. Gallagher wrote to Fox and asked to be consulted on the film because she felt "the pilgrimage was very sacred to us and we may not wish to see it commercialized."[93] Perhaps Gallagher worried that Hollywood might dishonor the sanctity of the real pilgrimages by portraying fictional pilgrims behaving badly on the silver screen.

The construction of the rest houses helped the army successfully execute the pilgrimage program and its goals. The Quartermaster Corps employed female hostesses and attendants to take care of the buildings, host the pilgrims, and serve them lemonade and American coffee.[94] A 1930 medical report highlighted the positive benefits provided by the rest houses and the hostesses who staffed them:

> French coffee as a rule was not acceptable to the pilgrims and the serving of American coffee was greatly appreciated. Box lunches put up by the hotels in Verdun were served to the pilgrims at noon in the rest house of the Meuse-Argonne Cemetery. The serving of box lunches at this cemetery proved to be most satisfactory in that they were well prepared, were apparently relished by the pilgrims and obviated the necessity of an additional bus trip, affording more time for rest.[95]

This medical report concluded that the rest houses and their hostesses formed an integral part of the endeavor to keep the pilgrims healthy and emotionally stable.

The rest houses, the hostesses, and the American coffee they served proved popular with the pilgrims and the officers. Letters of thanks from the pilgrims to the officers who led their trips repeatedly mentioned their gratitude to the hostesses. In a 1930 letter to Colonel Ellis, Hattie B. Bisbee and Sarah Parker pointed out how the hostesses eased their cemetery visits. After expressing their thanks for the trip, they stated, "We also wish to speak of the Hostess Mrs. Abbot[m] and Madam Juliette who in their sweet sympathetic manner made each visit to the cemetery much easier to bear."[96] Another 1930 letter to Ellis from Ettie M. Brown and Mrs. George Ingersoll commended the hostesses and the cemetery superintendent at St. Mihiel on a job well done. They explained how the hostesses "were so kind and thoughtful and served us coffee and iced lemonade; and everything we wanted done."[97]

Visitors like Eleanor Barnes further illuminated the effectiveness of the rest houses. In her article in the Women's Overseas Service League's magazine, *Carry On,* she wrote that the rest house at St. Mihiel "did much towards bracing up the mothers after their difficult visit. They all voiced the same sentiments—they were quite satisfied to go back home leaving their boys in this lovely spot so carefully tended, and they were more than happy because of all the Government had done for them."[98] Having seen firsthand how they eased the strain of the pilgrimages, Barnes deemed the rest houses to be successful.

The officers themselves also commented on the usefulness of the rest houses. In Ellis's 1930 report, he noted that the construction of the rest houses "undoubtedly was for the good of the pilgrimage and received favorable commendation not only from official visitors but from the Pilgrims themselves."[99] In his final report on the pilgrimages written in 1933, Colonel F. H. Pope similarly remarked that "the temporary hostess houses proved to be of great value in caring for the pilgrims during their visits to the cemeteries. All hostesses performed their work in a very satisfactory manner."[100] Pilgrims, officers, and observers alike agreed that the rest houses protected the pilgrims' physical and emotional health and created a comfortable, moral, and home-like atmosphere at the cemeteries. As they encountered the graves of their loved ones or saw their names inscribed on the Walls of the Missing, the pilgrims had a familiar space of their own to which they could turn for comfort, shelter, and protection from the public. Among the stately monumental architecture of the ABMC cemeteries, these women found a sanctuary that enabled them to approach this emotional experience with the dignity and strength that would reflect positively upon the army, the government, and themselves.

Debate and Demolition: The Fate of the Gold Star Rest Houses

Despite the success of the rest houses, heated debate about them occurred among officers involved with the pilgrimages. While they all agreed on their usefulness, some officers wondered what should be done with them when the pilgrims were not visiting. The debate began with an August 21, 1931, memorandum to the Quartermaster General from Lieutenant Colonel E. B. Gregory, who received an assignment as a temporary observer of a pilgrimage. In this report Gregory offered recommendations to improve the pilgrimages based on his recent experiences on the trip. He seemed keenly aware of the need to reduce spending during the Great Depression, as he devoted the last section of his report to cutting the costs incurred by the rest houses. He believed the hostesses to be unnecessary, noting that "their functions could easily be performed by the nurses who accompany each cemetery group. . . . This would result in a monthly saving of $640."[101] Gregory argued that the rest houses should be used by other cemetery visitors apart from the Gold Star pilgrimages and suggested that they "should either be definitely closed while the pilgrims are not in the cemetery or their use by the small parties of visitors be allowed."[102]

Gregory's suggestions generated discussion among the officers involved with the pilgrimages. In response, Colonel Ellis sent a rebuttal to the Quartermaster General. He disagreed with Gregory's remarks about the rest houses and stressed that:

> the proper functioning of the hostess house at the cemeteries is one of the vital points of the pilgrimage and was given the most serious and lengthy consideration when the original plans were drawn . . . the Cemetery Superintendent is entirely too busy to attend to the running of a host-

ess house for the Pilgrims. . . . to place the Hostess Houses in charge of nurses accompanying the Pilgrims is impracticable. It takes a day or so to prepare for the arrival of a Party of Pilgrims . . . and similarly a day or so is necessary for cleaning up purposes.[103]

Ellis explained that nurses might not be properly qualified or have the appropriate personality to operate the rest houses. More nurses would be required if they also ran the rest houses in addition to their other duties. This would create an even greater expense since nurses received higher wages than hostesses. Most importantly, Ellis feared that the environment of the houses would be compromised under the charge of nurses. He emphasized that "the most complimentary remarks have been received by this office concerning the operation and the 'home-like' atmosphere of each of the Hostess Houses and it is felt that to substitute nurses for the Hostess would be most unsatisfactory."[104]

In reference to Gregory's suggestions about closing the houses when they were not being used by the pilgrims or allowing them to be used by other tourists, Ellis again dissented. He explained that closing the houses would create more work, since staff used the time in between visits to clean and prepare the buildings for the next group. Allowing tourists to use the houses would require more supervision and cleaning. Ellis emphasized that "pilgrimage funds are not available for use for purposes other than those connected with the Pilgrims and the personnel on duty therewith. It is not felt that any material change is warranted in the operation of the Hostess Houses."[105]

After their superiors in the Office of the Quartermaster General reviewed Ellis's and Gregory's conflicting comments, Ellis prevailed. An officer with the surname Shannon explained the Quartermaster General's office concluded the "functioning of the hostess houses during the two years of the pilgrimage have been satisfactory, and the small amount of savings that might possibly be made would not justify a change to the methods that might not prove nearly as satisfactory."[106] Despite the economic pressures of the

Great Depression, the quality of the pilgrimage experience took priority over frugality because of the value of the rest houses and their hostesses.

This debate helps explain the eventual demolition of the rest houses, for it demonstrates that the Quartermaster Corps always considered the rest houses to be impermanent structures intended only for use by the Gold Star pilgrims. Their temporary nature was affirmed when the rest house at the Aisne-Marne Cemetery was dismantled and moved to the Somme Cemetery in 1933 before the last summer of pilgrimages. In a letter to Mr. F. Santi, head of the French construction firm hired to carry out the move, Lieutenant Colonel R. H. Jordan gave detailed instructions including specifications to remove the brick fireplace but not reerect it at the Somme, to remove all electrical wiring and transport it to the Somme but not reinstall it, and to completely rebuild the porch at the building's new location. In addition to receiving payment for this work, whenever the rest house went up for sale, Santi would be given preference in purchasing it.[107]

That this rest house could be completely dismantled, moved, and rebuilt demonstrated the short-term structural nature of these buildings. No plans included permanently retaining the rest houses on the grounds of the ABMC cemeteries. Rather, the ABMC seemed keen to get rid of the buildings at the termination of the pilgrimage program. In a letter to the Quartermaster General on January 31, 1933, Jordan reported that the ABMC was

> anxious to have the Pilgrimage Rest Houses at Aisne-Marne and Meuse-Argonne Cemeteries removed as soon as practicable in order that they may complete the planting which will go on the present sites of these houses. It is therefore requested that I be authorized to demolish these houses as soon as they are no longer required for Pilgrimage purposes.[108]

Jordan received approval to demolish the rest houses on February 10, 1933, although he soon supervised the move of the rest house at Aisne-Marne instead of its demolition.

The cemeteries remained under construction during the pilgrimages, justifying the eagerness of the ABMC to remove the rest houses so they could complete these large projects.[109] With the exception of the rest house at St. Mihiel, the final fate of each rest house remains unclear. It cannot be determined whether Santi purchased the rest house at the Somme or when the other rest houses were either moved or demolished. The St. Mihiel rest house was certainly gone by December 10, 1932, before the end of the Gold Star pilgrimage program, because a document regarding an electric line that had run to the rest house stated the electric line was of no further value to the U.S. government, since the rest house had been demolished.[110] It is likely most of the rest houses were demolished rather than relocated, as no surviving examples have been discovered.

The desire of the ABMC to demolish the rest houses and the Quartermaster Corps' concurrence with its wishes demonstrate how both groups excluded women from the permanent landscapes at the cemeteries. Built as distinctively female spaces, the rest houses served as additions to the cemeteries to temporarily include women in military commemoration. Even though the ABMC commissioners included one Gold Star mother and although the ABMC cemeteries contained the graves of at least sixty women who served overseas during the war, the government did not intend women to be a major or visible parts of the permanent landscape of memory created at the cemeteries.[111]

By learning about the rest houses and figuratively reinserting them into the ABMC cemeteries, the Gold Star pilgrimages can once again become part of the interpretation of these sites. The story of the rest houses demonstrates the important role of women in American commemorative culture after World War I and reveals women's often overlooked impact on America's landscapes of memory overseas. Yet the demolition of the rest houses reflects the partial and often fleeting role accorded to women in commemorative culture after World War I. Once the pilgrims' roles as official female mourners at the cemeteries concluded, the government no longer needed the rest houses. The cemeteries reverted back to male-dominated landscapes, and the government erased the physical traces of women's influence and roles at the cemeteries. Whether through exhibits, tours, virtual reality renderings, or publications, opportunities exist to revive the memory and legacy of these rest houses and the Gold Star pilgrimages. Such projects will help educate the public about American women's involvement with military commemoration and their long history of influencing the military even before they were officially allowed to enter all arenas of military service and policy making.

AUTHOR BIOGRAPHY

Allison S. Finkelstein earned her PhD in U.S. history with a minor and certificate in historic preservation from the University of Maryland–College Park and is a historian for the federal government.

NOTES

For their support of this article, I thank Donald Linebaugh, Saverio Giovacchini, Michael Ross, Robyn Muncy, Jennifer Wingate, Cynthia Falk, Marta Gutman, Anna Andrzejewski, Jonathan Casey, Stacie Peterson, Kristine Krueger, Carroll Van West, Britta Granrud, David Bedford, Jason Blount, Geoffrey Fournier, Michael Shipman, Richard Hulver, Walter Frankland, Alec Bennett, Michael Knapp, General John S. Brown, Monique Ceruti, Gerald Torrence, Robert Dalessandro, Manon Bart, Kristin Britanik, and the entire staff of the American Battle Monuments Commission.

1. American Battle Monuments Commission, *Meuse-Argonne American Cemetery and Memorial* (Arlington, Va.: American Battle Monuments Commission, 2008), 10–15.

2. Jay Winter's assertion that "remembrance is part of the landscape" and Pierre Nora's concept of *lieux de mémoire* informed the author's concept of landscapes of memory in this article. Jay Winter, *Sites of Memory, Sites of Mourning: The Great War in European Cultural History* (Cambridge: Cambridge University Press, 1995); Pierre Nora, "Between Memory and History: Les Lieux de Mémoire," *Representations* 26 (Spring 1989): 7–24; and Pierre Nora, ed., *Rethinking France: Les Lieux de Mémoire*, vols. 1–3, trans. David P. Jordan (Chicago: University of Chicago Press, 2009).

3. Ron Theodore Robin, *Enclaves of America: The Rhetoric of American Political Architecture Abroad, 1900–1965* (Princeton, N.J.: Princeton University Press, 1992), 45–46. Cecilia Elizabeth O'Leary argues World War I was a turning point in the development of American patriotism at which a more militaristic form of patriotism overpowered more egalitarian ones. This could account for the marginalization of personal losses in favor of national sacrifices at the time. Cecelia Elizabeth O'Leary, *To Die For: The Paradox of American Patriotism* (Princeton, N.J.: Princeton University Press, 1999), 3–10.

4. Popular after World War I and World War II, living memorial buildings were public structures such as community centers that were intended to serve as utilitarian memorials. They were used as an alternative to traditional statuary memorials. Andrew M. Shanken, "Planning Memory: Living Memorials in the United States during World War II," *Art Bulletin* 84, no. 1 (March 2002): 130–47; and Allison S. Finkelstein, "Carry On: American Women, and the Veteranist-Commemoration of the First World War, 1917–1945" (PhD diss., University of Maryland, 2015), 3–5.

5. Rebecca Jo Plant provides a detailed assessment of women's political activism during the interwar period in the context of the pilgrimages. Rebecca Jo Plant, *Mom: The Transformation of Motherhood in Modern America* (Chicago: University of Chicago Press, 2010), 57.

6. Sally McMurry, "Women in the American Vernacular Landscape," *Material Culture* 20, no. 1 (Spring 1988): 33–49; Angel Kwolek-Folland, "Gender as a Category of Analysis in Vernacular Architecture Studies," in *Gender, Class, and Shelter: Perspectives in Vernacular Architecture, V,* ed. Elizabeth Collins Cromley and Carter L. Hudgins (Knoxville: University of Tennessee Press, 1995): 3–10; Joan W. Scott, "Gender: A Useful Category of Historical Analysis," *American Historical Review* 91, no. 5 (December 1986): 1053–75.

7. During the Spanish–American War the United States repatriated remains of the fallen, but the number of dead was much smaller than in World War I. Lisa M. Budreau, *Bodies of War: World War I and the Politics of Commemoration in America, 1919–1933*

(New York: New York University Press, 2010), 21; and Dean W. Holt, *American Military Cemeteries: A Comprehensive Guide to the Hallowed Grounds of the United States, Including Cemeteries Overseas* (Jefferson, N.C.: McFarland, 1992), 3.

8. The total U.S. World War I dead varies by source. "World War I Burials and Memorializations," American Battle Monuments Commission website, https://www.abmc.gov/node/1273; "America's Wars," Department of Veterans Affairs Office of Public Affairs website, http://www.va.gov/opa/publications/factsheets/fs_americas_wars.pdf; Budreau, *Bodies of War,* 21; Michael Sledge, *Soldier Dead: How We Recover, Identify, Bury, and Honor Our Military Fallen* (New York: Columbia University Press, 2005), 135; George Brown Tindall and David Emory Shi, *America: A Narrative History,* brief 8th ed. (New York: W. W. Norton, 2012), 765. *America: A Narrative History* lists the number at 126,000, whereas the ABMC and the Veterans Administration list it as 116,516.

9. Sledge, *Soldier Dead,* 136; "World War I Burials and Memorializations," American Battle Monuments Commission website. Including the missing, 33,717 Americans are buried or memorialized at ABMC World War I cemeteries.

10. Drew Gilpin Faust, *This Republic of Suffering: Death and the American Civil War* (New York: Vintage Civil War Library, 2008), xiv, 61–63.

11. Faust, *This Republic of Suffering,* xiv, 61–63, 86–87, 96–101.

12. *History and Development of the National Cemetery Administration,* U.S. Department of Veterans Affairs website, January 2014, http://www.cem.va.gov/docs/factsheets/history.pdf.

13. Budreau, *Bodies of War,* 27–36; Sledge, *Soldier Dead,* 25–36.

14. "Roosevelt Objects to Removal of Son," *New York Times,* November 18, 1918, 11; quoted in Budreau, *Bodies of War,* 70.

15. Elizabeth Conley to the Quartermaster Corps, February 20, 1921, folder 293 "Conley, Francis X.," box 1008 "Burial Cases Files, 1915–39," RG 92, Records of the Office of the Quartermaster General, National Archives, College Park (NACP). These burial files were located at NACP when the author conducted her research but have been moved to the National Personnel Records Center, St. Louis, Mo.

16. Elizabeth Conley to the Quartermaster Corps, February 20, 1921, NACP.

17. Katherine M. Gallagher to Captain A. D. Hughes, June 21, 1931, folder "Gallagher, Edward," box 1784 "Burial Cases Files, 1915–1939," RG 92, NACP.

18. "History," American Battle Monuments Commission website, http://www.abmc.gov/about-us/history.

19. Sledge, *Soldier Dead,* 136; Budreau, *Bodies of War,* 22.

20. The ABMC replaced two earlier government entities that regulated the creation of overseas memorials: the War Department's War Memorials Council and later the Battle Monuments Board. The government wanted to prevent the erection of substandard memorials and the oversaturation of the battlefields with monuments and gave the ABMC this first mission to fulfill. Budreau, *Bodies of War,* 108–11.

21. American Battle Monuments Commission, *American Memorials and Overseas Military Cemeteries* (Arlington, Va.: American Battle Monuments Commission, 2009), 3; "The Commission: Intro," American Battle Monuments Commission website, http://www.abmc.gov/about-us/.

22. American Battle Monuments Commission, *American Memorials,* 3, 6–14. During the interwar period, the ABMC included a Historical Section, staffed in part by Major Dwight D. Eisenhower. The Historical Section published guidebooks to the U.S. World War I battlefields and individual publications that summarized the operations of each AEF division. Steven Trout, *On the Battlefield of Memory: The First World War and American Remembrance, 1919–1941* (Tuscaloosa: University of Alabama Press, 2010), xv–xxxiii, 6–14.

23. American Battle Monuments Commission, *American Memorials,* 3, 6–14; "American Battle Monuments Commission to Assume Control of Clark Veterans Cemetery," American Battle Monuments Commission website, December 16, 2013, https://www.abmc.gov/news-events/news/abmc-assume-control-clark-veterans-cemetery#.VyFcxvkrKoo.

24. Faust, *This Republic of Suffering,* 248–29; William Blair, *Cities of the Dead: Contesting the Memory of the Civil War in the South, 1865–1914* (Chapel Hill: University of North Carolina Press, 2004).

25. Faust, *This Republic of Suffering,* 249, 271. Michele H. Bogart, *Public Sculpture and the Civic Ideal*

age Gold Star (Europe 1930, 1931, 1932, 1933PILG),” box 360, RG 92, NACP.

95. “Medical Report of Pilgrimage Gold Star Mothers and Widows in Europe 1930,” 12–13, folder 319.1 “Pilgrimage Gold Star (Europe 1930, 1931, 1932, 1933PILG),” box 360, RG 92, NACP.

96. Hattie B. Bisbee and Sarah Parker to Colonel Ellis, n.d., folder 330.1 “Pilgrimage Gold Star 1930,” box 376, RG 92, NACP.

97. Ettie M. Brown and Mrs. George Ingersoll to Colonel Ellis, n.d., folder 330.1 “Pilgrimage Gold Star 1930,” box 376, RG 92, NACP.

98. *Carry On,* 10, no. 1 (February 1931): 13–14, folder 1931, box 1922–1932, Women’s Overseas Service League (WOSL) *Carry On* Collection, Gift of Nelda P. Bleckler, Women’s Memorial Foundation Collection.

99. “Col. Ellis Report of 1930 Pilgrimage in Europe. Submitted March 7, 1931,” NACP, 17.

100. Final Report of the American Pilgrimage Gold Star Mothers and Widows to the Quartermaster General, September 13, 1933, 3.

101. Memorandum, LTC E. B. Gregory to the Quartermaster General, August 21, 1931, 2, folder 319.1 “Pilgrimage Gold Star (New York 1930 Appendix A),” box 361, RG 92, NACP.

102. Instead of hiring a hostess paid four thousand francs per month, Gregory proposed the rest houses should be under the direct supervision of the cemetery superintendents. Memorandum, LTC E. B. Gregory to the Quartermaster General, August 21, 1931, 2.

103. Colonel Ellis to the Quartermaster General, “Subject: Replies to the Remarks Contained in the Pilgrimage Observers Reports,” September 30, 1931, 3, folder 319.1 “Pilgrimage Gold Star (New York 1930 Appendix A),” box 361, RG 92, NACP.

104. Colonel Ellis to the Quartermaster General, NACP, 2–3.

105. Colonel Ellis to the Quartermaster General, NACP, 2–3.

106. “Memorandum for the Quartermaster General,” signed by Shannon, n.d., folder 319.1 “Pilgrimage Gold Star (New York 1930 Appendix A),” box 361, RG 92, NACP.

107. LTC R. H. Jordan to F. Santi, March 3, 1933, box 100, RG 92, NACP; John S. Pantelis, Superintendent of the Somme Cemetery, to Colonel R. H. Jordan, February 21, 1933, folder 319.1 “Pilgrimage Gold Star (New York 1930 Appendix A),” box 361, RG 92, NACP.

108. Colonel Jordan to the Quartermaster General, January 31, 1933, folder 319.1 “Pilgrimage Gold Star (New York 1930 Appendix A),” box 361, RG 92, NACP.

109. American Battle Monuments Commission, *Aisne-Marne American Cemetery and Memorial* (Arlington, Va.: American Battle Monuments Commission, 2009), 7; American Battle Monuments Commission, *Somme American Cemetery and Memorial* (Washington D.C.: American Battle Monuments Commission, n.d.), 8.

110. “Abstract of Proposals Opened,” Captain Henry S. Evans to Societ d’ Electricite du Rupt de Mad, December 10, 1932, folder 1930 “AGRS Paris 3400 Reports of Procurement Authorities & Etc.,” box 353, RG 92, NACP.

111. Budreau, *Bodies of War,* 115. The number of women buried in ABMC’s World War I cemeteries varies by source. “Women in ABMC World War 1 Cemeteries,” ABMC Headquarters Collection, Arlington, Va,; “List of Women Buried in World War I American Military Cemeteries,” ABMC Headquarters Collection, Arlington, Va.

HEIDI DODSON

Race and Contested Rural Space in the Missouri Delta

African American Farm Workers and the

Delmo Labor Homes, 1940–51

ABSTRACT

In 1940 the Farm Security Administration, as part of the New Deal, embarked on an experimental housing program in the Missouri Delta when it constructed the Delmo Labor Homes. Although classified as migratory labor camps, the FSA designed the ten communities as permanent housing projects for the growing workforce of farm laborers. The Delmo communities were segregated, and the experience of African American farm workers in the North Wyatt and South Wardell projects during the 1940s illustrates the interconnectedness of housing and education struggles in this Border South region. In 1941 black farm workers in Pemiscot County fought for the right to live in the South Wardell project when local white residents campaigned the government to keep them out. During this battle the workers stressed the importance of living in housing off plantations, where landowners were in control. The increased autonomy provided by the Delmo projects also facilitated residents' ten-year struggle for a public school in the African American Delmo community of North Wyatt. The community center, at the heart of the project, was a staging ground for this battle. Both of these examples demonstrate the importance of interrogating the spaces in which rural black freedom struggles took place.

In 1940 the Farm Security Administration (FSA) constructed ten rural housing projects for agricultural workers in the Missouri Delta, a region of six lowland counties in the far southeast corner of the state (Figure 1).[1] Collectively called the Delmo Housing Projects, or Labor Homes, three of the communities were built for African American workers, and seven, for white workers. Finished in 1941, they were part of the federal government's attempt to address the crisis of rural poverty and unemployment in the South during the Great Depression. Farm mechanization and the Agricultural Adjustment Acts (AAA) of 1933 and 1938 contributed substantially to this crisis. The AAA, which sought to raise the price of cotton by paying farmers to take part of their acreage out of production, encouraged landowners to evict sharecroppers from plantations and use day laborers during peak cotton picking and chopping seasons. Because housing was often tied to sharecropping arrangements, many farm families found themselves evicted and homeless.[2]

Scholars have explored the ideologies of New Deal planners who administered federal programs and resettlement projects and debated the extent to which they made a difference in the lives of poor rural people. Less work has been done on the lived experience of residents within these communities, particularly that of African Americans.[3] At the same time, historians like John Dittmer, Charles M. Payne, and Hasan Kwame Jeffries have turned attention to the grassroots struggles of rural African Americans during the twentieth century. This work has emphasized activism in the Deep South, where voting rights and education were focal issues, but it has left aside questions about the nature of struggles in rural regions of the Border South, where African Americans could legally vote.[4]

This article examines the relationship between black freedom struggles and the built environment by looking at African Americans' educational and labor activism during the New Deal in the Missouri Delta, a Border South region on the northern edge of the cotton South. The expansion of housing and community space independent of white-owned plantations was an important part of black freedom struggles in the region. The relative autonomy of such spaces, including the Delmo projects, facilitated residents' ability to strike for higher pay and fight for equal educational resources without fear of eviction.

The experiences of black workers also demonstrate that in this Border South region white supremacy operated through a combination of discriminatory practices enforced by law, violence, policy, and custom. For example, school segregation was mandated by the state constitution, as was the case in other southern states. African Americans in the Missouri Delta also could not eat at white-owned restaurants or enter public libraries. These latter exclusions were not enshrined in state law, but the consistency of their enforcement through the threat of violence meant that segregation resembled southern practices more than northern practices. This southern form of racial control was more prevalent in the counties along the Mississippi River, where slavery was the dominant labor system before the Civil War.[5]

In some parts of the Missouri Delta where slavery had been minimal, however, whites excluded African Americans from entire towns, townships, and larger rural areas, thus creating sundown areas. The term *sundown* refers to African Americans not being allowed in these places after dark, thus preventing them from living there. In most cases this exclusion was enforced by custom or violence, but some communities passed ordinances. Often, African Americans could enter such towns and shop, but they had to leave by sundown or they risked white violence. Sundown towns existed across the United States, but they were most prevalent in the bor-

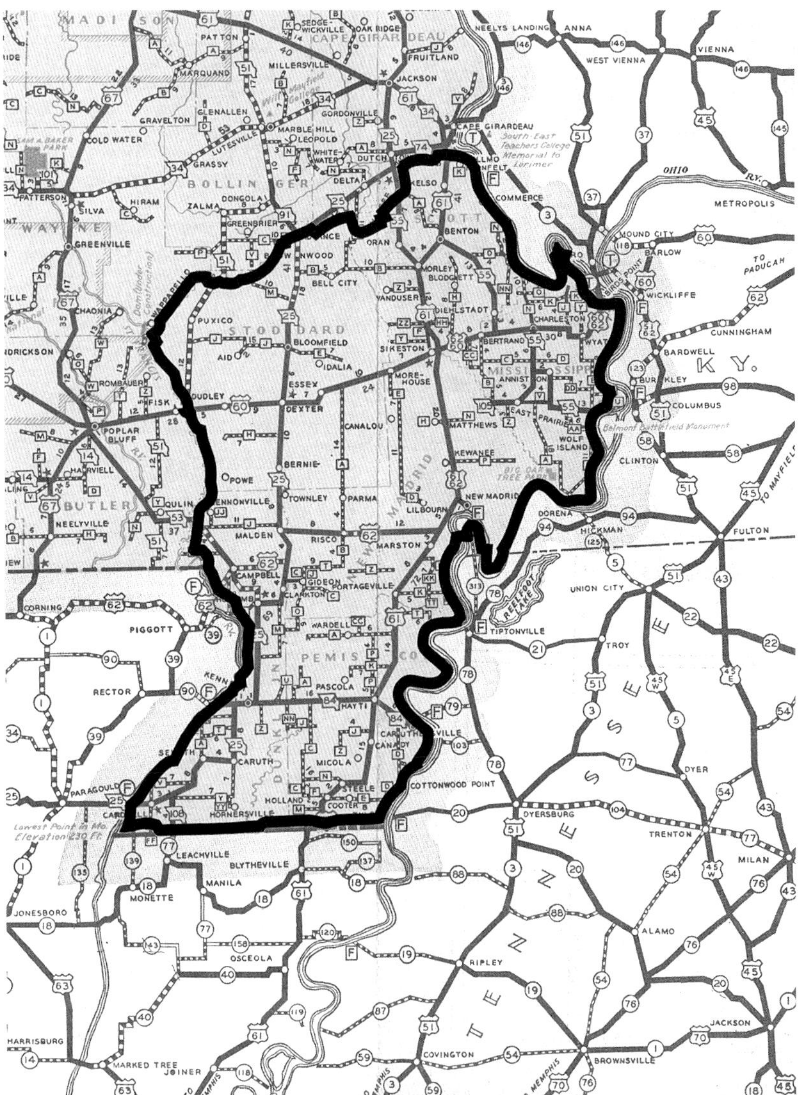

Figure 1. Outline of the Missouri Delta, or Bootheel, Missouri (Official) Highway Map, 1939. This region comprises the northern edge of the Mississippi River Alluvial Plain. Courtesy of the Missouri Highway and Transportation Commission and Davis Library, University of North Carolina-Chapel Hill; image cropped with additional labels by Heidi Dodson.

der regions, the Midwest, and the West. In most of the South, whites depended on black labor, so segregation, rather than complete exclusion, was more common. There were, however, sundown towns in upland areas of the South, such as the Missouri and Arkansas Ozarks, where the black population was relatively small.[6]

Residents of the African American Delmo projects had to contend with legal segregation and exclusion by non-legal means as they fought for expanded community and educational space in the Missouri Delta. In 1941 whites from the Wardell area opposed African Americans' occupation of the South Wardell project because they did not want the black population to increase in an area they deemed "white man's country."[7]

Black workers successfully fought back through a letter-writing campaign and threatened to leave the area if they could not move into South Wardell. Residents' stories illustrate that gaining access to housing was only one part of workers' ongoing battle. Families had to defend themselves from potential violence from whites and challenge the paternalism of well-meaning government officials and philanthropists.

The design of the Delmo projects, which brought together groups of residents and was influenced by the region's Border South geography and labor conditions, facilitated residents' autonomy as well as labor and educational activism by providing space for community interaction and organizing. In the black community of North Wyatt, the community building located at the center of the project was the focal point of residents' ten-year battle for a public school. Residents refused to let the school district use the space for classes, simultaneously maintaining pressure on public officials to build new facilities while reserving the space to map out strategies for this educational battle.

The experiences of residents in North Wyatt and South Wardell highlight the intersection of black labor and civil rights struggles, and they reveal the ways in which black farm workers shaped the built environment in order to advance freedom and full citizenship rights. Black freedom struggles did not just play themselves out on the landscape but were an integral part of the production of the vernacular built environment in this evolving rural region. Expanding access to housing as well as community and educational space was the goal of black activism, but at the same time, these spaces were central to further labor and educational activism, illustrating a sociospatial dialectic.

The Missouri Delta Becomes a Housing "Laboratory for the Cotton South"

The crisis of sharecropper evictions that took place in the 1930s affected most of the cotton South, but the Federal Emergency Relief Administration (FERA) designated the Missouri Delta as one of six "problem areas" in the county.[8] By 1938 labor conditions had worsened, and share-croppers expected a massive round of evictions in early January 1939. In order to force the situation into the public eye, Reverend Owen H. Whitfield, an African American sharecropper, preacher, and Southern Tenant Farmers' Union (STFU) organizer, planned a roadside protest that took place on January 10, 1939. Nearly 1,500 people moved their belongings to makeshift camps along U.S. Routes 60 and 61 in Missouri (Figure 2).[9]

The highway locations were strategic partly because of their visibility but also because the right of way where sharecroppers camped was public space under state government jurisdiction (Figure 3).[10] Privately owned land dominated rural areas; thus, sharecroppers found it difficult to organize and carry out protests while living on plantations. Landowners exercised social and economic control by keeping laborers on plantations under their surveillance and out of public sight. The obstacles African Americans faced when trying to collectively organize were particularly daunting because they owned less private property than whites and were often excluded from public buildings in towns. Even in public or black-owned spaces, retaliatory violence was an ever-present threat. By moving to the roadside in 1939, workers challenged geographies of labor and race that planters sought to create and enforce.[11]

Roads also held symbolic meaning because they led out of the region. If sharecroppers and laborers could not find housing or earn enough wages to make a living, they would hit the road, just as thousands in the Midwest and Great Plains had done in their exodus to California earlier in the decade.[12] Arthur Rothstein's photograph captured an image of Missouri highway officials moving protesters away from the roadside after the state inspector of public health declared their camps a health hazard. The intersection of county roads H and N with U. S. Route 61 in New Madrid County suggests workers along the roadside were at a junction in their lives as well as at a literal crossroads in this region (see Figure 3). They had to decide whether to stay and fight for a place to live and fair wages or leave the region and make a life elsewhere.

The demonstrators succeeded in garnering national attention, but state and federal governments responded slowly with viable solutions. The following year workers threatened another roadside demonstration, and this time Missouri governor Lloyd Stark took action, inviting landowners, sharecroppers, and government officials to a conference in St. Louis. The meeting drew widespread attention because, as FSA assistant administrator R. W. Hudgens noted, "the problem was one for all the South where cotton is produced, but the conference might herald a new era, might provide the prescription to bring the solution."[13] Thus, while the meeting had the short-term goal of addressing the shortage of housing and work for farm laborers in the Missouri Delta, the bigger issue was the transformation of agriculture, which was fundamentally restructuring the landscape of the cotton South. The Delmo Housing Projects were one proposed solution to the crisis of sharecropper displacement that emerged as a result of the roadside demonstration.[14]

The federal government viewed the Missouri Delta as a "laboratory for the cotton South" because it was experiencing the effects of agricultural mechanization and federal policy more acutely and at a faster rate than many areas farther south. Cotton as the primary cash crop and sharecropping as the dominant system of labor had taken hold in this region only during the early 1920s. Prior to this time, farmers produced small amounts of cotton, but agriculture more closely resembled that of the Midwest in its production of corn and wheat. Production patterns changed when the price of wheat dropped after World War I. In counties that had been producing little or no cotton, farmers decided to experiment with the crop. While the boll weevil was devastating cotton crops in the Deep South, the Missouri Delta was just far enough north that the insect had little effect.[15]

Landowners turned to cotton for their cash crop in 1922–23, and approximately fifteen thousand African Americans and smaller numbers of white farmers moved into the Missouri Delta from Mississippi, Arkansas, and Tennessee. During the 1920s it seemed as though landowners

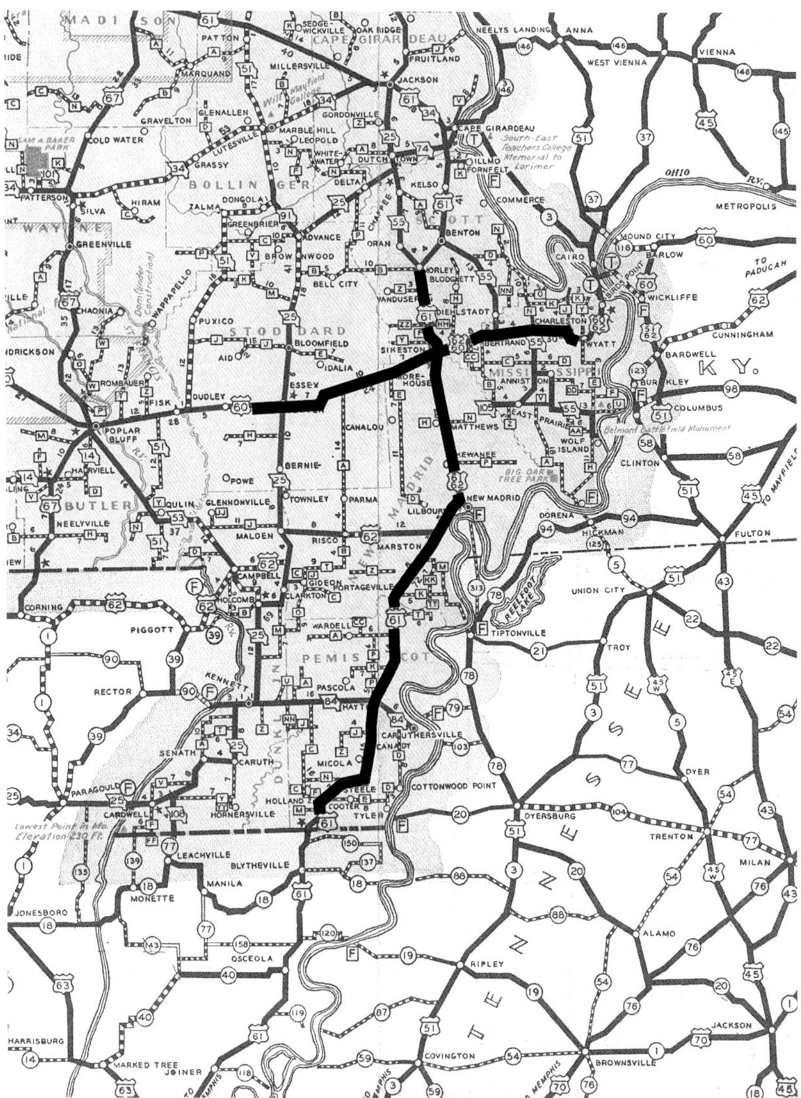

Figure 2. U.S. Route 60 (east/west) and U.S. Route 61 (north/south), Southeast Missouri, where sharecroppers staged their protest, Missouri (Official) Highway Map, 1939. U.S. Route 61 was a major cross-continental thoroughfare, dating back to the Spanish colonial period. Courtesy of the Missouri Highway and Transportation Commission and Davis Library, University of North Carolina–Chapel Hill; image cropped with additional labels by Heidi Dodson.

could not get enough labor for the expansion of this crop. With the onset of the Depression, however, the price of cotton dropped. The federal government mandated a reduction in cotton acreage, thus reducing the need for labor.[16] The Missouri Delta, then, by virtue of its adoption of cotton as a cash crop, southern migration, and its history of slavery and segregation, shared many characteristics with the South, specifically the cotton South. As a place of cultural confluence,

Figure 3. "New Madrid County, Missouri. State highway officials moving sharecroppers away from roadside to area between the levee and the Mississippi River." Photograph by Arthur Rothstein, January 1939. Courtesy of the Library of Congress, Farm Security Administration—Office of War Information Photograph Collection, LC-USF33-002975-M2.

however, it was distinctly a Border South region, also shaped by midwestern influences.[17]

When the FSA built the Delmo projects, they were classified as migratory labor camps, even though the houses were designed for workers who permanently resided in the area. This permanence reflected the difference between labor conditions in the cotton South compared with those of the East and West Coasts. According to FSA administrator Frank Haverly, "the Delmo Labor Homes differed from other labor supply centers in that its primary function was to provide better housing for farm labor families more or less permanently resident in the project areas, whereas other farm labor centers were established to house migrant workers following the crop cycles throughout the country."[18] Farm laborers rented the homes, paying three dollars per month and working up to four hours per week on project maintenance, as a way of supplementing their rent.[19]

The Delmo communities were also the first federal group housing projects in the Lower Mississippi Valley designed specifically to house farm laborers rather than sharecroppers. Sharecroppers, on the one hand, farmed land year-round for employers and received a share of the crop as payment. Housing, equipment, food, and other supplies were provided to the sharecropper, but the costs of this "furnish" were subtracted from the money each family received for its crop at the end of the harvest. Laborers, on the other hand,

did not farm land but worked for wages seasonally, picking or chopping cotton. In some cases housing was available on a plantation, but often it was not. The workforce landowners needed during peak seasons was much larger than their year-round labor force.

Up until the Delmo communities were built, most of the FSA's efforts in the South were geared toward resettling sharecroppers on cooperative farm projects, with land and quality housing, or building individual housing for laborers in a scattered pattern across plantations. If successful, FSA officials hoped group housing projects for farm laborers, like Delmo, might be expanded throughout the cotton South.[20]

The distinction between the permanent housing of the Delmo projects and the temporary housing of farm labor camps on the East and West Coasts was evident in the size and quality of the Delmo homes. Each was 640 square feet, with three bedrooms, a kitchen that connected to the combination living room and dining room, and a pantry and storage closet (Figure 4). There was a small screened-in porch and a stoop outside the front door. There were four different floor plans, so the location of the porch and the internal arrangement of rooms varied. Each house was of frame construction, was set off the ground on concrete piers, and had a brick chimney and shingle roof. The exterior walls were of finished pine and were painted white. The houses were intended to endure well into the future.[21]

The quality of housing construction and the incorporation of green space was consistent with working-class housing the federal government was building in urban areas, such as the greenbelt cities.[22] The push for better housing was connected to urban planner Catherine Bauer's vision of "modern housing," which was affordable, useful, and incorporated into planned neighborhoods with social amenities.[23] Modern housing for rural workers followed urban efforts. Initially, the federal government responded to an increase in seasonal and migrant day labor by building labor camps on the East and West Coasts as emergency measures. Shelter consisted of platform tents or metal shacks. By the late 1930s, farm labor housing had evolved to incorporate elements of the garden home, which emphasized green space and permanence. The Delmo projects exemplified this evolution and were experiments designed to remedy the housing and subsistence needs of growing numbers of farm laborers in the South.[24]

Unlike most sharecropper shacks on plantations, the Delmo houses were planned so residents could economically support themselves year-round despite the fact most worked seasonally. There was a concrete food storage area under each house that could be accessed from within the house (Figure 5). Having a storage space that protected food from the elements and from animals was critical for helping families get through the winter, when there was little work. It also meant they would not have to spend meager funds to purchase food at high interest rates from plantation and country stores. Another significant part of the community's design was the inclusion of surplus land that could be rented out or used for cooperatively grown crops. This land comprised about two-thirds of the acreage in each community and was separated from the large yard allotted to each house for a family garden.[25]

Finally, two other aspects signaled the FSA's intention that these housing projects would provide permanent homes: the absence of schools in the projects and the projects' locations near existing towns. The FSA anticipated the residents were either already embedded in local communities, having lived in the area before, or would become integrated after they moved there. The children would attend nearby schools. Residents would shop in existing nearby towns, and they would participate in the social life of the area as well as in their own community.[26]

This differed from most other FSA cooperative projects in the South, designed for sharecroppers, where the government typically built a school on project land. For example, the FSA built a seven-room school for African American children at the Mileston, Mississippi, farm resettlement project.[27] According to historian Donald Holley, school construction was done "when necessary."[28] Most resettlement communities were farm projects where each family had around sixty acres of land. The government had to prioritize

Figure 4. One of the group labor homes in the Morehouse Delmo community, New Madrid County, Missouri. Photograph by John Vachon, 1941. Courtesy of the Library of Congress, Farm Security Administration—Office of War Information Photograph Collection, LC-USF34-061854-D.

Figure 5. "Interior of group labor home at Grayridge, New Madrid County [sic] Missouri." Grayridge was one of the Delmo housing projects erected for white residents in Stoddard County (although its location is misidentified in the photograph's title). The concrete food storage can be seen in the floor of the kitchen, just to the right of the door. Photograph by John Vachon, November 1940. Courtesy of the Library of Congress, Farm Security Administration—Office of War Information Photograph Collection, LC-USF34-061841-D.

finding an appropriate tract to purchase, and often there were not adequate existing school facilities, particularly for African Americans.

Although FSA officials wanted the Delmo housing project residents to have relationships in nearby towns, they planned the communities such that they would spur internal cooperation and community interaction. This ideology had roots in the Progressive movement of the early twentieth century, which saw the built environment as a way to effect social change. The FSA designed the community to promote cooperation among residents as a method of empowering poor tenant farmers and laborers and facilitating democracy in a region where the white elite had control over most resources.[29]

Prior to building the Delmo projects, the FSA constructed individual worker houses in the Missouri Delta that were scattered across privately owned plantations.[30] Robert W. Hudgens, the deputy administrator of the FSA, and Phil Beck, the regional administrator, found this option unsatisfactory because, according to Hudgens, "there was no provision for community facilities, no plumbing, no schools, no crossroads, nor all the other things that make a community a decent place to live." Beck believed a "much more effective job can be done in the close settlement type because of the possibilities of getting people

together frequently and teaching them to work out their own problems."[31] In order to promote community decision making, each project had a community council, elected by the residents, that functioned in many ways like a town council.[32]

The community mind-set was also reflected in the inwardly oriented layout of the Delmo community. Each Delmo project had from thirty to eighty houses that surrounded a central utility, or community, building, which housed communal laundry facilities, meeting space, and offices (Figure 6). The East Prairie community was rectangular, with one entrance and exit. The streets encircled a central public green space (Figure 7). North Wyatt and North Lilbourn were also rectangular, but the South Wardell community resembled a baseball diamond with two branching culs-de-sac. These designs reflected the influence of European and American urban planners, who thought residents would benefit from open recreational space and "face-to-face relationships."[33]

Quality Housing and the Battle against Sundown Exclusion and Paternalism

While some aspects of the Delmo projects were designed to encourage year-round resident and community cooperation, others were intended to improve daily health and general quality of life and provide a step up from typical sharecropper shacks. The poor quality of plantation shacks affected black and white workers alike, but there was a racial hierarchy of housing, whereby white workers occupied the best housing available. The Delmo houses, through their standardization, were intended to eliminate this hierarchy.

Photographer John Vachon documented farm laborer A. J. Hunter and his family sitting on the front porch of the shack they occupied before moving into a Delmo home (Figure 8). Many of the sharecropper shacks in Missouri were built quickly around 1922–23, when thousands of sharecroppers moved into the area, and by 1940 they were nearly two decades old. Most were constructed with untreated wood that was permeable to insects like bed bugs. As the wood expanded and contracted through the seasons, it warped and cracked. These cracks were often stuffed with newspapers or whatever material could keep the

Figure 6. Group labor homes at the Delmo community of Morehouse, New Madrid County, Missouri. Photograph by John Vachon, November 1940. Courtesy of the Library of Congress, Farm Security Administration—Office of War Information Photograph Collection, LC-USF34-061853-D.

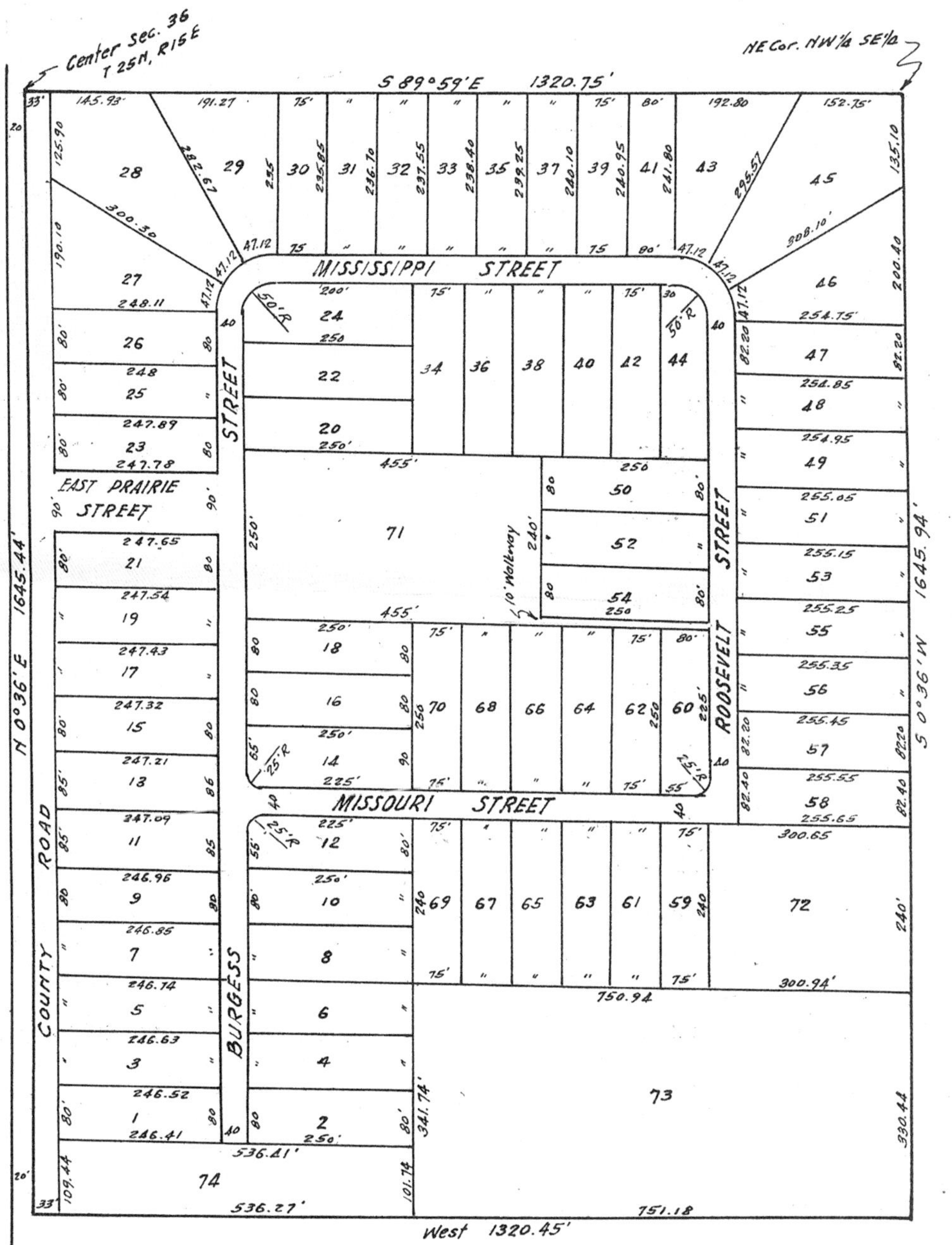

Figure 7. East Prairie Delmo community plat map, circa 1948. Courtesy of Mississippi County Recorder of Deeds, Charleston, Missouri.

wind out. Families covered windows with paper, tin, or cotton sacks or, as in the case of the Hunter family, did without. As Vachon's image reveals, some houses had to be built fairly high off the ground because of their flood-prone location. The Missouri Delta's rich farmland was reclaimed from bottomland swamps, and many areas were still subject to periodic flooding.[34]

Quality of housing had a significant impact on family health, especially in a region where bayous and flooding attracted mosquitos. The lengths that black families were willing to go in order to live in decent housing are illustrated by the experience of the Speller family. Bud and Nicula were sharecroppers and renters in Mississippi County, Missouri. Eugene Speller, their son, recalls they moved off the Goodin Plantation in 1934 and then lived in the rural neighborhoods

of Samos and Windyville. Near Windyville, his father rented land that was still wooded. Part of the arrangement with the owner was that they could keep all of their crop the first year if they cleared some of the timber and built a house.

They built a one-room cabin with a stove and two beds. Five kids slept in one bed, and the parents, in the other. They did not have much money to buy building materials, so they scouted around the town of East Prairie and found some tin for fifteen dollars. Eugene recalled how he prayed they would not have enough money to get the tin: "You know what it's like in the rain with a tin roof? It's worse than the wood owls. But when it rains on a tin roof, of course, it's terrible. And of

course it would get terribly hot in the summertime." His father was able to purchase the tin, but they could not afford glass or screen for windows, so they had to improvise by covering a hole in the wall with a piece of cotton sack.[35]

Eventually they left that land and moved into a slightly better, or "so-so," house. Next, they rented land recently purchased by several black farmers that had a very nice house. According to Eugene, it had "rooms for everybody, pump on the back porch, another one out at the barnyard. I mean that's up there." At the time the black farmers purchased the land, a white family was renting the house. This family told Bud Speller the white people in the nearby town of East Prairie would not stand for having blacks so close to their town. East Prairie was a sundown town; African Americans could come into town to shop but could not live within the city limits. Bud Speller told the white family, "You get out and I'll take care of the neighbors." He had his brother bring him a .32-20 Winchester rifle, which he "slept with beside the bed." His son Eugene was "thankful that nobody did anything. Nobody came round or else daddy was going to prison because he would have shot them. We had the chance to live in a decent house, after what we come in with."[36]

Bud Speller's willingness to defend the home with his life reflects the importance of a decent home to a family's survival and its quality of life. Having two water pumps, one for animals in the barnyard and one on the porch of the house for human use, saved valuable time hauling water. After moving in, his father built a fruit closet for his mother, a place to store the food she canned. Speller's actions were significant because they defied the boundaries of exclusion informally enforced by white residents of East Prairie. In the Missouri Delta, if a town excluded African Americans, the boundaries of such exclusion often extended about two miles from the town into the surrounding countryside.[37]

Like the home Bud Speller and his family rented, the Delmo homes were a significant improvement over typical tenant farmer abodes. The change is visible in the photograph of A. J. Hunter and his family moving into their new house in North Wyatt (Figure 9). Their house was built with wood coated with three layers of paint, sharply differentiating it from sharecropper shacks, which were often made of unfinished wood. Glass windows provided light as well as protection from the elements. The screened-in porch, while small, offered a place to sit while being protected from mosquitoes. The houses were intended to be aesthetically pleasing and comfortable, encouraging workers to stay long term, but many of their features were designed by the FSA also to improve the health of their occupants.

Although the FSA constructed these homes so that they would benefit workers, the agency was also paternalistic in how it managed communities. The project manager in each community, for example, had the power to override community council decisions. There was an assumption on the part of the agency that residents had to be taught how to work together, ignoring contemporary examples of working-class collective organization such as the STFU. This paternalism was also evident in the rules governing buildings in the projects. Residents had to obtain permission before they made any alterations to their homes. Reverend John Mack, one of the first occupants of the South Wardell project, was in charge of monitoring the community for any unauthorized changes. In 1945 the FSA was particularly conservative about allowing changes because, as a result of political backlash against the New Deal, Congress ordered all FSA resettlement projects liquidated.[38]

It was in 1944 that Mozetta and Lewis Henry moved into South Wardell with their family after their previous home on a plantation burned. Mrs. Henry quickly became frustrated with some of the limitations of their house. As she explained, "You had this little black pot stove and you couldn't brown no biscuits or nothing. . . . I just got so sick of that." The smoke from the heater also meant she constantly had to wash and iron the blackened curtains. She did not like the built-in cabinets nor the fact that there were no closets in the house. Her neighbors informed her "that Rev. Mack was gonna make me move if I . . . made any changes. I said, well, he got to do it cause I'm gonna make 'em." According to Mrs. Henry, "he would come every month and check

Figure 9. "Hugh Edwards, colored assistant camp manager, presents key to new home to Hunter family, Southeast Missouri." The Hunter family moved into one of the North Wyatt Delmo homes. Photograph by John Vachon, 1941. Courtesy of the Library of Congress, Farm Security Administration—Office of War Information Photograph Collection, LC-USF34-007635-ZE.

to see if you done anything to the house." One morning, she got fed up. Her son was at home, so she enlisted his help. They removed the pot stove and replaced it with a gas one, added a table and some chairs, and took out the cabinets with a hammer. Mrs. Henry's next-door neighbor watched the whole process anxiously, sure that Henry would be evicted. When Reverend Mack and a government official came by to inspect the house, however, they complimented her on how nice it looked. Neighbors who had gathered to see what would happen soon started making changes to their homes.[39]

Mrs. Henry, by refusing to ask permission for the changes she made, asserted control over her family's living space. For most of their lives, residents of the Delmo communities, as laborers and sharecroppers, had rented homes from employers. Landowner neglect, low wages, and the constant threat of eviction limited the control they had over their living conditions, including the quality of their housing. Delmo housing, however, was stable, up until the congressional order to sell the homes.

In 1945, in response to the FSA's liquidation announcement, a group of religious leaders, philanthropists, and businessmen in St. Louis formed the Delmo Housing Corporation in order to purchase the homes from the FSA and resell them to residents on reasonable terms. It is likely when Mrs. Henry made some of the changes to her home she was inspired by the possibility she would soon own it. According to Mrs. Henry's daughters, she had always been a trendsetter; in this case she helped change the culture of fear that permeated the community and gave courage to others who wished to make changes to their homes. Mrs. Henry's house at the time she was interviewed in 2013, juxtaposed with one of the original homes in the Morehouse project from 1941 (see Figure 4) demonstrates how residents individualized what were originally standardized homes and adapted them to meet their family's needs (Figure 10).[40]

Black Workers' Struggle for "Places to Live"

Mrs. Henry lived in her home until she passed away at the age of 103 in 2015, but her situation might have been vastly different if white residents in the area had their way in 1941 when the community was built. When local whites discovered that eighty newly constructed houses, located two miles from Wardell, would be homes for black families, they were outraged. Representatives of the local school board, the Rotary Club, churches, and other white community institutions wrote letters of protest to U.S. representative Orville Zimmerman and Senators Harry S. Truman and Bennett Champ Clark.[41]

One factor feeding this opposition was resistance to expanding black educational facilities. Landowners did not think African Americans needed to attend school beyond the elementary grades, because they wanted an adequate labor force to work in their fields.[42] Working- and middle-class whites resented paying for black school facilities. O. A. Knight, a member of the Wardell Board of Education, was worried the district would have to build a black high school. The state of Missouri, while maintaining school segregation, was more responsive to African Americans' pressure to improve educational opportunities than many Deep South states and, in some cases, put pressure on local districts to pass bond issues for black schools.[43]

African Americans also had some political leverage because they could vote in Missouri. A few years before, in the nearby Hayti School District, black World War I veterans had helped organize sharecroppers to vote for a school bond issue that would expand their high school to twelfth grade. Some white landowners tried to intimidate black voters by threatening to evict them if they voted, but a small number of black landowners offered sharecroppers a place to live if this happened. Attempts at intimidation occurred periodically throughout the region because black voters in some cases could swing the vote in one direction or another. Such attempts were not as widespread as in the Deep South, however, where African Americans were a demographic majority and posed a greater political threat. Wardell residents likely knew about the educational activism of African Americans in the Hayti area and were worried something similar could happen in their district.[44]

A second factor informing white opposition to South Wardell was the belief black workers should not have good-quality housing as long as there were white workers living in worse conditions. W. H. Foster, superintendent of schools and president of the Rotary Club of Wardell, argued, "We are not adverse to a housing project for Negroes, but we do feel that in our particular situation, and since we have a four to one greater need for White labor housing than we have for Colored, and since we have that White-Colored population ratio in this community, we

Figure 10. Home of Mozetta Henry from 1944 to 2015, in Homestown (formerly South Wardell), Missouri. Mrs. Henry chose to enclose her porch and stoop, and she added the lean-to section on the left side of the photo onto the house. Photograph by Martha Dodson, August 2015.

should entertain no other plan but insist that these houses be occupied by White labor."[45] Other residents complained to FSA regional director Phil G. Beck that there was such a visible difference in quality between Delmo homes and those of many white laborers they "consider[ed] the situation as serious as any the community has ever faced."[46]

The houses built for the Delmo projects were the same across white and black projects, but for many whites this very sameness was an affront to white supremacy and signified African Americans' aspirations to equality with whites. Although it was after World War II that single-family housing became most closely identified with social mobility and achievement of the American Dream for working- and middle-class whites, this connection began in the 1930s with the creation of the Federal Housing Administration (FHA), which backed private, financially accessible loans. The FHA did not want to insure mortgages in racially mixed neighborhoods, because they were deemed "inharmonious" and unstable, so it recommended whites use restrictive covenants as a way to ensure racial homogeneity. This endorsement reduced African Americans' access to loans and solidified the connection among quality housing, home ownership, and whiteness.[47]

A final source of opposition to African American workers' access to South Wardell came from landowners. They were not opposed to the presence of black workers, since many landowners depended on a steady supply of labor in the area. Instead, they were hostile to the fact workers would be living in a cooperative project on federal land rather than scattered across their plantations, where they would have had more control over workers' lives and labor. They feared that black workers living in close proximity to one another would organize for better wages and other issues, like education, and that they would become "uppity" or "clannish."[48] This was a source of consternation for landowners across the Missouri Delta where the projects were located. It was directed toward black and white projects, but there was more forceful resistance to black projects because any organizing would represent a challenge to white supremacy.

These concerns were not misplaced. Houses were built close to each other, which facilitated neighborly communication. The community, or utility, building, located at the center of each project, housed laundry facilities where women visited with each other while doing this domestic chore (Figures 11 and 12). The community building also contained a meeting room, which could be used for organizations such as the Women's Club or for recreation. Perhaps most important, the meeting room was where the elected community council met to discuss issues that affected the welfare of the residents.[49]

The FSA hoped the design of the Delmo projects would facilitate cooperation among the residents, economically and socially. However, black workers did not need the FSA to show them how to work and organize collectively. Cooperative practices were a core part of black culture, politics, and community building. Notably, black towns and independent farming communities were examples of "planned communities" that existed long before the federal government established its own under the New Deal. Prominent examples include Mound Bayou, Mississippi;

Figure 11. "Front view, utility building, Wyatt unit. Southeast Missouri." The utility building functioned as a community center. After World War II, residents expanded the building. Photograph by John Vachon, 1941. Courtesy of the Library of Congress, Farms Security Administration—Office of War Information Photograph Collection, LC-USF34-007645-ZE.

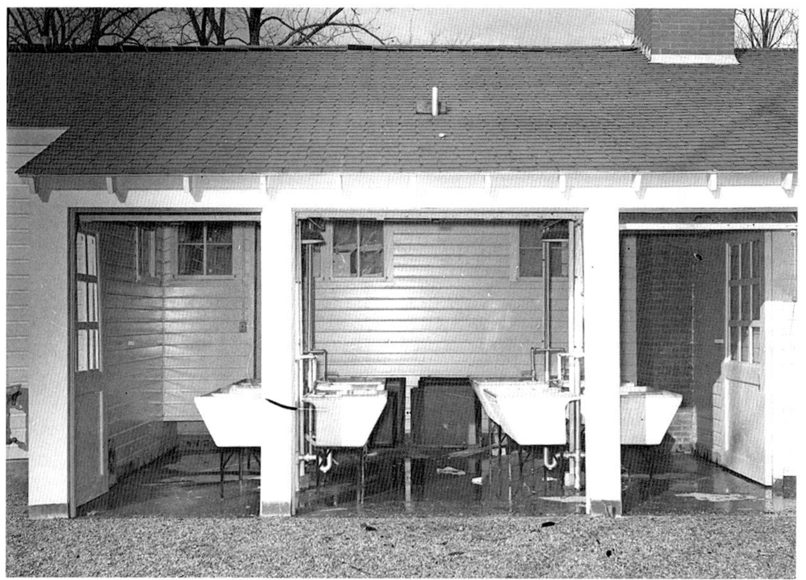

Figure 12. Laundry room in the utility building at one of the Delmo housing projects. Photograph by John Vachon, 1941. Courtesy of the Library of Congress, Prints and Photographs Division, Reproduction number LC-USF34-007643-ZE.

Brooklyn, Illinois; and Nicodemus, Kansas. In the Missouri Delta in 1940, the Christian Era Association, a corporation of fifty black tenant farm families, implemented its own solution to the crisis of displacement when it established a farming community called Pinhook.[50]

The federal housing projects, such as South Wardell, like black communities that came before them, provided an alternative to plantation living when African Americans did not have the financial resources to purchase land. They facilitated cooperation and collective action among black farm laborers by providing affordable housing and community space that offered some protection from the control of local whites because it was under federal jurisdiction. They also contributed educational resources that enabled survival on seasonal, low wages, such as classes on canning and food preservation. These were "live-at-home" programs, designed to enable farm worker families to be as self-sufficient as possible in a depressed economy.[51]

The autonomy of residents was not total. They had to contend with requirements of the FSA. One stipulation was that at least one wage earner in each family had to register as an agricultural worker with the U.S. Employment Service. Another was that family size had to be between four and seven people, although some exceptions were made for eight. Those living in the federal housing projects also had to contend

with the oversight of the project manager, who could override decisions made by the community council. Despite these constraints, residents had more autonomy in the Delmo projects than they would have had on plantations.[52]

The importance of decent housing free from the control of planters became a rallying point for black workers, particularly those who were already organized through the Missouri Agricultural Workers' Council, when whites near Wardell launched a political attack against black residency in South Wardell. Through a letter-writing campaign, over one hundred black men and women launched their own protest by signing a petition that demanded access to housing.[53] Another group of five black tenant farmers wrote a letter of protest making the same demands. Their correspondence refuted the notion that black workers did not need housing and pointed out that because very few African Americans owned housing, they were "placed in a very subservient position, subject to the personal whims of the land owning class. Negroes who reside in this section are forced to inhabit the worst tenement houses which are *merely places to stay and not places to live.*"[54]

They emphasized the crowded conditions of housing, particularly when several families had to share one shack, and they pointed out that proportionally their need was greater than that of white workers and tenants. As the signers of the petition reminded the government, "We have suffered most, we have suffered longest."[55] In making this statement, black workers referred not to the demographics of the general population, which local whites and the FSA used to determine resource allocation, but the demographics of need. White laborers experienced homelessness and hunger, yet comparatively, black workers earned the lowest wages, lived in the worst housing, and comprised a greater proportion of the lowest income bracket. For example, a government survey in 1935 revealed the average annual income for white sharecroppers was $415, and for white laborers it was $264. The average income of black sharecroppers and laborers, together, was only $251 each year.[56] Moreover, African Americans were often undercounted because, as NAACP field representative William Pickens noted, many lived in the backwoods.[57]

Black workers in the Missouri Delta recognized they had a right to federal assistance. Proportionally, compared with white workers, they had the most acute need because they experienced racial as well as class discrimination in every aspect of their daily lives. They were also intensely aware of the unfulfilled promises of Roosevelt's New Deal. Their disillusionment with the government's treatment of African Americans as well as the regional scale of their solidarity came through in the closing statement of their petition. If they were ignored, they would "depart from this county in a body on March 20, 1941," taking workers from other counties with them, and "*once again* this great American nation and the World shall know that this government of our United States of America, that preaches Democracy so loudly, has failed to practice its own preaching."[58] With World War II raging in Europe at the time of the petition, farm workers articulated sentiments that informed A. Philip Randolph's March on Washington Movement (MOWM) and that would coalesce into the national Double V campaign the following year, emphasizing victory at home and abroad.

The FSA took into account the worker protests, met with white Wardell complainants at a public meeting, and met with landowners at a private meeting. Representatives decided to go forward with their original plan to make South Wardell a black project, but they appeased whites by promising to seek money for a white project, which ultimately became North Wardell.[59]

North Wyatt: Protecting Community Space and Fighting for a Public School

Sixty-five miles away in Mississippi County, the residents of North Wyatt, a black project similar in size to South Wardell, also faced white resistance. White residents in Wyatt did not threaten the construction of the black housing project, but their unwillingness to fund a school meant that for a decade after the housing project was built, African American schoolchildren had to attend classes in a variety of overcrowded buildings, including the Church of God in Christ, Sanders

Chapel AME Church, the back of a segregated bus depot, and even a local tavern.[60]

After workers moved into North Wyatt in 1941, the FSA met with local and county school officials to encourage them to build a school for African Americans in the area. The Wyatt School District thought the FSA should help pay for the school, since it was responsible for bringing new families to the area through the housing project. African Americans had been living in the area since the 1920s, however, and while the North Wyatt project increased the black population, a school had been needed long before its construction.[61]

The white grade school was already overcrowded, and a state-imposed limit on school bonds meant the Wyatt School District could not build any more schools—white or black—unless it raised a significant amount of private money. Referring to whites in the Wyatt School district, FSA manager Carl D. Hudson wrote to a colleague, "They . . . insist that it is their desire to erect two buildings of exact construction, but cannot finance the Project, and will therefore meet the needs of white families first."[62]

When the Wyatt School District decided not to build a school for African Americans in 1941, county school superintendent J. Abner Beck suggested the housing project use its community building for classes. North Wyatt's community council rejected Beck's proposition and held fast to this decision for the next seven years.[63] In refusing to allow the school district to co-opt their community building, the residents of North Wyatt were asserting control over their community space while maintaining pressure on white education officials to build a public school building.

Black schoolchildren in the area, meanwhile, continued to attend school in local churches, and parents and teachers made the best of trying conditions. Sanders Chapel AME Church, one of the school locations, was typical of many rural, one-room churches built during the early twentieth century that functioned as public schools because black schools were underfunded in the South. Building size varied, but in Mississippi County a church such as Sanders Chapel was around 1,100 to 1,250 square feet (Figure 13).[64] Having to use religious buildings for public education was part of the double tax African Americans had to pay. Not only did private spaces have to function as public educational spaces, but the buildings were paid for by African Americans, while their taxes were directed toward white schools.[65]

The North Wyatt community council did not want its community building co-opted by the school district, because it needed the space for other activities, including labor and civil rights organizing. Churches were often important spaces for organizing, but conservative church leaders, fearful of retribution from whites, sometimes barred such activities. Using community spaces such as the North Wyatt community building sidestepped conflict with religious leaders and provided an important degree of autonomy from the local white power structure.[66]

The residents' increased independence prompted complaints from employers and politicians. Prominent businessmen E. F. Raffety, a cotton gin and alfalfa processing plant owner near Wyatt, argued for disposing of the Delmo program because "it has been a disappointment to this community, practically the whole project have signed up in the unions, which is very much against the interest of farmers in Mississippi County." Senator L. Danforth Joslyn, from Charleston, complained, "Some of these people in this project are spending their entire time in labor agitation. This community has become a nucleus of discention [sic] and disorder among the working class. A spirit has gradually grown up that has endangered the people and the welfare of the community. Last Sunday in Wyatt there was a near race riot which I directly attribute to the existence of this enterprise."[67]

The "spirit" that Joslyn referred to also informed the fight for equal educational facilities, which in 1946 was spearheaded by members of the North Wyatt Women's Club. The issue of pressing for a public school building had been put on the back burner with the advent of World War II, but in the fall of 1946 community women asked Delmo Housing Corporation (DHC) business manager Harris D. Rodgers to raise the school issue with

Figure 13. Sanders Chapel AME Church, Wyatt, Mississippi County, Missouri. The church building also served as temporary quarters for elementary school classes for African Americans during the 1940s. Photograph by Martha Dodson, August 2015.

the rest of the Delmo board.[68] At this time the landscape of black protest in the Missouri Delta and the rural South was changing. Black veterans returned from the war determined to transform oppressive conditions at home. This followed an effort in the early 1940s by the NAACP to increase membership in the rural South. In the Missouri Delta the organization initially recruited members of the black middle class: teachers, ministers, and landowners. By the mid-1940s, however, the number of black working-class members had grown substantially. In 1946 the Charleston chapter in Mississippi County, consisting of 515 members, including some occupants of North Wyatt, was the largest in Missouri outside St. Louis and Kansas City.[69]

Over the next two years, DHC board members met with Wyatt and Mississippi County school officials, but they made no progress, because the Wyatt School District was still paying off a bond for the white school.[70] The Delmo Board of Directors (BOD) looked into the possibility that the Rosenwald Fund, which was well known for its rural school building program in the South, could provide assistance. Unfortunately, by that time the Rosenwald Fund had been liquidated. It had assisted in a minor way with a few schools in Missouri during the 1930s, but because Missouri was a border state with a relatively small black population, it did not receive much support from the organization.[71]

The Delmo BOD then sought a legal opinion from St. Louis attorney Victor B. Harris. He looked into whether the 1938 *Missouri ex. rel. Gaines v. Canada* decision or the 1945 state constitution provided legal grounds to force the local school board or the state to provide a school.[72] Harris responded that according to state law, if the local school board did not comply with educational requirements for black schools, "such school district shall be deprived of any part of the public school funds."[73] This meant there were grounds to file a lawsuit. Moreover, the Wyatt School District would not be able to use lack of funds as a defense, since it was legally required to divide funds between black and white schools. The bond issue from 1941 thus should have resulted in funds being allocated equally.

Harris went on to note, however, "As a practical matter there are serious objections to bringing such an action [lawsuit]." He was undoubtedly referring to possible retribution from local whites. Harris suggested pressuring the state to withhold funds without going through the courts.[74] The Delmo board contacted the state department of education, but in June 1948 it responded there was nothing it could do unless the county implemented school district consolidation, which would make it eligible for additional construction funds.[75]

The people of North Wyatt grew increasingly frustrated that for years local, federal, and state governments cast blame on one another without action. Then, on September 20, 1948, Lucinda Crenshaw, Carryola Dickson, Georgia Jones, Otelia Scaife, and Rosie Holman, all members of the North Wyatt Women's Club, decided to take matters into their own hands. They walked their children from North Wyatt to the white elementary school, at the edge of the nearby town of Wyatt, and tried to enroll them in the school (Figure 14). They were denied permission on the grounds the state constitution of Missouri forbade African American and white children from attending school together.[76] The courageous action of these women was a direct challenge to white supremacy and risked physical and economic retribution. Notes from a Delmo board meeting suggest the women were threatened with arrest for disturbing the peace. When their efforts were reported in the local press, however, they ramped up the pressure on the Wyatt School Board.[77]

It is difficult to ascertain what type of planning preceded the actions of the Women's Club. Adam Holman, whose mother, Rosie Holman, participated in the integration attempt, recalled that the women made the decision on their own, without consulting with the community council or the NAACP.[78] What is certain is the women had been meeting in the community building for years and discussing issues of concern to their community. While such activities also took place in churches, the community building provided a space where women from different denominations could gather. It is likely the women had been discussing the education issue from the

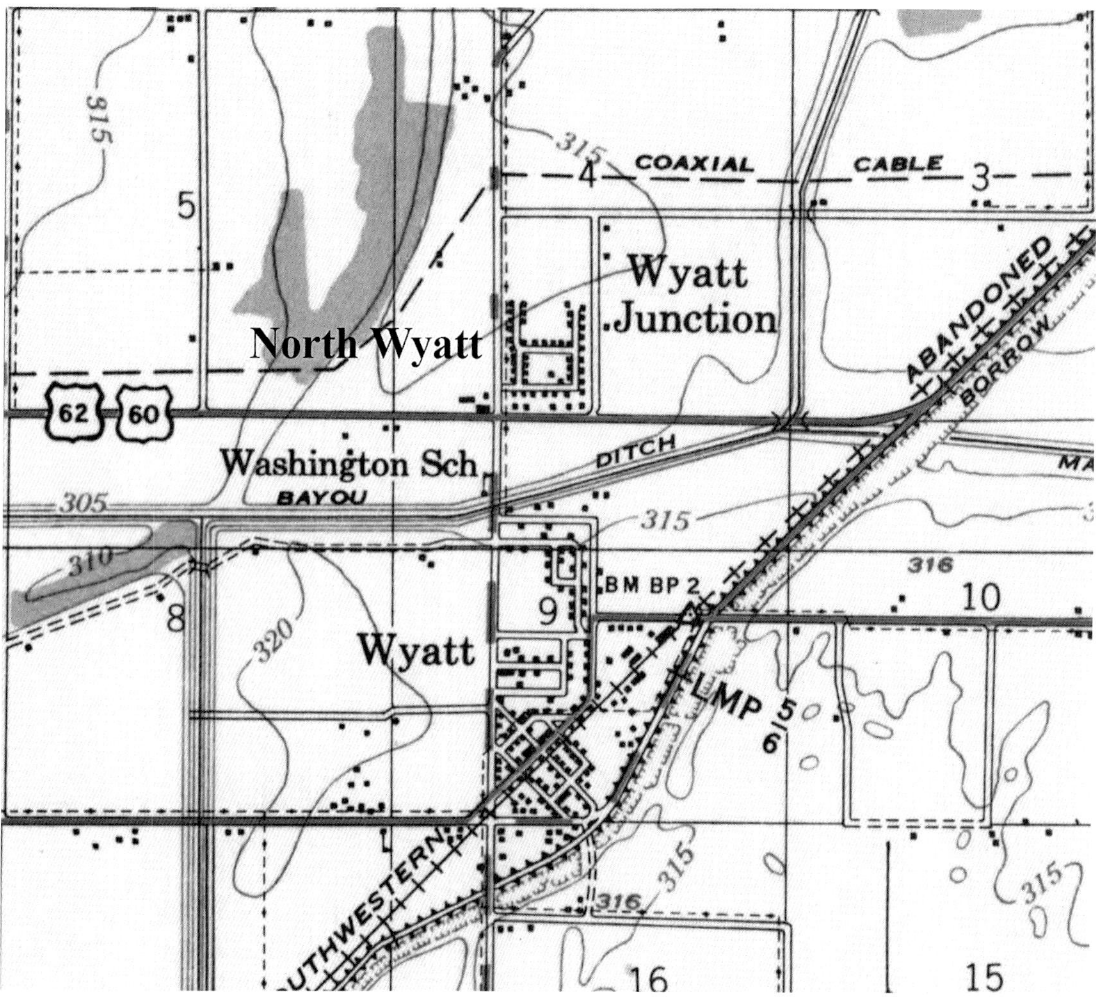

Figure 14. The Delmo project of North Wyatt (now Wilson City), Mississippi County, Missouri. Located just across Highway 60/62 from the town of Wyatt, North Wyatt was one of the Delmo projects created for African Americans. Wyatt was the location of several black institutions and businesses, but few African Americans lived within the town limits. U.S. Army Corps of Engineers, Mississippi River Commission, "Wickliffe quadrangle, Kentucky" 1:62,500 (Washington, D.C.: United States Geological Survey, 1952).

time they brought it to the Delmo BOD's attention in 1946. By 1948, seeing little progress had been made, they apparently decided it was time to move things along. After the women went to Wyatt, a white teacher told them the government was working on the issue, but Otelia Scaife commented to a newspaper reporter, "You know how long that takes."[79]

The women's attempt to integrate the white elementary school, six years before the *Brown v. Board of Education* decision, put their educational battle on the radar of the state and national NAACP. Two weeks later, over three hundred African Americans attended a NAACP meeting seven miles away in the small city of Charleston, where they raised money to file a lawsuit to force the district to build a school or integrate. Gloster B. Current, director of branches and field administration for the national NAACP office, was the keynote speaker. In a letter to the president of the Missouri State Conference of Branches, he indicated the National Office Legal Department was interested in the case.[80]

The national NAACP at this time was transitioning toward direct attacks on segregation, but a variety of political factors and differences of opinion among African Americans kept it from committing to this strategy. Instead, from 1948 to 1950, the NAACP decided to attack discrimination while leaving the remedy open to either equal facilities or desegregation. In other communities across the country, at that same time, similar cases were developing that would ultimately become part of the landmark *Brown v. Board of Education* case.

The threat of a lawsuit maintained pressure on the local school board. In 1950 the Wyatt School District finally passed a bond issue to build a black school, and legal action against the district was abandoned. The Booker T. Washington School was built in 1951, and according to Preston Heard, a former teacher at the school, the building was deliberately constructed outside the city limits of Wyatt because locals feared school desegregation was on the horizon (Figure 15). Around the time the Washington School was being built, the House Education Committee of the Missouri General Assembly approved a bill, by a significant margin, to end segregation in public schools. It was not the first time such a bill had been written, but it was the first time it was approved and sent to the floor. Ultimately, it failed, but there was some political support for school desegregation in Missouri, unlike in the Deep South.[81]

The fact that the North Wyatt case did not make it to court in no way diminishes the importance of the residents' grassroots activism. Often, battles like this, which were tied to the everyday built environment of black community life, did not garner much visibility beyond the local level. They remain central, however, to understanding the origins of broader social movements that did make national newspaper headlines. Although the plaintiffs in *Brown v. Board of Education* have received the most public and scholarly attention, battles for equal school facilities and, ultimately, desegregation were forged through the small campaigns of working people like Lucinda Holman and her fellow Women's Club members who decided to challenge the status quo. These battles were often repressed or truncated in some manner, but they reveal the spirit of civil rights activism that was burgeoning in the rural South. This activism did not take place evenly across the landscape but was shaped by the power dynamics of particular spaces. In the Missouri Delta the Delmo housing projects fostered collective action by supporting community cooperation and providing black farm workers an important degree of independence from plantation owners.

Reframing a Narrative of Black Rural Community Decline

The 1940s are often depicted as years of decline for black communities in the rural South, marked by the acceleration of agricultural mechaniza-

Figure 15. Former Booker T. Washington Grade School, Wyatt, Missouri, established in 1951. Photograph by Martha Dodson, August 2015.

tion and the migration of African Americans to northern cities. Yet as the intertwined housing and educational struggles of South Wardell and North Wyatt residents reveal, African Americans in the Missouri Delta pressured the federal government and mobilized labor and civil rights organizations to forge new community geographies off plantations. The increased autonomy farm workers gained in the Delmo projects and the social networks they formed through a rich civic life in the community center at the heart of the projects fueled further activism.

The activism and planning associated with these communities have been overshadowed by white-centered narratives of development and poverty that tend to depoliticize rural black history. Similarly, the spaces associated with rural black freedom struggles, such as the South Wardell community center, have literally disappeared. Their physical absence renders them invisible to the general population and, often, to historians, and it contributes to historical narratives that underrepresent African American agency.

It is vitally important, then, to ask questions about presences and absences in the landscape, to excavate the power struggles undertaken for and through the vernacular spaces of rural black community life. There are clues that help us unearth these forgotten stories, such as the entry to Wilson City, formerly North Wyatt. There, a sign

Figure 16. Entrance to Wilson City, Missouri (originally North Wyatt). This sign symbolizes community pride and the central role the Women's Club played over the years in planning and development. Photograph by Martha Dodson, August 2015.

stands prominently, indicating that Wilson City, established in 1941, is the "Home of the Women's Club" (Figure 16). As geographer Doreen Massey notes, social and economic changes do not just mark "reorganization of relations *in space,* but *the creation of a new space.*"[82] In the case of North Wyatt and South Wardell, the mechanization of agriculture, labor activism, and federal assistance created community spaces from which distinct new collective identities and political mobilizations emerged, shaped by the particularities of place and region.

AUTHOR BIOGRAPHY

Heidi Dodson recently received her PhD from the Department of History at the University of Illinois at Urbana–Champaign.

NOTES

1. The Missouri Delta region is also known as the Bootheel because the portion of the state that extends into Arkansas looks like the heel of a boot. The boundaries of the Bootheel are subjective, but the area is most commonly assumed to include the six counties of Pemiscot, Dunklin, Scott, Mississippi, Stoddard, and New Madrid.

2. B. Mildred Nelson Smith, *Delmo: Threshold of Freedom* (Mount Ayr, Iowa: Paragon Publications, 2003), 22; Jarod Roll, *Spirit of Rebellion: Labor and Religion in the New Cotton South* (Urbana: University of Illinois Press, 2010), 116. The African American projects were North Wyatt (renamed Wilson City), South Wardell (renamed Homestown), and North Lilbourn. The white projects were South Wyatt (renamed Pecan Grove), Grayridge (called Circle City), Morehouse (called "The Colony"), North Wardell, Kennett, South Lilbourn, and East Prairie. The original names of these projects refer to towns or villages that existed before the housing projects were built. The housing projects were usually located adjacent to the village or within a mile or two. Gobler, originally a black farm-owning community, was incorporated as a Delmo project in the 1950s.

3. Sidney Baldwin, *Poverty and Politics: The Rise and Decline of the Farm Security Administration* (Chapel Hill: University of North Carolina Press, 1968); Donald Holley, *Uncle Sam's Farmers: The New Deal Communities in the Lower Mississippi Valley* (Urbana: University of Illinois Press, 1975); Jess Gilbert and Carolyn Howe, "Beyond 'State vs. Society': Theories of the State and New Deal Agricultural Policies," *American Sociological Review* 56, no. 2 (April 1991): 204–20. Spencer D. Wood has explored the importance of land ownership to civil rights activism at Mileston Farms, an African American FSA community in Mississippi. See "The Roots of Black Power: Land, Civil Society, and the State in the Mississippi Delta, 1935–1968," (PhD diss., University of Wisconsin–Madison, 2006).

4. For studies of grassroots struggles in the rural Deep South, see, for example, John Dittmer, *Local People: The Struggle for Civil Rights in Mississippi* (Urbana: University of Illinois Press, 1995); Robin D. G. Kelley, *Hammer and Hoe: Alabama Communists during the Great Depression* (Chapel Hill: University of North Carolina Press, 1991); Nan Elizabeth Woodruff, *American Congo: The African American Freedom Strug-*

gle in the Delta (Cambridge, Mass.: Harvard University Press, 2003); and Hasan Kwame Jeffries, *Bloody Lowndes: Civil Rights and Black Power in Alabama's Black Belt* (New York: New York University Press, 2009). In *Spirit of Rebellion,* Jarod Roll examines the intersection of labor and religion among black and white workers in the Missouri Delta. For an understanding of urban black freedom struggles in the Border South, see Clarence Lang, *Grassroots at the Gateway: Class Politics and Black Freedom Struggle in St. Louis, 1936–1975* (Ann Arbor: University of Michigan Press, 2009); and Tracy E. K'Meyer, *Civil Rights in the Gateway to the South: Louisville, Kentucky, 1945–1980* (Lexington: University Press of Kentucky, 2009).

5. Gerald W. Heaney and Susan Uchitelle, *Unending Struggle: The Long Road to an Equal Education in St. Louis* (St. Louis: Reedy Press, 2004), 58–59, 62; Pauli Murray, ed., *States' Laws on Race and Color,* rev. ed. (1951; repr., Athens: University of Georgia Press, 1997), 251–54 (citations refer to the University of Georgia Press edition); W. Wilder Towle, *Delmo Saga* (Lilbourn, Mo.: Delmo Housing Corporation, 1983), 35; Preston Heard, interview by Heidi Dodson, January 23, 2013. Public spaces were most commonly segregated through custom, but in 1939 the state of Missouri passed state statute 10474, which permitted boards of education to establish segregated libraries, parks, and playgrounds in school districts.

6. In the Missouri Delta and in parts of northeast Arkansas and southern Illinois, there was a "deadline" that divided territory where African Americans could live from areas where they were excluded. See James W. Loewen, *Sundown Towns: A Hidden Dimension of American Racism* (New York: New Press, 2005), 3–5, 76–77, 99–103. There are places within the South where blacks have been excluded. They tend to be upland areas like the Missouri and Arkansas Ozarks.

7. P. E. Bussert to Orville Zimmerman, February 15, 1941, folder "AD-MO-21-911-045 Delmo Labor Hms. 1941 Reg. 3 Applicants-Selection," box 414 "FSA & Predecessor Agencies Project Records, 1935–1940," Records of the Farmers Home Administration (FmHA), Record Group (RG) 96, National Archives at College Park, College Park, Md.

8. Charles S. Aiken, *The Cotton Plantation South since the Civil War* (Baltimore, Md.: Johns Hopkins University Press, 1998), 126; "SE Missouri Study," box 1, Report File on the Southeast Missouri Study, 1937,

Records of Region 3, Indianapolis, Ind., Records of the Farmers Home Administration (FmHA), Record Group (RG) 96, National Archives and Records Administration (NARA)—Great Lakes Region (Chicago).

9. Louis Cantor, *A Prologue to the Protest Movement: The Missouri Sharecropper Roadside Demonstration of 1939* (Durham, N.C.: Duke University Press, 1969), 3, 63–64; Roll, *Spirit of Rebellion,* 132–37. This was an interracial demonstration, although most of the protesters were African American.

10. Harry F. Parker to Governor Lloyd Stark, January 19, 1939, folder 1938, Lloyd Crow Stark Papers, C0004, State Historical Society of Missouri. Highways 61 and 60 were U.S. highways, but it was Harry F. Parker, inspector from the state board of health, who declared the camps a public health hazard. Parker collaborated with Colonel Marvin Casteel, superintendent of the Missouri State Highway Patrol, to remove the protestors.

11. Don Mitchell, *Lie of the Land: Migrant Workers and the California Landscape* (Minneapolis: University of Minnesota Press, 1996), 26–28, 40 44.

12. James N. Gregory, *American Exodus: The Dust Bowl Migration and Okie Culture in California* (New York: Oxford University Press, 1991), 1–19.

13. "Move to Assist Farm Workers," *Southeast Missourian* (Cape Girardeau, Mo.), January 6, 1940.

14. Roll, *Spirit of Rebellion,* 156–57; "New FSA Plan for Semo Farmers Gets Under Way," *Enterprise-Courier* (Charleston, Mo.), March 7, 1940.

15. U.S. Department of Agriculture, U.S. Farm Security Administration, *Southeast Missouri: A Laboratory for the Cotton South* (Washington, D.C., 1940), 1.

16. Roll, *Spirit of Rebellion,* 56–59, 71–77, 116.

17. African Americans in the Missouri Delta retained the right to vote. They also experienced less direct supervision in the fields, compared with African Americans in the Deep South, and had more autonomy in making farming decisions. Adam D. Holman, interview by Heidi Dodson, September 30, 2012.

18. Smith, *Delmo,* 152–54. For an understanding of the Atlantic Coast migrant labor force, which included African Americans from the South, see Cindy Hahamovitch, *The Fruits of Their Labor: Atlantic Coast Farmworkers and the Making of Migrant Poverty, 1870–1945* (Chapel Hill: University of North Carolina Press, 1997).

19. Smith, *Delmo,* 46. The rental rates increased in

1943 when the War Food Administration temporarily took over management of the camps.

20. Roll, *Spirit of Rebellion*, 175–76; Paul K. Conkin, *Tomorrow a New World: The New Deal Community Program* (Ithaca, N.Y.: Cornell University Press, 1959), 93–213; Holley, *Uncle Sam's Farmers*, 17–29.

21. Smith, *Delmo*, 22–24.

22. Conkin, *Tomorrow a New World*, 305–25.

23. Gail Radford, *Modern Housing for America: Policy Struggles in the New Deal Era* (Chicago: University of Chicago Press, 1996), 59–69.

24. Cindy Hahamovitch, *The Fruits of Their Labor*, 151–81; Greg Hise, "From Roadside Camps to Garden Homes: Housing and Community Planning for California's Migrant Work Force, 1935–1941," *Gender, Class, Shelter: Perspectives in Vernacular Architecture*, 5 (Knoxville: University of Tennessee Press, 1995): 243–58.

25. Towle, *Delmo Saga*, 18; Smith, *Delmo*, 22–24.

26. Joseph Francis Xavier Paiva, "A Study of Unplanned Effects of Planned Change in Community Development" (PhD diss., Brandeis University, 1968), 74.

27. Wood, "The Roots of Black Power," 95–100.

28. Holley, *Uncle Sam's Farmers*, 136.

29. Hise, "From Roadside Camps to Garden Homes," 243.

30. P. G. Beck to Dr. W. W. Alexander, May 2, 1940, folder "AD-MO-21-540 Delmo Security Homes," box 414 "FSA & Predecessor Agencies Project Records, 1935–1940," FmHA, RG 96, National Archives at College Park, College Park, Md.

31. Towle, *Delmo Saga*, 18; Philip G. Beck to Walter E. Packard, November 29, 1939, folder "060—July 1939–June 1940," box 229 "Region 3—General Correspondence, 1935–1942," FmHA, RG 96, NARA–Great Lakes (Chicago).

32. Smith, *Delmo*, 53.

33. Radford, *Modern Housing for America*, 69.

34. Thad Snow, *From Missouri* (New York: Houghton Mifflin, 1954), 157.

35. Eugene Speller, interview by Heidi Dodson, June 11, 2012, interview U-0856, Southern Oral History Program Collection #4007, Southern Historical Collection, Wilson Library, University of North Carolina at Chapel Hill.

36. Eugene Speller, interview by Heidi Dodson, June 11, 2012. White resistance to African Americans living near East Prairie also obstructed the FSA's plan to build a cooperative project in the area. "Club Objects to FSA Project," *Enterprise-Courier* (Charleston, Mo.), January 29, 1942; "East Prairie Men Tell FSA Officials Objections to Colony," *Enterprise-Courier* (Charleston, Mo.), February 5, 1942; "Two Houses and Barn Destroyed on Colony Site," *Enterprise-Courier* (Charleston, Mo.), February 5, 1942.

37. Eugene Speller, interview by Heidi Dodson, June 11, 2012. Sources do not specify why this exclusionary buffer existed, but residents of East Prairie did not allow African Americans to live within city limits, and they likely anticipated future town growth and the expansion of these boundaries. Specifically, white resistance to financing black education was one of the motivations for excluding African Americans from towns.

38. Mitchell, *Lie of the Land*, 184–86; Holley, *Uncle Sam's Farmers*, 134–36; Mozetta Henry, Juanita Henry, and Toni Powell, interview by Heidi Dodson, October 28, 2013; Smith, *Delmo*, 142.

39. Mozetta Henry, Juanita Henry, and Toni Powell, interview by Heidi Dodson, October 28, 2013. Mrs. Henry could not recall the exact year she made the changes to her house, but she did remember that one of the reasons the owners could not make changes was because the houses were going to be sold. This narrows the time frame to 1945, when the Delmo projects were liquidated by the FSA.

40. Roll, *Spirit of Rebellion*, 175–76; Mozetta Henry, Juanita Henry, and Toni Powell, interview by Heidi Dodson, October 28, 2013.

41. "Mozetta (Hull) Henry," Carter Funeral Home website, http://www.carterfuneralhomemo.com/obits/obituary.php?id=639969; P. G. Beck to Thomas S. Terry, February 27, 1941, folder "RP-MO-21-160-02 Complaints," box 414 "FSA & Predecessor Agencies Project Records, 1935–1940," FmHA, RG 96, National Archives at College Park, College Park, Md.

42. "SE Missouri Study," box 1, Report File on the Southeast Missouri Study, 1937, Records of Region 3, Indianapolis, Ind., FmHA, RG 96, (NARA)—Great Lakes (Chicago); Alex Cooper, interview by Heidi Dodson, October 25, 2012.

43. O. A. Knight to Orville Zimmerman, February 17, 1941, folder "AD-MO-21-911-045 Delmo Labor Hms. 1941 Reg. 3 Applicants-Selection," box 414 "FSA

& Predecessor Agencies Project Records, 1935–1940," FmHA, RG 96, National Archives at College Park, College Park, Md.; Peter William Moran, "Border State Ebb and Flow: School Desegregation in Missouri, 1954–1999," in *With All Deliberate Speed: Implementing "Brown v. Board of Education,"* ed. Brian J. Daugherity and Charles C. Bolton (Fayetteville: University of Arkansas Press, 2008), 177–78; "Information Regarding the Proposed Bond Issue of $56,000," *Missouri Herald* (Hayti, Mo.), August 7, 1931. In 1931 the state department of education threatened to withhold financial aid for the construction of a white high school in Hayti if the district did not build a four- to five-room brick school building for African Americans. At that time, 155 students were being taught in a one-room school.

44. Alex Cooper, interview by Heidi Dodson, October 25, 2012. Will Sarvis, *J. V. Conran and Rural Political Power: Boss Mythology in the Missouri Bootheel* (Lanham, Mass.: Lexington Books, 2012), 22–33; "Warned Negroes from Polls," *Kansas City Star,* November 9, 1922; "Strife Marks Election Day in Pemiscot," *Missouri Herald* (Hayti, Mo.), November 9, 1934.

45. W. H. Foster to Hon. Harry S. Truman, February 15, 1941, folder "AD-MO-21-911-045 Delmo Labor Hms. 1941 Reg. 3 Applicants-Selection," box 414 "FSA & Predecessor Agencies Project Records, 1935–1940," FmHA, RG 96, National Archives at College Park, College Park, Md.

46. P. G. Beck to C. B. Baldwin, March 21, 1941, folder "RP-83-MO-21-432 Budgets," box 414 "FSA & Predecessor Agencies Project Records, 1935–1940," FmHA, RG 96, National Archives at College Park, College Park, Md.

47. Dianne Harris, *Little White Houses: How the Postwar Home Constructed Race in America* (Minneapolis: University of Minnesota Press, 2013), 1–2; *Encyclopedia of African American History, 1896 to the Present: From the Age of Segregation to the Twenty-first Century,* s.v. "Buchanan v. Warley," by James W. Loewen, Oxford African American Studies Center, http://www.oxfordaasc.com.proxy2.library.illinois.edu/; Kenneth T. Jackson, *Crabgrass Frontier: The Suburbanization of the United States* (New York: Oxford University Press, 1985), 203–13.

48. "Fairness of FSA Brought Opposition," *Atlanta Daily World,* May 5, 1945.

49. Smith, *Delmo,* 22–25; "80-House Labor Settlement Nears Completion," *Missouri Herald* (Hayti, Mo.), October 25, 1940; F. Brown, interview by Heidi Dodson, October 28, 2012.

50. Sundiata Cha-Jua, *America's First Black Town: Brooklyn, Illinois, 1830–1915* (Urbana: University of Illinois Press, 2000), 1–10; and "Fifty Negro Families Purchase 2,000-Acre Tract for Colony," *Southeast Missourian* (Cape Girardeau, Mo.), January 23, 1940.

51. Constance E. H. Daniel, "Security for Farmers," *Crisis,* April 1940, 106; Smith, *Delmo,* 30–31.

52. Smith, *Delmo,* 30–31.

53. Petition, March 1941, folder "AD-MO-21-160-02 Delmo Labor Home," box 414 "FSA & Predecessor Agencies Project Records, 1935–1940," FmHA, RG 96, National Archives at College Park, College Park, Md. Many of the petitioners were members of the Missouri Agricultural Workers Council (MAWC), which was a subsidiary of the United Cannery, Agricultural, Packing, and Allied Workers of America (UCAPAWA). See Roll, *Spirit of Rebellion,* 160.

54. Thomas S. Terry et al. to P. G. Beck, February 2, 1941, folder "RP-MO-21-160-02 Complaints," box 414 "FSA & Predecessor Agencies Project Records, 1935–1940," FmHA, RG 96, National Archives at College Park, College Park, Md. (emphasis added).

55. Petition, March 1941, folder "AD-MO-21-160-02 Delmo Labor Home," box 414 "FSA & Predecessor Agencies Project Records, 1935–1940," FmHA, RG 96, National Archives at College Park, College Park, Md.

56. Roll, *Spirit of Rebellion,* 95.

57. Max R. White, Douglas Ensminger, and Cecil L. Gregory, U.S. Department of Agriculture, U.S. Farm Security Administration, *Rich Land, Poor People,* research report no. 1 (Indianapolis, Ind.: U.S. Department of Agriculture, U.S. Farm Security Administration, 1938), 5; Walter White to C. B. Baldwin, March 12, 1941, folder "AD-MO-21-911-045 Delmo Labor Hms. 1941 Reg. 3 Applicants-Selection," box 414 "FSA & Predecessor Agencies Project Records, 1935–1940," FmHA, RG 96, National Archives at College Park, College Park, Md.

58. Petition, March 1941, folder "AD-MO-21-160-02 Delmo Labor Home," box 414 "FSA & Predecessor Agencies Project Records, 1935–1940," FmHA, RG 96, National Archives at College Park, College Park, Md. (emphasis added).

59. P. G. Beck to C. B. Baldwin, March 21, 1941,

folder "AD-MO-21-911-045 Delmo Labor Hms. 1941 Reg. 3 Applicants-Selection," box 414 "FSA & Predecessor Agencies Project Records, 1935–1940," FmHA, RG 96, National Archives at College Park, College Park, Md.

60. Smith, *Delmo*, 22; "Negro Children Ask to Be Admitted to White School at Wyatt Last Monday Morning," *Enterprise-Courier* (Charleston, Mo.), September 23, 1948; "No Fund to Build School for Negroes," *Southeast Missourian* (Cape Girardeau, Mo.), September 22, 1948; Towle, *Delmo Saga*, 62.

61. Frank K. Ashby to Sen. Harry S. Truman, March 27, 1941, folder "AD-MO-21-615 Delmo Project," box 414 "FSA & Predecessor Agencies Project Records, 1935–1940," FmHA, RG 96, National Archives at College Park, College Park, Md.

62. Carl D. Hudson to Marvin M. Gray, April 29, 1941, folder "AD-MO-21-615 Delmo Project," box 414 "FSA & Predecessor Agencies Project Records, 1935–1940," FmHA, RG 96, National Archives at College Park, College Park, Md.

63. Hudson to Gray, April 29, 1941, National Archives at College Park, College Park, Md.; Smith, *Delmo*, 33.

64. The dimensions of Sanders Chapel A. M. E. are not readily available, but similar churches in the county that functioned as schools include New Bethlehem Missionary Baptist Church, previously the Blue School, and Mt. Zion Missionary Baptist Church. See Gary Kremer and Brett Rogers, *African American Schools in Rural and Small-Town Missouri*, Office of Historic Preservation, Missouri Department of Natural Resources, Mississippi County, 2002, no. IV-8, no. IV-13. This is a survey of extant African American school buildings, including churches that functioned as schools.

65. James D. Anderson, *The Education of Blacks in the South, 1860–1935* (Chapel Hill: University of North Carolina Press, 1988), 154–56.

66. Dittmer, *Local People*, 76–77, 146. When Owen Whitfield was organizing the roadside demonstration, the last large organizational meeting took place at the First Baptist Church in Sikeston, an African American church. The editor of the white newspaper criticized this event in a threatening manner but mistakenly said it took place at a different African American church, the Second Baptist Church. Reverend S. D. Woods, pastor of the Second Baptist Church, published a response the following week reassuring the white elite in Sikeston he never would have hosted such a meeting "without consulting the officials of our city." Charles L. Blanton, "The P.C. Editor Says," *Sikeston (Mo.) Standard,* January 13, 1939; Rev. S. D. Woods, *Sikeston (Mo.) Standard,* January 20, 1939.

67. Smith, *Delmo*, 131–32.

68. Roll, *Spirit of Rebellion*, 176.

69. Patricia Sullivan, *Lift Every Voice: The NAACP and the Making of the Civil Rights Movement* (New York: New Press, 2009), 82–84; Lucille Black, membership report, October 25, 1946, Missouri State Conference of Branches, Papers of the NAACP, microfilm, part 26C, roll 10.

70. Towle, *Delmo Saga*, 62.

71. Minutes, Board of Directors, November 21, 1947; Minutes, Board of Directors, January 23, 1948, series 1, box 1, Delmo Housing Corporation Records, University Archives, Department of Special Collections, Washington University Libraries; Mary S. Hoffschwelle, *The Rosenwald Schools of the American South* (Gainesville: University Press of Florida, 2006), 1–6, 139, 283.

72. Memorandum, Harold C. Hanke to Victor B. Harris, November 24, 1947, folder "Wyatt School District," series 1, box 3, Delmo Housing Corporation Records, University Archives, Department of Special Collections, Washington University Libraries.

73. Victor B. Harris to Henry V. Putzel, March 17, 1948, folder "Wyatt School District," series 1, box 3, Delmo Housing Corporation Records, University Archives, Department of Special Collections, Washington University Libraries.

74. Harris to Putzel, March 17, 1948, Delmo Housing Corporation Records.

75. Memorandum, Hanke to Harris, June 30, 1948, Delmo Housing Corporation Records.

76. "Ask Negro Pupils be Permitted to Attend White School at Wyatt," *Southeast Missourian* (Cape Girardeau, Mo.), September 21, 1948; "No Fund to Build School for Negroes," *Southeast Missourian* (Cape Girardeau, Mo.), September 22, 1948; "Negro Children Ask to Be Admitted to White School at Wyatt Last Monday Morning," *Enterprise-Courier* (Charleston, Mo.), September 23, 1948; "The Constitution and Separate Schools," *Enterprise-Courier* (Charleston, Mo.), February 15, 1945. Technically, the Missouri state constitution, revised in 1945, stated, "Separate schools shall

be provided for white and colored children, except in cases otherwise provided for by the law." The latter part of this statement was added to accommodate the U.S. Supreme Court decision in *Missouri ex. rel. Gaines v. Canada*, which in 1938 ruled that Lloyd Gaines should be admitted to the University of Missouri Law School because the state did not provide an equivalent school for African Americans. See Constitution of the State of Missouri, art. IX, 1(a), p. 119, Lloyd L. Gaines Collection, University of Missouri Digital Library, http://digital.library.umsystem.edu.

77. Committee Minutes, October 5, 1948, series 1, box 1, Delmo Housing Corporation Records, University Archives, Department of Special Collections, Washington University Libraries.

78. Adam D. Holman, interview with Heidi Dodson, September 30, 2012.

79. "No Fund to Build School for Negroes."

80. "To Take Wyatt Case to Court," *Southeast Missourian* (Cape Girardeau, Mo.), October 5, 1948; "Negro School Problem May Go to Court," *Enterprise-Courier* (Charleston, Mo.), October 7, 1948; Gloster B. Current to Reverend L. L. Haynes, October 6, 1948, Missouri State Conference of Branches, Papers of the NAACP, microfilm, part 26C, roll 10.

81. Committee Minutes, October 5, 1948, Delmo Housing Corporation; Minutes, December 11, 1949, Missouri State Conference of Branches, Papers of the NAACP, microfilm, part 26C, roll 10; Minutes, Board of Directors, November 20, 1950, series 1, box 1, Delmo Housing Corporation Records, University Archives, Department of Special Collections, Washington University Libraries; Gary Kremer and Brett Rogers, *African American Schools in Rural and Small-Town Missouri*, no. IV-9, 2002; "Lawmakers Again Tackle Mixed School Issue," *Norfolk (Va.) Journal and Guide*, March 3, 1951. Toward the end of 1948, the North Wyatt community council did allow the Wyatt School District to rent its community building, while still pursuing legal action, but it negotiated for advantageous terms.

82. Doreen Massey, *Spatial Divisions of Labor*, 2nd ed. (New York: Routledge Press, 1995), 4.

Reviews

Vittoria Di Palma
Wasteland: A History

New Haven, Conn.: Yale University Press, 2014.
xi + 266 pages, 107 black-and-white and color
illustrations.
ISBN: 978-030-019779-2, $45.00 HB

Review by Louis P. Nelson

Every now and then, a gifted scholar produces a book that simultaneously reimagines some broad dimension of everyday life in the early modern British world and situates the telling of that experience in the physicality of material culture. One of the most important of these for me was John Crowley's *The Invention of Comfort,* which provided a rigorous historical frame for the shifting conceptions of comfort, directly challenged our contemporary assumptions about the primacy of physical comfort, and gave new meanings to all kinds of everyday material culture, from mirrors to fireplaces.[1] Crowley taught us that comfort had a history. In her new book, *Wasteland: A History,* Vittoria di Palma reminds us that "nature" has a history—we've already learned this, of course, from William Cronon and others—but Di Palma adds to that discourse a critical theological/social/aesthetic condition as yet underdeveloped if not flatly ignored.[2] And for historians of places, material culture, and vernacular architecture, she situates the wasteland in actual territories of the British world and gives us a new frame for understanding not only cartographic representations and landscape paintings but also fences, embankments, ditches, windmills, and sawmills. All scholars of the early modern British world should read this book.

She begins by grappling with the difficult task of defining her subject. A wasteland is "a landscape that resists notions of proper or appropriate use," is "defined not by what it is or what it has, but by what it lacks," and is a "threatening, challenging, and perilous place" (3–4). The earliest manifestations of the word in English are biblical. The Latin term *desertus* becomes "wasteland" in early translations of the Old and New Testaments, referring to spaces of desolation, isolation, and wandering. But, Di Palma argues, "a particular convergence of beliefs, technologies, institutions, and individuals in seventeenth- and eighteenth-century England, Scotland, and Wales" transformed the early biblical understanding of wasteland as immutable antithesis into a very real physical (and social) problem with potential solutions. The early modern British view of wasteland took on something greater than theological significance partly in response to the reformulation of aesthetic theory that gave sensory perception and emotional response greater significance in the definition of beauty. The production of a theory of the beautiful made room also for the rise of its aesthetic antithesis, the disgusting. The picturesque found its antithesis in the wasteland, a place in which theology and aesthetics comfortably cohabitate. But this aesthetic reformulation took place alongside the enclosure of the countryside, the agricultural revolution, the expansion of empire, and the early Industrial Revolution. Wasteland arises as a convenient trope in the remaking of early modern Britain.

Di Palma's telling unfolds in six chapters. The initial two—"Wasteland" and "Improvement"—very carefully unpack the historical usage and evolution of each word. The first undertakes a careful etymology, following the term from the Old English *westen* to the English *wasteland* and its early association with the notion of common lands: those fields made available by the nobility to commoners for gleaning and pasturing and those forests available for foraging for wild fruit and firewood. This understanding is deeply enmeshed in the legal framework of a commonwealth. The prominence of wastelands in John Bunyan's enormously popular *The Pilgrim's Progress,* first published in 1678, cemented the meaning of *wasteland* as "wilderness" in the popular imagination. Simultaneously, a new political economy—articulated most clearly by John Locke—reframed the commons not as a landscape of provision for the commoner but as land that is unproductive, unimproved. As a result, the end of the seventeenth century brought with it the demise of one land-dependent collective political economy and the rise of private property claims and the concomitant imagination of the wilderness as improvable. Without improvement, wasteland was, well, wasted. The solution, privatization of property and the resulting diminution of common lands, was generally understood to be a moral good in that it introduced far greater productivity. Furthermore, privatization necessitated enclosure, which diminished the visibility of poverty in the newly improved landscape. Late eighteenth-century parliamentary Acts of Enclosure permanently reorganized rural Britain. This narrative of improvement is, of course, well rehearsed. But it is an important part of the story of wasteland, and it is well represented in the book's second chapter.

The next three chapters are all of a set: swamp, mountain, and forest. "Swamp" recounts the extraordinary draining of England's bogs and fens. If enclosure is well studied, the massive transformation of swamplands is less recognized. In this chapter the author returns to the theme of visceral disgust and its common association with bogs and fens. Quagmires, moors, fens, bogs, these were all repulsive and unhealthy—both physically and morally. The solution was draining. The chapter narrates the repeated experiments of mapping and subsequent reclaiming, increasingly larger territories of the motherland. The greatest of these projects was the draining of the Great Fens, formerly ranging across Lincoln, Northampton, Norfolk, Suffolk, and Cambridge, with the goal of transforming the bog into land fit for year-round pasture and capable of sustaining wheat and other industrial crops. In the space of thirty years, ten thousand square miles of England were transformed in this way. Not surprisingly, the disappearance of fens corresponds to the rise of decoys—little artificial fens—in the picturesque gardens of the elite.

"Mountain" explores the aesthetic reframing of the dangerous and threatening landscape of mountains as the stage of the sublime. In this way, disgust generated delight, and wasteland became art. The practical extension of this was, of course, tourism and the increasing value of heretofore ignored districts like northern Wales and the Lake District, as landscapes commodified. "Forest" returns to etymology by examining the early legal framework of the term as physical territory—heavily wooded or not—set aside for the exclusive purpose of staging the royal hunt. A forest was a sanctuary for the king's venison and a space demarcated for his recreation. Trespassing the forest came with consequences enacted by a forest court. By the seventeenth century, forests became associated with dense stands of trees because these were increasingly rare except in these preserves as the housing revolution and the expanding navy consumed trees from common lands. At times these pressures even led to deforestation of forest lands. Charles I, in fact, generated significant income from selling off rights to the trees in his forests. After the Restoration the widespread popularity of John Evelyn's *Sylvia* popularized the notion of tree plantations and the management of forests. This management ethic reinforced the already expanding emphasis on huge gar-

dens, and by the early eighteenth century, the boundaries between garden and forest were often blurred. Naturally, planters of these new forests worked very hard to institute the wildness that was increasingly absent from the landscape.

The book's final chapter, "Wilderness, Wasteland, Garden," is a brief musing on the emerging Industrial Revolution and the generation of an entirely new kind of wasteland in the early nineteenth century: the industrial wasteland of the city and metropolis. By then the wilderness had become romanticized as pure, uncorrupted. The city had become the wasteland.

The broad scope of *Wasteland: A History* is its greatest appeal. While there are certainly some discussions that readers will find familiar, the critical frame holds together throughout, and readers new to the topic will find the retelling useful. There are some larger problems, however. The title is misleading; one might be surprised to discover the book's focus on early modern Britain as the title gives no clues to either place or time. This absence led me to wonder about Asian expressions of the same idea, for example. The disappearance of any theological considerations after the opening chapter ignores the continuing significance of religion in eighteenth-century Britain. The evidence is uneven, and the chapters are thematic and only loosely chronological. And last, Di Palma too frequently ignores her images, preferring the historian's dependence on text over the art historian's capacity for exploiting visual evidence. But I hope that my colleagues will read this book and come to their own conclusions, because *Wasteland* is a fruitful read.

AUTHOR BIOGRAPHY

Louis P. Nelson is professor of architectural history at the University of Virginia, where he is also the associate dean in the School of Architecture and the director of the program in historic preservation.

NOTES

1. John E. Crowley, *The Invention of Comfort: Sensibilities and Design in Early Modern Britain and Early America* (Baltimore, Md.: Johns Hopkins University Press, 2001).

2. William Cronon, *Uncommon Ground: Toward Reinventing Nature* (New York: W. W. Norton, 1995).

Marta Gutman
A City for Children: Women, Architecture, and Charitable Landscapes of Oakland, 1850–1950

Chicago: University of Chicago Press, 2014.

xxi + 453 pages, 116 black-and-white illustrations, 11 plans, 3 maps.

ISBN: 978-022-6311128-9, $45.00, HB

ISBN: 978-022-615615-6, $7.00–$45.00, EB (various formats)

Review by Paula Lupkin

The focus of *A City for Children* is a phenomenon nearly erased from view today: the landscape of charitable institutions built by middle-class women to serve the needs of working-class children within the industrial nexus of Oakland, California, in the late nineteenth and early twentieth centuries. At the intersection of histories of architecture, cities, race, gender, and urban planning, this study uncovers and reconstructs the everyday world created by women of diverse religious and racial backgrounds as they sought to define themselves and their society by carving out space, ordinary and sometimes extraordinary, for the care and education of children. With great skill, creativity, and meticulous research, Marta Gutman offers vernacular architecture studies and many related fields an innovative and important model of scholarship that helps us recover the past, understand the present, and advocate for the future.

Gutman's book is built on and embedded within an important growing national and international literature on the role of women and children in shaping urban landscapes, built environments, and institutional architecture in the modern city. Like Abigail Van Slyck, Annmarie Adams, Daphne Spain, Jessica Sewell, and Despina Stratigakos, Gutman focuses scholarly attention on women as active agents of change as advocates, policy makers, builders, designers, and caregivers who carved out private and public spaces for themselves in the industrial-era city.[1] Using an impressively interdisciplinary range of sources and methods, Gutman contributes to this history and significantly expands it, uncovering and interpreting the dense and diverse network of charitable spaces women designed, built, and operated for children, including orphanages, settlement houses, day nurseries, playgrounds, and kindergartens.

Carefully situated in Oakland, California, Gutman's narrative broadens the history of reform movements, which in the United States has tended to focus on major metropolises like New York, Boston, and Chicago. Working at the finely grained scale of the block and neighborhood, while also telling a story about the city, region, and nation, she successfully presents the importance of Oakland, its economy, its physical and social morphology, its history, its people, and the particular nuances of race and place, including the struggles faced by its Chinese immigrant community. Readers will come to know not only Oakland and the particular neighborhoods and people Gutman studies but also the city's connections to the state policies of California and to Progressive reform movements around the country.

Perhaps more important for students of vernacular architecture than her geographical expansion of the topic of urban reform is the author's attention to what she calls the "repurposed." In contrast to much scholarship on architecture and the built environment, which focuses on purpose-built structures, Gutman directs our attention to the way that the women of Oakland salvaged and transformed existing buildings, opening a fasci-

nating window into the gradual processes of change that shape communities over time. *A City for Children,* in this sense, constitutes a rich piece of detective work. The selection of photographs, official documentation, interviews with grown children once served by this landscape, and redrawn maps and plans allow the reader a spatial and social understanding of a world that was constantly changing and is now largely destroyed.

Gutman breaks new ground by demonstrating the importance, as well as the centrality, of repurposing as an architectural process. Carving out space from the existing cityscape, redesigning it for alternative use, and making new meanings in the process have not been valorized in previous histories of the built environment. Recently, attention has been paid to creative destruction, the constant building up and tearing down that often characterizes the development of central business districts and urban renewal areas. Less attention, however, has been paid to the creative act of salvage, adaptive reuse, and redecoration—at least outside historic preservation circles—and Gutman deserves much credit for foregrounding them.

Of equal interest is the role of nonprofessional actors. Architects and planners, including Charles Mulford Robinson and Julia Morgan, played a role in Oakland's constant state of repurposing and transformation, but they are not the central characters of Gutman's tale. Instead, major figures are the enterprising women of diverse religion, race, and background who reclaimed the gridded streets and adjacent railyards of West Oakland from the free market to create private and, later, public spaces dedicated to the needs of society's most vulnerable citizens.

While it is true that strained finances often prevented the women of Oakland from building homes for their institutions from scratch, reuse was also, for them, a practice loaded with symbolic significance and creative power. The selection of sites and buildings for repurposing could be extremely meaningful, as Gutman points out in her chapter

"The Saloon That Became a School," about a kindergarten built in what had been a bar. She teases out the significance of such choices by paying close attention to context and site. Through careful work with Sanborn maps, she demonstrates the importance of the kindergarten/saloon's footprint on a prime corner in a neighborhood dense with corner saloons, a linkage that would surely have been clear to the neighborhood's children. It was through the transformation and rebirth of the space, rather than the design of the building or the choice of materials, that reformers communicated their message of uplift and education. Interior design was equally important in this schema. Women not only selected sites but also redesigned buildings using their skills as decorators to create the home-like environments that they believed would suit their missions. In Gutman's account, interior decoration, often defined and dismissed as a ladies' pastime, becomes as important as building in creating a city for children.

A real strength of the book is the use of oral history: accounts of life in the kindergarten or on the playgrounds and memories of the spaces and their use. These enliven and animate the sometimes dry and overly detailed institutional records that, over nine chapters, Gutman uses to recover the complex, multifaceted West Oakland that was razed to make way for an ammunition plant, public transportation systems, and low-income housing in the mid-twentieth century.

What makes this book so important, ultimately, is the contribution it makes, as a work of history, to our present and our future. Through its consideration of the everyday landscape, the interconnections between buildings and people, it recovers the past, warts and all, peopled by intensely human, hopeful, and dedicated women, flawed figures who supported and worked within structures of inequality and racism. It is a story of success and failure, of conflict and change, of the relationship between private effort and public responsibility. *A City for Children* provides a framework for understanding the importance and possibilities of preservation, repurposing, and grassroots reform.

AUTHOR BIOGRAPHY

Paula Lupkin is assistant professor of art history at the University of North Texas. She is the author of *Manhood Factories: YMCA Architecture and the Making of Modern Urban Culture* (Minnesota, 2010).

NOTE

1. Abigail Van Slyck, *Free to All: Carnegie Libraries and American Culture, 1890–1920* (Chicago: University of Chicago Press, 1998); Annmarie Adams, *Architecture in the Family Way: Doctors, Houses, and Women, 1870–1900* (Montreal: McGill-Queen's University Press, 1996); Daphne Spain, *How Women Saved the City* (Minneapolis: University of Minnesota Press, 2000); Despina Stratigakos, *A Women's Berlin: Building the Modern City* (Minneapolis: University of Minnesota Press, 2008); Jessica Sewell, *Women and the Everyday City: Public Space in San Francisco, 1890–1915* (Minneapolis: University of Minnesota Press, 2011).

Micheline Nilsen

The Working Man's Green Space: Allotment Gardens in England, France, and Germany, 1870–1919

Charlottesville: University of Virginia Press, 2014.

xiv + 232 pages, 41 black-and-white illustrations and 4 tables.

ISBN: 978-081-393508-9, $39.50 HB

ISBN: 978-081-393537-9, $39.50 EB

Kindle, $30.81

Review by Marie Warsh

The first time I encountered an allotment garden, I had no idea what it was. I was visiting Europe and staying on the outskirts of Zurich. I was wandering one night after missing the last tram when I came upon an extensive allotment garden along a hillside. I marveled at the neatly gridded landscape filled with late summer's harvest, each plot containing its own tiny cottage. To my impressionable eyes, the place seemed truly magical—a miniaturized rural utopia. When I began to study the history of gardens years later, I found myself returning to the memory of this hillside often: there, a spark of curiosity, an inchoate realization that a garden was more than a place of recreation or source of food but a profound expression of place and culture.

I remembered this scene and reflected on the multivalent garden while reading Micheline Nilsen's *A Working Man's Green Space*, which focuses on allotment gardens created in England, France, and Germany between 1870 and 1919. Nilsen, an urban historian, begins by defining the allotment garden: small in size, in a location separate from a dwelling, and used to cultivate food for the gardener. At the turn of the twentieth century, these gardens became a widespread urban phenomenon, one of the many new types of landscapes and institutions devised to help the urban poor in response to the unprecedented upheavals of the Industrial Revolution. A range of individuals and groups created—and advocated for—these gardens, including philanthropic organizations, employers, landowners, religious leaders, and ultimately city and national governments. As Nilsen deftly illustrates, "Much more was at stake in these gardens than the provision of vegetables and a few flowers" (1).

Interweaving landscape history and social history, Nilsen investigates three main areas of inquiry: the use and effectiveness of allotment gardens as a social program; their relationship to other landscapes and forms of land use; and the experiences of the gardeners. The study ends with World War I, during which the governments of the countries in question promoted allotment gardening as essential to the war effort to supplement food supply. This support contributed to their lasting presence in many European cities after the war, despite some interruptions and shifts in purpose. Nilsen concludes the book discussing their enduring impact, including their current status.

Nilsen approaches this history by first presenting primary motivations for creating allotment gardens, and she outlines common features and organizational structures shared among the three countries under study. This initial chapter is followed by one on each country offering a detailed history of its allotment garden movement, including local antecedents and specific examples. Most previous scholarship on the topic has focused on individual places, making Nilsen's a novel approach that reinforces overarching themes while drawing out regional variations. (A comparably ambitious study worth noting is Laura Lawson's *City Bountiful* on the history of community gardening in America.)[1] What Nilsen finds is that most allotment gardens were conceived as a way to help the poor, and while food was a major part of this assistance, their creators and supporters also hoped gardens would provide a number of other less tangible benefits.

The chapter on Germany presents several examples. There were gardens that industrial concerns created for employees as a benefit—a way to retain workers—and also to potentially quell subversive political activity. Other gardens were created by private philanthropies to promote health and relieve the stresses of urban life but also to distract workers from its allures, such as drinking. As the allotment garden movement grew, a number of associations were formed to support gardeners and acquire land; in some cases they managed the rental of the land from municipalities and other owners. During World War I the associations banded together to promote gardening to supplement food supply and to increase production. As a response to war—a new crisis—gardening became associated with new forms of relief and therapeutic values.

Through these examples and those from England and France in other chapters, Nilsen argues that the allotment garden became a powerful force for stability and domestic harmony by providing a connection to rural life and values. In this sense the allotment garden challenged and informed ideas about urban planning and land use. Although the creation of the gardens was often motivated by a desire for social control, as suggested in the book's title, Nilsen argues that for the working classes, who lived primarily in overcrowded, rented multistory tenements, allotment gardens offered a chance to connect to, and control, land.

Perhaps because of the broad geographical scope, on the one hand, and the great detail about particular gardens, on the other, I often lost track of the larger context, both historical and physical. Although most readers will be familiar with the impact of industrialization and urbanization on Europe at the turn of the twentieth century—and this background material can be found scattered throughout the book—providing a concise introduction would have reinforced why allotment gardens became such a widespread and multifaceted response to urbanization. The book also left me with questions about the location of these gardens, which Nilsen often does not indicate. It seems that gardens were mostly located on the outskirts of cities on land that was not valuable for development, but the lack of analysis is surprising considering her interest in land use. How far away were gardens from where the gardeners lived? Were gardens near other facilities created to help the poor? How did location and/or size influence the longevity of gardens? In photographs allotment gardens often appear as a grid of individual plots, but was that always how they were laid out? Providing maps or other forms of graphic information to spatialize the gardens also would have afforded deeper insight into their relationship to urban development. In general, the narrative would benefit from more summary and synthesis.

Nilsen's most compelling investigation is into the question of whether allotments were primarily utilitarian or engendered a form of "aesthetic experience." While it is clear what typically motivated the creation of gardens, how did the gardeners respond? Answering this question presents a methodological co-

nundrum, as the voices of the gardeners are almost impossible to find. They are rarely extant, and when they are, they are mostly obscured by promotional rhetoric found in the records of advocates and sponsoring groups. Nilsen offers theoretical frameworks and more recent examples to help illuminate more generally how we experience nature and gardening and give them meaning in an urban context. Allotment gardens were clearly very popular, one indication that they had relevance beyond the utilitarian. There were waiting lists, and turnover was low. There were various forms of support for gardeners to help them succeed and that aimed to sustain the gardens. After exploring various ways of "being" in a garden from historical and phenomenological perspectives, Nilsen concludes that the gardens provided opportunity for individual expression, community and familial engagement, and respite from urban life, all of which had the potential to contribute to a dynamic, aesthetically charged experience.

By way of clarification, the American community garden movement, which Nilsen does not reference, is worth a brief mention. Contemporary American community gardens, which have origins in the 1960s, often include areas gardened collectively and more ornamental features. There are, however, many intriguing similarities between allotment gardens and the gardens created for children during the early twentieth century in American cities. These gardens were motivated by markedly similar agendas of social reform and environmental determination; they were promoted as offering relief from urban problems and a mode of inculcating moral values associated with rural life.

Nilsen ends the book by discussing the evolution of the allotment garden after World War I. Following World War II, the purpose of allotment gardens shifted from the primarily social and utilitarian to the recreational, and many of these later gardens were called "leisure gardens." As a result, this working-class practice became popular with many affluent urban dwellers. Despite this transformation,

the endurance of these gardens, as well as the growing interest in nutrition, sustainability, and urban ecology in both Europe and the United States, makes this volume particularly timely. Nilsen's well-researched and ambitious cross-cultural perspective provides insight into the origins of the urban garden movement and into the social and political value of the allotment garden that is both deeply connected to but also transcends time and place. I look forward to the next installment of this history, the topic of Nilsen's next book.

AUTHOR BIOGRAPHY

Marie Warsh is a landscape historian and the Director of Preservation Planning for the Central Park Conservancy in New York.

NOTE

1. Laura J. Lawson, *City Bountiful: A Century of Community Gardening in America* (Berkeley: University of California Press, 2005).

Lawrence J. Vale
Purging the Poorest: Public Housing and the Design Politics of Twice-Cleared Communities

Chicago: University of Chicago Press, 2013.

xvi + 428 pages, 55 black-and-white illustrations, 8 maps, 4 charts.

ISBN: 978-022-601231-5, $91.00 HB

ISBN: 978-022-601245-2, $30.00 PB

ISBN: 978-022-601259-9, $7.00–$30.00 EB (various formats)

Kindle, $16.50

Review by Jennifer Hock

Lawrence J. Vale's goals for *Purging the Poorest* are set out clearly in the book's first pages. Much of the literature on public housing, he argues, has conceived of it as a single, failed building program that consolidated the poorest urban residents in segregated, poorly designed, ill-maintained "projects." A broader, more compelling approach, he writes, would describe public housing as a succession of distinct social experiments, encompassing clearance as well as construction and governed by policies favoring the dispersal of the poor as well as their concentration in isolated projects. Over eight decades public housing has adapted to respond to the changing ambitions—and prejudices—of urban elites and has addressed the needs of very different segments of the low-income population. One theme remains constant: the United States has always been ambivalent about its responsibility for those unable to afford decent housing in the private market. Nowhere is that ambivalence more evident than in the long history of the "twice-cleared" communities that are Vale's focus in this book.[1]

Purging the Poorest documents the transformation of two urban neighborhoods: Atlanta's Techwood Flats, which became the Techwood/Clark Howell public housing project and more recently the mixed-income Centennial Place, and Chicago's "Little Hell," which became the Cabrini-Green public housing project and is today a part of the gentrifying Near North Side. Their stories run parallel. In the early 1930s, both sites were impoverished but adjacent to more valuable real estate; Techwood Flats was near the Georgia Institute of Technology and Coca-Cola's headquarters, and Little Hell was just west of Chicago's wealthy Gold Coast. During the early days of the public housing program, both places were targeted for clearance by an interested elite of social reformers, businessmen, and political leaders intent on using federal money to build low-cost housing.

The modern housing projects constructed on both sites transformed these neighborhoods physically and socially. Hundreds of poor families were displaced, and housing officials made few provisions for their return. Instead, projects like Atlanta's low-rise Techwood Homes (which opened as the nation's first public housing project in 1936) and Clark Howell (opened in 1941) and Chicago's low-rise Frances Cabrini Homes

(1942) and high-rise Cabrini Extension (1957) and William Green Homes (1962), in accordance with federal priorities, were tenanted primarily by upwardly mobile working-class white families, many of whom saw their time in public housing as a stepping stone to better apartments or homeownership.

By the 1950s and 1960s, however, the public housing population was changing. Desegregation of public housing and expanded housing opportunities for whites in the suburbs transformed the racial composition of most projects. Federal reforms and pressure from civil rights leaders also opened public housing to new constituencies, including single mothers and welfare recipients. The effects of these new policies were profound; household income at Cabrini-Green, for example, dropped from approximately 70 percent of the Chicago area median in the early 1940s to only 20 percent of the area median by the end of the 1970s. Few housing authorities were prepared to offer the services these new tenant populations would need or to address the long-term effects of declining operating budgets and structural unemployment.

By the 1980s and 1990s, these public housing projects housed each city's poorest and least advantaged, and urban elites viewed Techwood/Clark Howell and Cabrini-Green with the same fear and disdain they had reserved for Techwood Flats and Little Hell fifty years earlier. In Atlanta the promise of international attention during the 1996 Olympic Games sparked a series of proposals for the demolition and redevelopment of Techwood, and housing officials turned to HOPE VI, a new federal program set up to address deferred maintenance in public housing by making grants for renovation. Hoping for a more fundamental transformation and to disperse public housing tenants—in part in response to widely held beliefs that earlier policies had created a dangerous concentration of poverty in socially isolated housing projects—Atlanta proposed something more radical: complete redevelopment. Federal officials were convinced and awarded Atlanta the first HOPE

VI grant. Techwood/Clark Howell's modernist row houses were demolished, and the site was rebuilt as the mixed-income, neotraditional Centennial Place.

The transformation of Techwood/Clark Howell into Centennial Place served as a model for the city and the nation. In the early 1990s, 13 percent of Atlanta's population lived in public housing, but during the late 1990s and early 2000s, the city used HOPE VI to demolish virtually all of its family public housing (that is, housing not restricted to seniors) and to redevelop the sites with a mixture of subsidized and market-rate housing. Other cities followed suit, including Chicago, which in 1999 announced the fifteen-year-long Plan for Transformation, which also recommended the demolition of the majority of its family public housing units. (The more politically palatable senior housing was retained.) At Cabrini-Green, where gentrification pressures at the edges of the neighborhood were making the area attractive again, the city envisioned extensive demolition and the construction of several thousand new units of low-rise, mixed-income housing, as well as a commercial center, a library, a school, and a police station. Protest by the Cabrini-Green tenants and a lawsuit on their behalf led to a consent decree that mandated greater tenant involvement in the planning process and a number of replacement public housing units in the new developments, but the agreement could not ensure that displaced Cabrini-Green residents would be the ones to live in the new units, which were subject to more rigorous qualification requirements. As had happened two generations earlier, the poorest were deliberately driven away by new development.

Supporters of HOPE VI would be quick to point out that today's displaced tenants are not left to their own devices, as earlier residents had been; federal guidelines ensure they are granted at least a nominal role in the planning process, and they are offered preferential eligibility for new housing units if they qualify to stay and relocation support and Housing Choice (Section 8) Vouchers if they leave. In fact, many HOPE VI supporters argue the move out of isolated, stigmatized public housing and into market-rate housing elsewhere in the city is an optimal outcome, and Vale's thoughtful, evenhanded account considers these arguments carefully. Ultimately, however, he concludes the experience of displacement has not changed significantly. Powerful interests retain the desire and ability to reclaim valuable real estate and protect the image of the city by redeveloping impoverished neighborhoods, and the poor themselves have very little to say in the process. Arguments about the potential for vouchers to expand opportunities for public housing residents, Vale adds, are not that different from the older arguments about the power of slum clearance to destroy unsafe and unsanitary environments. Whatever marginal benefits might accrue to those displaced are far outweighed by the heavy costs of displacement.

Purging the Poorest is one of a number of recent studies that revisit the familiar narrative of catastrophic policy failure, granting more agency to a greater variety of historical actors and expanding our understanding of poverty and public housing. Rhonda Y. Williams's and Roberta Feldman and Susan Stall's accounts of the struggles and achievements of black women living in public housing in Baltimore and Chicago, Nicholas Dagen Bloom's investigation of the New York City Housing Authority's effective management practices, D. Bradford Hunt's examination of the Chicago Housing Authority's slow unraveling, and filmmaker Chad Friedrichs's documentary on Pruitt-Igoe all, like this book, seek to challenge the easy assumption that public housing was a bad idea, destined to fail.[2]

Purging the Poorest has a more complex relationship with the previous generation of public housing history, particularly Arnold R. Hirsch's seminal 1983 study of housing in Chicago.[3] In bringing the story of Techwood/ Clark Howell and Cabrini-Green up to the present, Vale adopts a much broader historical vantage point, surveying seven decades rather than two and forcing us to confront the historical specificity of Hirsch's claims about the postwar period. Hirsch focused on the role of white oppression—both overt violence and institutional racism—in constructing the "second ghetto." Vale, meanwhile, emphasizes our changing paternalistic and revanchist attitudes toward the poor as expressed in urban space and housing policy. While the two categories clearly intersect, Vale's emphasis on class over race occasionally obscures key issues. For many contemporary housing officials and policy makers, for example, it is not just neoliberal faith in housing markets that drives their desire to demolish public housing but a firm conviction that midcentury housing projects institutionalized, isolated, and disempowered black residents.

Meticulously researched and lucidly written, *Purging the Poorest* presents significant new research, including several dozen interviews with tenant leaders, lawyers, housing officials, and developers and substantial work in the archives, most notably on the early history of the Housing Authority of Atlanta. It also draws on an array of newspaper accounts, planning reports, and market and sociological studies. Surprisingly, in a book that opens with a powerful introductory argument about the significance of design, the two case studies convey a much stronger sense of local politics and local actors than spatial transformation. In vivid prose Vale shows us the idealism of Chicago affordable housing developer Peter Holsten; the political acumen of Cabrini-Green resident leader Carol Steele; the prejudices of Charles F. Palmer, a real estate executive who later became the founding chairman of the board of the Housing Authority of Atlanta; and the tough-mindedness of Atlanta housing chief Renée Lewis Glover, who presided over the dismantling of the city's public housing stock. More sustained discussion of the politics of design and development will appear in a companion volume currently under way, one that will investigate various approaches to rebuilding public housing in HOPE VI projects nationwide.

AUTHOR BIOGRAPHY

Jennifer Hock is assistant professor of art history at the Maryland Institute College of Art.

NOTES

1. In earlier work on public housing, Vale observes that attitudes toward housing for the poor inform two very different traditions: public housing as a reward for the hard-working and upwardly mobile and public housing as a last resort for the most vulnerable. See especially Lawrence J. Vale, *From the Puritans to the Projects: Public Housing and Public Neighbors* (Cambridge, Mass.: Harvard University Press, 2000).

2. See Rhonda Y. Williams, *The Politics of Public Housing: Black Women's Struggles against Urban Inequality* (New York: Oxford University Press, 2004); Robert Feldman and Susan Stall, *The Dignity of Resistance: Women Residents' Activism in Chicago Public Housing* (New York: Cambridge University Press, 2004); Nicholas Dagan Bloom, *Public Housing That Worked: New York in the Twentieth Century* (Philadelphia: University of Pennsylvania Press, 2008); D. Bradford Hunt, *Blueprint for Disaster: The Unraveling of Chicago Public Housing* (Chicago: University of Chicago Press, 2009); *The Pruitt Igoe Myth*, directed by Chad Freidrichs (Columbia, Mo.: Unicorn Stencil, 2011), DVD.

3. Arnold Hirsch, *Making the Second Ghetto: Race and Housing in Chicago, 1940–1960* (Cambridge: Cambridge University Press, 1983).

Andrew M. Shanken

Into the Void Pacific: Building the 1939 San Francisco World's Fair

Berkeley: University of California Press, 2014.

248 pages, 144 black-and-white and color illustrations, 3 maps.

ISBN: 978-052-028282-7, $60.00 HB

Review by Robert W. Rydell

The 1939–40 Golden Gate International Exposition (GGIE) is usually regarded as the "other" world's fair—the, smaller, poorer, West Coast cousin of the grander, sleeker 1939–40 New York World's Fair. In this beautifully illustrated and printed book produced on the occasion of the GGIE's seventy-fifth anniversary, Andrew Shanken rejects this standard perception of the fair's otherness and challenges another viewpoint as well—namely, the argument that the fairs of the 1930s are best regarded as modernistic extravaganzas of imperialism and mass consumerism informed by East Coast architects and their European counterparts. For Shanken what makes the San Francisco fair so interesting and important is that it showcased the work of a number of West Coast architects who embraced regionalism as the core of their design ethos, not European and East Coast modernist aesthetics.

Imaginatively titled (drawing on a clever phrase coined by D. H. Lawrence to describe California's idiosyncratic relationship to the rest of the world), Shanken's book moves through the fair's contested planning and design phases and offers marvelously detailed chapters about some of the fair's major buildings: the Federal Building (Timothy Pflueger), the Yerba Buena Club (William Wurster), and the Tower of the Sun (Arthur Brown, Jr.). Many structures were clustered into thematic zones—for instance, Ernest Wiehe's Portals of the Pacific, which featured the two massive, cubistic Elephant Towers designed by sculptor Donald Macky that the author wryly describes as "Californian in their own way" (91). As with any good history of world's fair designs, Shanken also addresses some of the ideas not implemented, including a colossal sculpture appropriately named *Colossus* that sprang from Bernard Maybeck's fertile mind—one that combined with William Merchant's to produce the Redwood Empire Building, one of many buildings dedicated to representing multiple regions of California. Also noted are several structures designed by architects who remain anonymous (for instance, the loosely Internationalist-style buildings dedicated to the U.S. Coast Guard and the state of Illinois).

So much happens in this book. We learn about the siting of the fair on the human-built Treasure Island, annexed to Yerba Buena Island in the middle of San Francisco Bay and originally intended as the site of San Francisco's new airport. We learn about the debates among architects and designers about how the fair should be designed. In addition, Shanken masterfully discusses the color schemes of the fair, contrasting GGIE colorist Jesse Stanton's ideas with those of Joseph Urban for the 1933–34 Chicago Century of Progress Exposition, noting that Urban's schematics "resembled a Mondrian painting, while Stanton's looked like paint samples in a Benjamin Moore catalog" (83). Shanken also does a superb job of situating Miguel Covarrubias's famous *Peoples of the Pacific* mural in the complex mix of designers' thinking about the relationship between regionalism and imperialism.

As good as it is, Shanken's book has three gaps. First, only the briefest mention is made of the vernacular structures on the Gayway, the fair's midway, which counted among its many shows Sally Rand's Nude Ranch, a Chinese Village, and Billy Rose's Aquacade featuring Johnny Weissmuller and Esther Williams. Were these shows designed in regionalist idioms as well, or did they reflect national and corporatist branding strategies? Second, greater attention to exhibit design within the interior spaces of exposition buildings would have made a fascinating addition to the book. For instance, in his monumental *East Is East and West Is West* (a book Shanken notes), Carlos E. Cummings, director of the Buffalo Science Museum, visited both the San Francisco and New York fairs and recorded his impressions of exhibits at both expositions, noting that displays generally had a "billboard" effect.[1] Did the exhibit areas within exposition buildings reflect the regionalist idioms of the buildings themselves, or did they too reflect more standardized design aesthetics?

The third gap concerns the financing of the fair's architects. The people who poured considerable resources into this show were men of wealth and influence. A. P. Giannini, for one, president of Bank of America, led the effort to secure funds from his friends to get federal support for the fair. That support materialized in terms of both financial and human resources—notably, when George Creel, former head of the Creel Commission, which led U.S. government propaganda efforts during World War I, became head of the Federal Commission for the GGIE and turned his considerable influence toward securing representations of indigenous people from the Americas and Asia. How did the flow of money affect the design process? Did the architects have free hand? Or did the architects feel compelled to keep their regionalist desires in sync with the globalist desires of their clients in both the corporate and the government sectors?

These criticisms notwithstanding, *Into the Void* is a very important book. Grounded in a body of scholarship that argues fairs were jumbles of often hastily assembled designs that despite the best intentions of their managers and funders, often impressed visitors with their incoherence, this book makes for compelling reading—especially on the matter of how best to understand American modernism in the 1930s. Whereas some scholars (myself, for instance) argue that international exhibitions held during the 1930s used modernistic idioms to advance the imperial ambitions of exposition sponsors (both corporations and national governments), Shanken, without denying that the GGIE had imperialistic overtones, subsumes them under what he argues was the overriding preoccupation of the architects to popularize a regionalist aesthetic. In many respects he is certainly right that regionalism deserves greater consideration. Matthew Bokovoy's history of the San Diego fairs of 1915–16 and 1935–36 makes a similar point about California's "other" fairs.[2] But as passionate as the architects of these fairs may have been about regionalism, what I find striking about the Golden Gate show is that the exposition's planners, from the moment of the groundbreaking ceremonies in 1936, conceived of their region in broadly international terms that would advance both their own and U.S. economic and political interests overseas. The region imagined by Golden Gate International Exposition planners was transpacific in its orientation and not limited to California or even to the Western Hemisphere, like the fairs Robert González discusses in *Designing Pan-America*.[3] No doubt, the Elephant Towers had a California inflection, but they also made clear the power and eagerness of the fair's organizers to represent nations and cultures on both sides of the Pacific Rim to nearly ten million visitors. This interplay of regionalism and globalism is central to Shanken's analysis, and he is certainly right to suggest that no history of modern American architecture would be complete without understanding the complex negotiations about the meanings of regionalism and modernism that resulted in the designs for the GGIE.

To sum up, this is a fine and thought-provoking study that puts the GGIE—and a cohort of California architects—into the broader scholarly conversation about architectural trends of the 1930s. With respect to the historiography of world's fairs, this book joins Lisa Rubens's as-yet-unpublished dissertation in providing another essential port of entry into the GGIE.[4] Perhaps most important, the author reminds us that when we think about exposition architecture in the 1930s, the New York fair is only one part of the story. In the United States, there were multiple fairs: Chicago (1933–34), San Diego (1935–36), Dallas (1936), Cleveland (1937), and, certainly, San Francisco. Each was distinctive, yet each was also part of a larger package of designs intended to realize what seemed like an impossible dream in the darkest days of the Great Depression—namely, restoring Americans' faith in the future and linking that future to sustaining an economy driven by the values of corporate capitalism.

AUTHOR BIOGRAPHY

Robert W. Rydell is professor of history at Montana State University. He has authored many books and articles on world's fairs, including, with Laura Schiavo, *Designing Tomorrow: America's World's Fairs of the 1930s* (2010), which accompanied an exhibition of the same name at the National Building Museum.

NOTES

1. Carlos E. Cummings, *East Is East and West Is West* (Buffalo, N.Y.: Buffalo Museum of Science, 1940), 367.

2. Matthew F. Bokovoy, *The San Diego World's Fairs and Southwestern Memory* (Albuquerque: University of New Mexico Press, 2005).

3. Robert Alexander González, *Designing Pan-America: U. S. Architectural Visions for the Western Hemisphere* (Austin, Tex.: University of Texas Press, 2011).

4. Lisa Rubens, "The 1939 San Francisco World's Fair: The New Deal, the New Frontier, and the Pacific Basin" (PhD diss., University of California–Berkeley, 2004).

Richard Longstreth
Looking beyond the Icons: Midcentury Architecture, Landscape, and Urbanism
Charlottesville: University of Virginia Press, 2015.
x + 271 pages, 158 black-and-white illustrations and drawings.
ISBN: 978-081-393643-7, $65.00 HB

Review by David Smiley

Richard Longstreth mourns the loss of the post–World War II ordinary built environment: the loosely defined modernist work that, as the title suggests, did not become iconic or canonic. Architecture, urbanism, and suburbanism of America's mid-twentieth century have proved easy to overlook, dislike, and misconstrue, making them difficult to understand, much less preserve. Modernism is rife with tensions, to say the least, and Longstreth is no defender of its exclusions and erasures, yet he does not want to throw the baby out with the bathwater. For the sake of continuity and a proverbial usable past, Longstreth argues for a more informed stewardship of the built world that honors not just the monuments by Frank Lloyd Wright and Skidmore Owings and Merrill but the ordinary, "vernacular" productions, the "matter-of-fact" work of our visual and experiential universe. We stop for the icons, but everything else, we drive by or redevelop. But for Longstreth these "cultural landscapes," the ecumenical (if sometimes wooly) term developed by J. B. Jackson—to whom Longstreth pays homage—are just as important. The stakes of Longstreth's argument are made plain in the very subject of the book, which devotes one chapter each to eight case studies. By the time of publication, five had been demolished, two were in of a state of flux, and only one was (for now) safe from redevelopment.

A collection of essays written between 1984 and 2008 (some revised for publication), the book offers a window onto the evolving ways in which arguments about the value of places are constructed and how such arguments are used—and by whom—to muster support for preservation, reuse, or rehabilitation of buildings or sites. The essays are united by a desire to challenge the standards—some now relics themselves—by which cultural, institutional, and regulatory bodies govern the built landscape, in particular through standards for landmarking. Make no mistake: this is not a project to merely protect more things. Instead, Longstreth seeks to change the perception of what is worth preserving and what preservation entails, especially in the threatened modernist landscape.

The first section of the book ("Style and Taste") consists of two essays in which Longstreth takes to task the sources of "mischief" in the mainstream practice of preservation. First and foremost is the overriding concern with style, as well as a preoccupation with taste as a form of history that usually serves the preferences of one social group at the expense of others. Buildings in such a schema become agents or purveyors of narrow, exclusive signifiers. While study of styles and forms is necessary, too often it becomes an exercise in classification for its own sake, without any connection to social or other contexts of which buildings or landscapes are a part. Taste, "just below the surface of numerous preservation efforts," leads to a selective antiquarianism providing a veneer of history and, at its worst, a "theme" for redevelopment (20). In this critique of aestheticized judgment, Longstreth finds operating what Pierre Bourdieu called the work of "taste cultures," in which claims to authenticity and value are anything but disinterested. But for Longstreth disinterestedness is essential: rigorous, analytical frameworks of scientific inquiry, not taste (as in many current instances), are all that stand between preservation and erasure or, worse, Disneyfication.

The second set of essays ("Some Challenges of the Recent Past") shows how mid-twentieth-century work is at risk of demolition despite its ubiquity because it is ignored in most preservation and professional discourses. Public spaces like Lawrence Halprin's Skyline Park in Denver, misunderstood pedestrian malls like Victor Gruen's and Garret Eckbo's Fulton Mall in Fresno, California, banal suburban subdivisions that suffuse the American imaginary, and seemingly disposable shopping centers may strike most Americans as unworthy of preservation (or even notice), but as Longstreth reminds us, all were designed and planned by architects, landscape architects, builders, and others acting in good faith and according to then-contemporary normative practices. Moreover, any example we look at has (or had) local inflections, socially embedded stories, and wider community connections that defy its popular characterization as generic. More provocative, Longstreth points out the open spaces of urban renewal—the much maligned plazas, walkways, and hardscapes in cities like Hartford and Baltimore—are not mere incidents among agglomerations of buildings but parts of "ensembles." The essays of this section thus point to the larger problem of evaluating not just midcentury buildings but also urban spaces and site plans. Set within complex fabrics and often responsible for resetting property and neighborhood boundaries, merely "seeing" these projects is difficult.

Helpfully, Longstreth also ponders in this section how the practice of preservation might be improved for such environments. His answer is not the usual one of restoration. Instead, he argues that such spaces must be adapted to make them economically vital again. He is critical, indeed, of a heritage industry that all too often simply commodifies old buildings and places. Rather, he cites projects such as Albuquerque's Nob Hill center where local initiative and smaller businesses managed change while retaining the project's original character. This nuanced approach, which recognizes the utility of market-based solutions, is pragmatic. But it is also slippery and left me hoping for more discussion about how preservation practice might work at planning and policy levels so that following the logic of the market is not our only option.

The third section ("Extraordinary and Unknown") focuses on great but obscure works of architecture: poorly recognized buildings with "intrinsic" merit in their syntheses of form, structure, program, and siting designed by well-known architects. The Cabrini Church in New Orleans by Curtis and Davis uniquely fused liturgical reform with structural and spatial vocabularies; Araldo Cossuta and I. M. Pei's Third Church of Christ, Scientist in Washington, D.C., demonstrated the integration of site planning, open space, and structural and material inventiveness; Richard Neutra's Gettysburg Cyclorama brilliantly integrated landscape, programming, culture, and form. Yet in all three cases the buildings have been demolished. Professional misjudgments, rigid institutional protocols, blinkered taste cultures, and business as usual defaults made these buildings "obsolete."

Each project in this section is a tour de force of thoughtful, beautiful design. Yet even Longstreth's discussion makes clear how questions of taste powerfully color interpretation of the past. He unfavorably compares, for instance, the "structural exhibitionism" of Marcel Breuer's St. John's Church to the "reserve" of the Third Church of Christ. The latter, he suggests, is an example of an "integral" work, organic and whole, whereas the former, with its more overt expression, is decorative and somehow the lesser for it. Are gender-coded categories hovering in the text?

The final section ("Commonplace and Taken for Granted") takes on a selection of sites in Washington, D.C. (Longstreth's academic home), and Savannah, which from their very inception have flown under the cultural radar. In chapters on a humble community-built victory garden, an unassuming shopping center along a commercial strip, and an ordinary suburban subdivision lacking the heroic scale of Levittown, Longstreth offers deeply contextualized readings. United by a disparaged, loosely modernist visual order, he explores their design histories, the motivations of those who built them, and how residents, businesses, and local officials have used and looked after them. His treatment of these places makes clear that daily life, local patterns, and social experience all serve as important criteria for evaluating historic worth. Here, we see most vividly how Longstreth aligns himself with J. B. Jackson and others in the cultural landscape tradition who believe the everyday matters. It is also where we see most clearly Longstreth's aspirations for how the nonmonumental can become operative in preservation. He does not merely remind us these kinds of sites are important. He points to the dearth of legal mechanisms, the development incentives, and, more fundamental, the lack of interest in such places on the part of most preservation professionals.

Resetting the course of preservation is demanding, and Longstreth sets an ambitious agenda, not only to expand our conception of worthy objects and ensembles but also to scrutinize the assumptions of preservationists, historians, and other like-minded practitioners. Examples of such new approaches are to be found. Several are included in the insightful *Cultural Landscapes,* a 2008 collection edited by Longstreth.[1] Another is a pedestrian mall that Randall Mason and others have written about that the city of New York devised in the 1970s to "clean up" Brooklyn's "once thriving" Fulton Street department store district. It was realized, in fits and starts and with considerable racial and economic tensions, over the next three decades. In the process Fulton literally became an odd hybrid of urban interventions—a bus lane, new signage and street furniture, new commercial tenants—and, through it all, continued to serve as a regional destination for the city's increasingly nonwhite working class. Starting in the mid-2000s, projects by various nonprofit groups and local organizations chal-lenged the view of the mall as blighted. Using interviews and archival work to find value in the unconventional scales, types, and tenures of business and in the importance of quasi-commercial activities and events, the agency of once invisible actors was recognized. The result was a new kind of plan that proposed neither restoration nor wholesale makeover but incremental enhancement. In this case, preservation found its way into socially situated planning proposals—that is, into political actions.[2]

In their clarity, rigor, and broad reach, the essays in *Looking beyond the Icons* confirm the wisdom Longstreth has gained through his distinguished career in preservation, landscape studies, and architectural history. But doing justice to such a legacy requires asking even more of preservation than the book seems to ask. Indeed, preservation must look beyond the icon, but it must also struggle further with conceptions of value, with the field's place among other discourses of the built environment, and with its role in a system almost wholly grounded in the marketplace.

AUTHOR BIOGRAPHY

David Smiley is assistant director of the Urban Design Program at Columbia University's Graduate School of Architecture, Planning, and Preservation and author of *Pedestrian Modern: Architecture and Shopping, 1925–1956* (Minnesota, 2013).

NOTES

1. Richard Longstreth, ed., *Cultural Landscapes: Balancing Nature and Heritage in Preservation Practice* (Minneapolis: University of Minnesota Press, 2008). See also Arnold R. Alanen and Robert Z. Melnick, eds., *Preserving Cultural Landscapes in America* (Baltimore, Md.: Johns Hopkins University Press, 2000).

2. Vicki Weiner and Randall Mason, *Fulton Street Mall: New Strategies for Preservation and Planning* (Brooklyn, N.Y.: Pratt Center for Community Development, 2006); Rosten Woo and Meredith TenHoor with Damon Rich, *Street Value: Shopping, Planning, and Politics at Fulton Mall* (New York: Princeton Architectural Press, 2010). See also Randall Mason, "Theoretical and Practical Arguments for Values-Centered Preservation," *CRM Journal* (Summer 2006): 21–48.

Henri Lefebvre; Łukasz Stanek, editor; Robert Bononno, translator
Toward an Architecture of Enjoyment
Minneapolis: University of Minnesota Press, 2014.
lxi + 248 pages, 22 black-and-white illustrations (black-and-white and color in the Kindle edition).
ISBN: 978-081-667719-1, $84.00 HB
ISBN: 978-081-667720-7, $29.95 PB
Kindle, $15.49

Review by Olga Touloumi

One of the most prolific and influential philosophers of the twentieth century, Henri Lefebvre transformed how we understand the built environment, discussing space as a social product. In his writings, he pioneered a widely influential Marxist perspective that called for a reconsideration of everyday life and the ordinary and a rejection of more conceptual and abstract approaches. The English translation of his seminal *The Production of Space* in 1991, in particular, provoked new discussions about the built environment throughout the humanities and especially in the social sciences. Yet while also widely employed by architectural and urban historians, these writings seemed to have surprisingly little to say specifically about buildings, framing architecture instead as inherently compliant to the forces of capitalism and the structural principles of division of labor, class hierarchy, and accumulation of wealth. *Toward an Architecture of Enjoyment* complicates these assumptions.

The core of the book is an unpublished eponymous essay written in 1973 and recently rediscovered by Łukasz Stanek, an architectural historian who has researched and written extensively on Lefebvre's theories and their impact on the post–World War II built environment.[1] Edited by Stanek and translated by Robert Bononno, who also did Lefebvre's *The Urban Revolution* (2003), the revived text illuminates a more expansive understanding of architecture as a spatial practice of the everyday, foregrounding individualized and vernacular approaches while highlighting the role of minor actors in the production of space.[2] Framing the essay is a forward by Stanek outlining the circumstances of his discovery entitled "A Manuscript Found in Saragossa" and an introduction in which Stanek explores, among other things, the historical conditions surrounding the production of the manuscript, bringing it in dialogue with its postwar French context of *grand ensembles* (modernist housing estates) and other architectural experiments, and the Programme commun du gouvernement (Common program of government) and the effort to include public opinion in urban planning—the subject of Kenny Cupers's recent *The Social Project* (2014).[3]

Toward an Architecture of Enjoyment began as a collaboration between Lefebvre and Mario Gaviria, a renowned sociologist who, like Lefebvre, dedicated his career to developing a Marxist theory of space. While researching touristic development in Spain, Gaviria commissioned Lefebvre to write an essay on "the architecture of pleasure." The two saw a revolutionary potential in leisure that the French left and in particular the Communist party dismissed as irrelevant to the Marxist social project. For Gaviria and Lefebvre, however, the concept of leisure as time spent outside the framework of capitalist production and consumption could radically unsettle class hierarchies and divisions of labor. But instead of a chapter on the particulars of the built environment of tourism, Lefebvre delivered a lengthy theoretical exposé on *jouissance,* or enjoyment—a concept that Bononno meticulously examines in a helpful translator's note as distinct and separate from its common psychoanalytic framings. Lefebvre separated the milieu of tourism from the idea of leisure while opening up the field of architecture to discussions of bodily experience, participation, and individual spatial interventions. Not knowing what to make of the text, Gaviria buried it within his personal archives, where Stanek unearthed it in 2008.

Lefebvre's critique starts where Gaviria's expectations ended. Unlike Gaviria, Lefebvre draws a hard line between mass tourism and spaces of leisure. For Lefebvre mass tourism and the architecture produced to serve it constitute products of capitalism. Building programs typically associated with leisure, such as nightclubs, discotheques, and casinos, obey and reinforce the principles of capital accumulation. He distinguishes the buildings, however, from spaces of leisure, which materialize only outside the framework of capitalism, when the act of enjoyment does not feed back into the loop of surplus value production. In short, Lefebvre asks his reader to "not confuse the enjoyment of a space and the space of enjoyment" (52). He maintains that places like cloisters, Buddhist monasteries, ancient Greek temples, and the Baths of Diocletian exemplify a true architecture of enjoyment, while condemning entertainment venues, countryside vernaculars, Nicholas Schoeffer's Center for Sexual Relaxation, and the works of Claude Nicolas Ledoux, Gustave Eiffel, and Auguste Perret as a "caricature of enjoyment" (101).

His theory employs a dialectical model of thinking. On the one hand, Lefebvre places technocrats, capitalism, urban development, consumption, functionalism, and knowledge production as the epiphenomena of modernity. At the opposite pole he situates nature, the human subject-as-body, and sensations. Nature holds an especially prominent position. As Stanek remarks, Lefebvre calls for a new conceptualization of our relationship with nature that resists the exploitation of touristic development. Most of the architectural examples he offers, by contrast, articulate new encounters with the environment, where the senses rather than thought drive the experience. Resonating with a long intellectual tradition that positions modernization as an act of alienation from nature, Lefebvre argues an architecture of enjoyment is more likely to take place at the countryside than in the city. Building on the myth of an unmediated nature, he articulates the natural environment in terms of a tabula rasa, where function and program are not already inscribed in form and where nature's "qualitative properties"—sun, water, sand, snow—are widely available (100).

Although conceived as an essay, Lefebvre's text maintains the structure of a book, with subchapters mapping out the concept of enjoyment in a variety of academic disciplines, including philosophy, anthropology, semiology, and economics, as well as architecture. Surprisingly, geography and urban studies are absent. The reason for this, according to Lefebvre, is scale. For him, furniture, buildings, and landscapes constitute potential sites of enjoyment, or leisure, in a way that cities and regions cannot. Behind these choices lies a belief that enjoyment constitutes primarily a personal affair that is in conflict with the interests of the commercial and industrial networks that inform centrally administered urban planning, or the "quantitative space of production and consumption" that drives urbanization (100). Instead, for Lefebvre the architecture of enjoyment is to be found in subjective encounters with nature, bodily experience, and bottom-up spatial practices, sites that often constitute the subject matter of anthropology, psychology, and philosophy.

The central preoccupations of the text are the meaning of "enjoyment," its role in shaping the built environment, and, paralleling Lefebvre's other writings, its potential as a liberating corrective to welfare-state modernism in architecture, at least as deployed in postwar Europe. This is apparent even in Lefebvre's title, which echoes Le Corbusier's celebrated manifesto *Vers une architecture.* Lefebvre's main critique centers on the myth of functionalism and the wide range of architectural programs it had permeated by the 1960s, from entertainment venues to social housing. "Function dominates, asserts itself, is on display; it is function that signifies," he claims, arguing that when the production of the built environment follows the directives of predetermined functions, then leisure and individuality succumb to the drives of capitalism (19).

But in the architecture of enjoyment, Lefebvre identifies an opportunity to challenge and evade modernism's deterministic model of spatial production. Lefebvre assumes that a focus on the rhythms of the body can unsettle the pace of capitalism, contaminating with operational ambiguity and uncertainty modernity's obsession with utilitarianism and functionality. He proposes the architecture of enjoyment as a type of utopia. For him the utopian impulse, the desire to install and implement an ideal social organization, imbues all attempts to produce space, including capitalistic ones. "There is no plan without utopia," he claims (147). Within this context Lefebvre distinguishes between the "abstract utopias" of postwar welfare state–led urbanization that aspires to install totalities and the "concrete" or "negative utopia" of the architecture of enjoyment that negates them, as well as "the State and the primacy of the political" (148).

Although untangling enjoyment from the tourism–entertainment complex is relevant to many debates today—for example, on the recent privatization of southern European coasts, access to the beachfront in places such as Malibu, California, and the Disneyfication of Times Square—in places Lefebvre's essay feels dated. He uses the female body, the exotic orient, and the fantasy of unspoiled nature to exemplify his vision of enjoyment, reinforcing the very same divisions he wishes to abolish. This orientalism and sexism highlights the problematic state of Marxist thought in the late postwar era and its complicated relationship with questions of race and gender. To focus on the trees, however, is to lose sight of the forest. When read as a historical artifact, *Toward an Architecture of Enjoyment* not only provides critical insight into Lefebvre, whose impact is still palpable, but reveals new connections between his ideas and design and, ultimately, capitalism and the built environment.

AUTHOR BIOGRAPHY

Olga Touloumi is assistant professor of art history at Bard College, where she teaches architectural history.

NOTES

1. For a more detailed analysis of Lefebvre's work on space, see Łukasz Stanek, *Henri Lefebvre on Space: Architecture, Urban Research, and the Production of Theory* (Minneapolis: University of Minnesota Press, 2011); Łukasz Stanek, Christian Schmid, and Ákos Moravánszky, eds., *Urban Revolution Now: Henri Lefebvre in Social Research and Architecture* (Burlington, Vt.: Ashgate Publishing, 2014).

2. Henri Lefebvre, *The Urban Revolution,* trans. Robert Bononno (Minneapolis: University of Minnesota Press, 2003).

3. Kenny Cupers, *The Social Project: Housing Postwar France* (Minneapolis: University of Minnesota Press, 2014).

Katherine A. Bussard, Alison Fisher, and Greg Foster-Rice, editors
The City Lost and Found: Capturing New York, Chicago, and Los Angeles, 1960–1980
Princeton, N.J.: Princeton University Art Museum, 2015. 272 pages, 250 black-and-white and color illustrations. ISBN: 978-030-020785-9, $50.00 HB

Review by Benjamin Holtzman

In the late 1960s on Chicago's West Side, an African American gang called the Vice Lords turned away from turf battles and street fights. Concerned about the example that members were setting for neighborhood youth and believing that gang infighting perpetuated larger racial and economic oppressions, the group sought to improve relations among neighborhood gangs while also participating in actions for civil and economic rights and developing black-owned businesses. It announced its transformation with a new name: Conservative Vice Lords, Inc. Social justice filmmaker DeWitt Beall's 1970 documentary *Lord Thing* chronicles this struggle for political viability in an illuminating representation of life during the decades of America's urban crisis.[1]

Lord Thing is just one of the dozens of projects undertaken by city dwellers from a variety of backgrounds in Chicago, Los Angeles, and New York during the tumultuous 1960s and 1970s discussed in the visually absorbing volume *The City Lost and Found*. The book, which complements an exhibit of the same name in 2014 and 2015 at the Art Institute of Chicago and the Princeton University Art Museum, includes 250 images (many in color), twenty-six short essays by an interdisciplinary array of scholars, and three longer essays. Together, they explore initiatives by urban artists, activists, and planners who aimed to transform, in the words of editors Katherine Bussard, Alison Fisher, and Greg Foster-Rice, "conditions of crisis into provocative and visually compelling statements about the culture, landscape, and politics of the three largest cities in the United States" (10).

The striking visual material—including photography, planning documents, popular media, community organizing publications, and stills from films (feature and documentary) and performance art—creates a fascinating collage of city life during the upending 1960s and 1970s. Collectively, it addresses three broad themes. The first, preservation, reflects the call made by many urban dwellers to prevent further social and physical disintegration of their neighborhoods. The second, demonstration, includes a range of politicized art along with photography and cinematic representations of protests and uprisings. The third, renewal, encompasses projects that proposed specific solutions to urban problems along with more sweeping reimaginations of urban life.

The City Lost and Found is hardly the first volume to highlight how residents of U.S. cities undertook creative initiatives to comment on, and remedy, the so-called urban crisis. In the 1980s and 1990s, historians such as Arnold Hirsch and Thomas Sugrue traced the roots of the crisis through local and federal policies, housing segregation, and deindustrialization and job loss.[2] And for well over a decade, the literature has explored how working-class people of color, in particular, used protest, community organizing, strikes, lawsuits, and political campaigns to attempt to remake their troubled environments. But scholars have generally overlooked the importance of art and other visual material in understanding these efforts.

The volume's greatest strength is its images. These include pictures of gritty street life of the sort often conjured up in public remembrances of this pregentrification era, such as Helen Levitt's and Martha Rosler's photos of New York in the 1960s and 1970s. The collection also depicts the period's protests and uprisings through, for example, Barton Silverman's and Fred McDarrah's stirring shots from the 1968 Democratic National Convention in Chicago. While photos of this type are familiar, several of those included were never widely seen or have long been forgotten. This arresting material is augmented by Bussard's essay arguing that the images of demonstrations and protests that filled newspapers, magazines, and television reports in the 1960s reflected "a shift in photographic, cinematic, and planning practices that privileged the close observation of streets, neighborhoods, and seminal urban events" while simultaneously shaping public understanding of the social and physical status of cities (100).

While the editors, who also curated the exhibition, emphasize photography, the volume includes significant examples of other media that artists and urban residents used to make sense of, and shape, city life. Foster-Rice highlights the work of artist Hans Haacke, who produced two mixed-media installations in 1971 that vividly illustrated how large-scale real estate developers in New York profited enormously from the urban built environment in part by not adequately maintaining their holdings. In a reflection of how unsettling this kind of critique could be to powerful interests, the Guggenheim Museum canceled a planned solo exhibit over concerns that Haacke revealed identifying information about specific owners. (One of these pieces, Shapolsky et al., *Manhattan Real Estate Holdings, a Real-Time Social System, as of May 1, 1971,* was later acquired by the Whitney Museum of American Art and featured in its recent landmark survey *America Is Hard to See* [2015].) Historian Eric Avila, meanwhile, discusses how Chicano artists such as David Botello and Judith Baca used paintings and murals to depict—and often critique—the transformative role freeway development had in the social, economic, and physical landscape of East Los Angeles.

In one of the volume's most compelling pieces, architectural historian Mariana Mogilevich looks beyond the art world to examine how city officials, community members, and civic organizations in New York in the late 1960s responded to the dual and, at first glance, paradoxical problem of a proliferation of vacant lots, on the one hand, and a lack of public open space, on the other, in many lower-income communities. Residents, alongside a number of officials in Mayor John Lindsay's administration, proposed transforming these refuse-filled lots into "vest pocket parks." Despite professed support from the city, without major commitments of funding these parks achieved only modest success. Mogilevich's contribution, alongside a few others', helps illustrate how, despite a reputation for profound change, the era was replete with initiatives that did little to disrupt social, political, and economic relations.

Ultimately, one of *The City Lost and Found*'s strongest features—its expansive focus—also results in a shortcoming: lack of cohesion. The wide range of materials—produced by individuals of diverse subjectivities, with disparate intents, in various mediums, that had significantly different receptions and outcomes—at times makes the volume read as a collage of tantalizing but somewhat disjointed examples. This scattered quality is compounded by the book's structure. Many of the essays are very short—fewer than 750 words—which often leaves room for little more than description. One result is that it is not always clear why projects were included. The three longer essays—on municipal planning and artistic responses by Foster-Rice, protest imagery by Bussard, and use of the megastructure by architects and planners by Fisher—could do more to clarify and tie threads together. While all offer astute analysis, they also might have been enhanced by more discussion of why specific materials were selected and how each item supports (or complicates) the larger arguments laid out in the editors' introduction.

The introduction, as noted, does do some important legwork in linking the materials. In addition to articulating the three broad themes, it introduces several frameworks for understanding this specific era of urban visual production. These include how—following extensive critiques of urban renewal—this was a period in which both city planning and art practices shifted away "from aerial views and sweeping panoramas . . . to in-depth studies of streets, pedestrian life, neighborhoods, and seminal urban events" as well as how photography, especially, helped to make "legible and knowable" key issues in "the politics and landscapes" of cities (10, 15). Nonetheless, readers, particularly scholars outside the fields of art history, might wish the volume addressed more explicitly what these images add to our understanding of these already richly documented decades and what individual and cumulative effects these projects had on the worlds of art, politics, and social movements and, ultimately, the built environment of our cities. In short, why did these projects and representations matter?

Overall, *The City Lost and Found* is a considerable achievement. Uncovering the vast array of materials was no doubt an extraordinary undertaking, and it is fortunate the editors could include so much of it in this publication. Readers interested in photography, urban studies, and the architecture of decay and renewal will be treated to rich imagery and shrewd, if often truncated, writing. Perhaps most of all, the collection reminds us of the importance of the visual in discussions of the social and political dynamics of metropolitan environments and in voicing aspirations for change. The authors reveal how city dwellers used a range of forums and mediums to initiate powerful statements, whose very production illustrates the resilience of cities and their residents, even at the nadir of the urban crisis.

AUTHOR BIOGRAPHY

Benjamin Holtzman is a PhD candidate in the Department of History at Brown University.

NOTES

1. *Lord Thing,* directed by DeWitt Beall (1970), 16 mm film.

2. Arnold R. Hirsch, *Making the Second Ghetto: Race and Housing in Chicago, 1940–1960* (Chicago: University of Chicago Press, 1983); Thomas J. Sugrue, *The Origins of the Urban Crisis: Race and Inequality in Postwar Detroit* (Princeton, N.J.: Princeton University Press, 1996).

D. Medina Lasansky, editor
ArchiPop: Mediating Architecture in Popular Culture

London: Bloomsbury Press, 2014.
x + 248 pages, 29 black-and-white illustrations.
ISBN: 978-147-253146-9, $34.95 PB

Review by Sara Stevens

In 1965 Reyner Banham wrote an article for J. B. Jackson's journal, *Landscape,* lamenting how the exuberant architecture of the American roadside was conspicuously missing from the Museum of Modern Art's recent show *Modern Architecture U.S.A.*[1] In typical Banham style he groaned that Americans refused to see what was flashing and neon before them when it came time to install something in a museum. For him the "emotional engineering" of mass-market roadside buildings and interiors indicated a spirit of innovation that led to some impressive forms only hinted at by exhibitions such as MoMA's. But the piece also included a prediction: just as the Beaux-Arts-oriented architecture literati of a century ago ignored the office towers of the Chicago school celebrated today for their structural and stylistic innovations, the postwar roadside motels and neon signs of Las Vegas would eventually earn similar respect.[2]

Fifty years later, this hope has not yet come to pass—at least not entirely. *ArchiPop: Mediating Architecture in Popular Culture,* a new collection of twelve essays edited by D. Medina Lasansky, shows both how far we have come and how far we still have to go. Lasansky introduces the volume by taking aim at the elitist aesthetics that still inform much architectural writing today. This target is a bit of a boogeyman, as plenty of recent research in the field crosses boundaries between high-style architecture and everyday buildings. But fortunately, the book does much more than rehearse old critiques. Rather, *ArchiPop* attempts to address the ways in which popular culture intersects with architectural production, asking how the mass mediation of architecture has given meaning to form. In doing so, the book offers more than a simple corrective to scholarship focused on the "known designer." Instead, it posits popular culture "has maintained active agency in defining and manipulating architecture"—of all sorts (4).

The flip performed by this formulation is interesting. It frees architectural scholarship from reliance on the active voice (the designer produces culture) and, perhaps perversely, convinces us of the benefits of the passive voice (culture has produced architecture). This sets up the volume to explore a variety of terrains in new ways, although it also raises many questions—often unanswered—about who is steering the ship called "popular culture." Thankfully, many of the pieces in the book offer provocative and compelling case studies on how to navigate these waters.

Certainly, scholars of vernacular architecture know that popular culture—defined by Lasansky as "everyday vernacular culture in its various forms"—is difficult to pin down (4). Ascribing agency is not as simple as it sounds. Rather, the idea deserves serious meditation on who drives popular culture, not least because scholars such as Gabrielle Esperdy, Barbara Penner, and Sarah Benson (all of whom appear in this volume) have revealed that an elite cadre of mostly white, male television producers, newspaper and magazine editors, and the like shaped offerings so strongly.[3] (In this respect the critique offered by hip-hop culture, discussed in two of the chapters, is all the more powerful.)

The book is divided into six thematic sections. The first, "Domesticating Behavior," looks at the house on Universal Studio's "Colonial Street," which served as the set for *Leave It to Beaver* (and, later, other TV shows); the material culture of shag carpet; and the "cineramic" architecture of John Lautner. The second section, "Playing," explores mass-produced dollhouses (Fisher Price and Playmobil) as a transition from bespoke toy culture into a mass consumer market promoting imaginative play, as well as a nationalist Thai theme park and its reframing of global history. "Profligate Profiles," the third grouping of essays, studies the Soprano's McMansion from the HBO series as a new kind of mob house in the suburbs, folding home renovations into the striving dream of the mob wife; another chapter examines the Playboy Club of London as media, design, and lifestyle, particularly against Banham's shifting position on the relationship between architecture and pop culture. The fourth section, "Cinematic Travels," studies the undomestic appearance of Frank Lloyd Wright's Ennis House in films and the appearance of Roman ruins, as madness inducing or monstrous, in two films from around 1960. The fifth section, "Road Space," looks at automobile interiors as containers for new technology and the contradictory editorial stance of Time Life magazines toward American roadway architecture. The final section, "Urban Critiques," studies early hip-hop as a reimagining of modernist housing towers, giving those landscapes new meanings unanticipated by those who built them.

Many of the pleasures of the book come from its exploration of particular, often obscure, histories of pop culture. Holley Wlodarczyk presents the *Leave It to Beaver* house as a cultural lodestone with an outsized effect on popular culture given its rather bland messaging. The strong link she draws out between the colonial revival and the character of June Cleaver (house as mom, mom as house) is mirrored in Merrill Schleier's reading of the Ennis House's appearance in the 1933 film *Female,* in which Wright's stark design is presented as an analog to the main character's aberration of gender norms. Modernist architecture, Schleier argues, underscores the deviance of a professionally successful female—a suspect condition in itself. (Patriarchy, in other words, appears to us through the buildings.) Chad Randl's reading of shag carpet connects to the décor of Hugh Hefner's Playboy Club as discussed by Barbara Penner and, even, Iain Borden's trek through the history of automobile interiors. The tastes of consumers, be they looking for the right dollhouse, a climb up a miniaturized version of Khmer ruins, or an iPhone dock that can drive them around (as Borden characterizes contemporary cars), can reflect new cultural meanings of the built environment and the forces that produce them.

The strongest contributions to the volume deal more directly with the production of popular culture as a window into understanding architecture. Esperdy's analysis of Time Life magazines shows their complicated and often contradictory stances on architecture and American highway landscapes. Jon Yoder's diagnosis of the antiocular bias in films and his theories about John Lautner's architecture find surprising commonality between Hollywood features and critical theory. Other chapters suggest unexpected connec-

tions and challenge common categorizations: Lawrence Chua in comparing public housing production and the birth of hip-hop and Denise Costanzo in studying Tony Soprano's house against the Palazzo Medici of Renaissance Italy, to name two.

For all its merits, many readers may find *ArchiPop* frustrating. Given the strong analyses of visual culture, it is a disappointment to have just twenty-nine illustrations, which shortchanges the richness of material evidence discussed in all of the essays. The breadth of popular culture is by its nature impossible to narrow down into one tightly coherent volume. The topics covered are broad in time frame and geography; the book's operative definition of architecture—as "landscapes, entire cities, roadways and parking lots, appliances and postcards, films, toys, and much more"—is catholic, and what connects the diverse topics, both within the articles and between them, seems hazy at times (4). More important, to frame the scholarship as antielitist retreads old territory, especially given the volume of serious scholarship on vernacular architecture produced since Banham's era. This work long ago made the point, once and for all, that meaning can be found in any physical form and that all buildings offer insights into larger questions of history and culture. Oddly, in reiterating this point, the book risks policing the old boundaries it questions. In the bracketing of the topic as "popular culture," *ArchiPop* threatens to trivialize its subject. Ultimately, the collection succeeds as a reminder that flipping the grammar of who-creates-what builds a richer understanding of our constructed environments by requiring us to interrogate all angles.

AUTHOR BIOGRAPHY

Sara Stevens is assistant professor of architectural and urban design history at the University of British Columbia in Vancouver and author of *Developing Expertise: Architecture and Real Estate in Metropolitan America* (forthcoming).

NOTES

1. Reyner Banham, "Unrecognized American Architecture: The Missing Motel," *Landscape* 15 (Winter 1965–66): 2, 4–6.

2. Banham, "Unrecognized American Architecture," 2, 4–6.

3. For example, see Gabrielle M. Esperdy, *Modernizing Main Street: Architecture and Consumer Culture in the New Deal,* Center Books on American Places (Chicago: University of Chicago Press, 2008); Barbara Penner, *Bathroom* (London: Reaktion Books, 2013).

Sarah Lynn Lopez
The Remittance Landscape: Spaces of Migration in Rural Mexico and Urban USA

Chicago: University of Chicago Press, 2015.

xiv + 315 pages, 64 black-and-white illustrations, 5 maps.

ISBN: 978-022-610513-0, $90 HB

ISBN: 978-022-620281-5, $30.00 PB

ISBN: 978-022-620295-2, $7.00–$30.00 EB (various formats)

Review by Helen Gyger

Sarah Lynn Lopez's *The Remittance Landscape: Spaces of Migration in Rural Mexico and Urban USA* makes a valuable contribution to the small but growing body of research into new patterns of architecture and urbanism financed long distance by migrant remittances. Much of the emerging scholarship on the topic in Latin America has been focused on the individual house, such as the research presented in the exhibition *Arquitectura de remesas* (Remittance architecture) organized in Guatemala City in 2010 by a team of anthropologists, architects, and photographers working across three countries in Central America;[1] the related exhibition held in Mexico City the following year;[2] and Christien Klaufus's work on provincial cities in Ecuador, Guatemala, and Peru.[3]

Many of these writers are concerned with

identifying the emerging forms and aesthetics of this architecture, which—with its imposing scale and assertive façades featuring an eclectic assemblage of decorative features, bold colors, and finishes—is seen as disruptive in multiple senses. According to its critics, its *estética de la sobrecarga* (overcharged or overloaded aesthetic) is needlessly disruptive of traditional vernacular building practices and is insensitive to its semirural environment.[4] For others it is deliberately disruptive of regimes of taste established by elites and, by extension, disruptive of the cultural authority of those elites, just as it disrupts prevailing economic and social relations. In this reading, hypercharged housing commissioned by rural residents forced into international migration as a marginalized, legally invisible, and nomadic work force marks a "challenge to a history of exclusion" and "a legitimate ostentation" that resists conventional categories of aesthetic analysis.[5] Finally, according to Klaufus, it can be disruptive of the architectural profession itself: while established architects remain disdainful of the nouveau riche overtones of remittance housing, Klaufus recounts the experience of a young architect accepting remittance commissions from her former domestic as well as from a construction worker she had met on a building site—clients who would never have been in a position to hire an architect before migrating. For this architect, herself from a modest background, these projects provided a means of developing an architectural practice that was less dependent on the "good social connections" required to win prestigious commissions or academic positions.[6] (Indeed, as Lopez notes, architects and engineers are increasingly employed on these projects, as migrants experience the limitations of entrusting the construction of their "dream homes" to lay builders who cannot be adequately supervised from a distance [55].)

Lopez's approach is to widen the focus in two directions. On the one hand, she moves from the individual house to the efforts of groups of migrants to organize public—or better said, semipublic—projects in their hometowns, focusing on the example of rural Jalisco, where she did her fieldwork. On the other hand, she examines projects undertaken by Mexican migrants in their current places of residence in the United States in order to suggest the contours of a transnational remittance landscape. While the book's subtitle (*Spaces of Migration in Rural Mexico and Urban USA*) gives equal weight to these two realms—perhaps at the behest of the publisher's marketing department rather than the author—in practice the three central chapters presenting case studies of communal projects in Mexico form the book's most compelling contribution, while the lone, final chapter on the U.S. context feels far less convincing.

The book opens with two chapters that effectively set the scene for readers new to the topic. Chapter 1 introduces the remittance house in both its social and architectural dimensions, including a detailed history of construction practices, tracing a line from the traditional rural house to the rapidly evolving forms of contemporary remittance residences. Particularly illuminating are the experiences of several members of one family who have, with varying degrees of success, built six remittance-funded houses over twenty years in their small town.

Chapter 2 discusses the recent efforts of the Mexican government to channel the immense resource of *migradólares* streaming into Mexico via a program that aims to foster migrant investment in communal development projects with the promise of matching funds from three levels of government (federal, state, and municipal or county). Called Tres por uno (Three for one or, alternatively, 3x1), this program posits an outsourced model of "remittance development" that mobilizes informal capital flows into productive investments. Supposedly compensating for long-standing government neglect of rural areas, 3x1 is promoted as a more democratic, grassroots mode of development, since representatives of migrant groups have input into deciding where funds are spent.

As Lopez's case studies in chapters 3, 4, and 5 make clear, however, the ambitions for hometown improvements proposed by migrants—distant in space and often in time from their places of origin—frequently do not align with the desires and needs of those who have stayed behind. Migrants' proposals evoke either an indistinctly recalled past version of the community or an imagined, "modernized" future that incorporates the physical amenities and social conventions they have observed in the United States. Lopez's detailed, carefully researched case studies examine three such projects in rural Jalisco: a rodeo arena for *jaripeo* (bull-riding events) in Lagunillas, population 800, seating 2,500 people and costing US$500,000; the Casa de Cultura (a community center for social events) in San Juan de Amula that effectively excludes local residents who cannot afford the entrance fees and bar prices or do not want to conform to the migrants' imposed ideals of behavior, which are patterned on life north of the border (no smoking indoors, no drinking on the balcony); and a retirement home in Los Guajes that stands vacant while conflicts between local interests leave the facility without a budget for staff or ongoing maintenance.

Once again, these are architectures that deliberately disrupt existing social patterns, this time under the banner of improvement, while also (unwittingly, but inevitably) disrupting migrants' efforts to reestablish a symbolic presence for themselves in the landscapes they have left behind. The transformations they propose can only further alienate them. Local residents resent migrants' efforts to direct these construction projects, flexing the power that comes from newfound wealth, while migrants in turn resent the locals' ingratitude at their benevolence and their failure to recognize that the money invested is hard won rather than the surplus of a luxurious life up north.

One frequent criticism of remittance houses among scholars and local elites is that their lavishness represents a wasteful and ill-advised use of resources, especially since the houses often remain vacant for substantial periods of time, waiting for their owners to return.[7] Theoretically, the 3x1 program solves this problem by directing *migradólares* toward more productive ends. As Lopez makes clear, however, 3x1 projects are not always selected with the necessary degree of critical review or managed with adequate oversight. In addition, the three-part funding model can break down at the local (county) level when officials stymie projects that bypass established patronage networks or that furnish rural hamlets with facilities more luxurious than those enjoyed by regional capitals. Lopez's research also suggests pulling informal remittances into formal capital networks can leave migrants vulnerable to the risks of investment; when budgets run over or local officials refuse to contribute their share, payments must still be made according to an imposed schedule that may not match the rhythm of migrants' ability to save. As a consequence migrants are sometimes forced to take on debt in order to salvage their dream projects. It would have been fascinating for Lopez to extend this analysis further, concluding with an in-depth assessment of the 3x1 program as development model, particularly since there are clearly parallels to be explored with contemporary debates around microfinance.

Lopez's final chapter turns to a discussion of three instances of migrant-funded spatial interventions (or spatial practices) in the Midwest: two community centers in Chicago (Casa Michoacán and Casa Jalisco); the infrastructures supporting a Mexican rodeo circuit; and a growing network of funeral homes catering to migrants wishing to organize the postmortem return of loved ones to Mexico. In contrast to the earlier case histories, these explorations feel quite cursory. Furthermore, while the concept of mapping a transnational remittance landscape in this way may seem compelling, it proves problematic in practice. First, it is not clear that these spatial practices constitute remittance landscapes as opposed to migrant landscapes;

Lopez's argument that the clubs and rodeos are often used to raise funds for remittance projects fails to convince. Second, while the desire to establish a pattern of mutual influence between Mexican and U.S. landscapes is understandable—thereby avoiding the narrative of outsized U.S. influence yet again reshaping spaces south of the border—the two settings selected are fundamentally incommensurable.

The analysis of Mexico is limited to rural sites in Jalisco which, despite inevitable class and racial differences, are essentially monocultural; these are also small population centers, where Lopez can clearly track the impacts of individual remittance-funded interventions. By contrast, Lopez's discussion of the United States ranges throughout a diverse region with a focus on Chicago—a city of multiple, overlapping racial, ethnic, and class identities, where Mexican migrants are one group among many. Lopez certainly alludes to the city's layering of identities, noting for example that funeral homes now catering to Mexicans were established by earlier migrant groups. Nonetheless, she makes the claim that these disparate interventions reach the level of creating "pervasive spaces that . . . fundamentally define urbanism in the United States" (248). This may be a useful area of study for future research, but the challenges of tracing the impacts of a "remittance urbanism" generated by any single migrant group within the densely interwoven fabric of "urban USA" should give pause. Despite these reservations, Lopez has produced a thought-provoking and compelling piece of scholarship that expertly guides readers through largely unexplored terrain.

AUTHOR BIOGRAPHY

Helen Gyger is coeditor, with Patricio del Real, of *Latin American Modern Architectures: Ambiguous Territories* (2012). She is currently a Mellon Junior Fellow in the Humanities+Urbanism+Design Initiative at the University of Pennsylvania.

NOTES

1. Ruth Piedrasanta et al, *Arquitectura de remesas* (Guatemala City: Centro cultural de España en Guatemala, 2010); "Arquitectura de remesas: Guatemala—El Salvador—Honduras," exhibition website, arquitecturadelasremesas.blogspot.com/.

2. *Arquitectura de remesas: Sueños de retorno, signos de éxito* (Mexico City: Centro cultural de España en México, 2011), www.ccemx.org/descargas/files/arquitectura_remesas_folleto_2011.pdf.

3. Christien Klaufus, "Globalization in Residential Architecture in Cuenca, Ecuador: Social and Cultural Diversification of Architects and Their Clients," *Environment and Planning D: Society and Space* 24, no. 1 (2006): 69–89; Christien Klaufus, "*Arquitectura de remesas*: 'Demonstration Effect' in Latin American Popular Architecture," *Etnofoor* 23, no. 1 (2011): 10–28.

4. Piedrasanta, *Arquitectura de remesas*, 191.

5. Manuela Camus and Santiago Bastos, "Arquitectura de migrantes, las caras contradictorias del orgullo contrahegemónico," in *Arquitectura de remesas: Sueños de retorno*, 14; Jorge Durand and Patricia Arias, "La arquitectura migrante," in *Arquitectura de remesas: Sueños de retorno*, 28.

6. Klaufus, "Globalization in Residential Architecture," 84.

7. For example, see Piedrasanta, *Arquitectura de remesas*, 200.

Joy Monice Malnar and Frank Vodvarka
New Architecture on Indigenous Lands

Minneapolis: University of Minnesota Press, 2013.

xi + 259 pages, 20 black-and-white illustrations, 175 black-and-white and color plates.

ISBN: 978-081-667744-3, $120.00 HB

ISBN: 978-081-667745-0, $39.95 PB

Review by Peter Nabokov

Some years ago my then–graduate student son tooled me around his University of Victoria campus until we ended up at one of the most gorgeous interior spaces I have ever experienced. I choose the word "experience" advisedly because the sensual *taking in* of a three-dimensional built environment is intrinsic to the creative transaction between its maker and visitor and, hence, to its artistic and cultural fulfillment. Yet that encounter remains one of the hardest reactions to convey in words. Verbiage doesn't cut it; "Architecture must be lived to be known," my stepfather drummed into me—a good excuse for lots of travel. Or as the Los Angeles architectural guru John Lautner used to insist, "Architecture is the art we live in." And hence, if one allows oneself to let the architectural experience rise (or deepen) into consciousness, one can come to feel the proper, or "right," proportions of height, width, depth, the fit of coloration and lighting and even smell, all through an inner receptive apparatus similar to that which tells our nervous system whether an orchestra's instruments are in tune or off-key.

This interior had it all: from the stepped benches filling one end of the room to the stylized uprights fully evoking the carved crest poles of older days, plus the cosmic tie between skylight and fire pit, pulsating with that gorgeous honey-colored palette, and all magnificently re-created as a huge holding basket through that woven cedar-withe walling. Its blended adaptations of Pacific Northwest traditions were not superficial; this was an eminently successful updating, on both intrinsic and extrinsic levels, of the seasonal ceremonial room of a Coast Salish Big House. I'd often been in doubt whether contemporary architects, with their emphases on design appearances over cultural substance, could ever realize the menu of modernity, technology, and tradition that their press releases so breezily claimed. But here was one successful example, and I was knocked out.

So it was with a déjà vu of that pleasure of experienced architecture that I cracked open *New Architecture on Indigenous Lands*, Joy Malnar and Frank Vodvarka's marvelously illustrated and comprehensively written survey of contemporary Native American buildings, to rediscover that very interior with a full-page color photograph and learn its

backstory. Opening in 2009 and designed by the Chipewyan architect Alfred Waugh, it was the "Ceremonial Hall" and centerpiece of the campus's First Peoples House, the spiritual heart of "a home away from home" for aboriginal students at U-Vic, "a place of culture, honour and spirit," in Waugh's words (74). Moreover, "in addition to symbolic qualities and use of materials, traditional building methods can actually drive current technologies," underscore Malnar and Vodvarka, as they introduce Waugh's detailed explanation of how the anodized aluminum louvers and mechanical damper and control system allowed fresh but unconditioned air into the rooms so that, claims Waugh, "it does not look like the technology is applied to the building but is a fully integrated element of the architecture" (75).

Such is the coverage throughout this ambitiously wide-ranging and invitingly designed book, which overflows with stunning color photos, color drawings, and project plans. It is to be savored for a great river of similar architectural narratives; it seems unfair to single out just one. Yet this example's marriage of tradition and technology illustrates but one of the work's continuous through lines that surface in all of the fifty-six architectural projects it investigates, largely selected from the Northwest Coast, Central Plain–Great Lakes, and Southwest of the United States, with Canadian projects ranging from British Columbia to Quebec. And each case study sets up its unique technological, aesthetic, cultural, and spiritual challenge, as Malnar and Vodvarka never fail from addressing—and fully explaining, with great quotes. Mostly institutional buildings found across Indian country, they include primary and secondary schools, cultural centers, administrative offices, and housing. But whether or not their design firms are Native American—and many if not most are—all are consumed by the unique focus on creating, in Malnar and Vodvarka's words, "first-class architecture that refers to, and reinforces, the values of a particular Native culture and its building traditions" (1).

To meet that challenge entails facing a multifaceted question: how does one steer around stereotypes, avoid the merely cosmetic, tap into a community's deep heritage and spiritual principles, and still emerge with a coherent, practical, and creative design that embodies the traditional while looking contemporary? Readers and viewers of this remarkable book will evaluate for themselves how this tall order is met to varying degrees. But they will always find it backed up by smart commentaries, provocative manifestos, and a seminar's worth of examples. They will discover that most of these projects could never have been realized without community consultation. They will also learn how such cooperative ventures with Native people rarely succeed as overnight wonders. They require of professional designers a patient saturation in human relationships and enough time to reach consensus and collectively make durable decisions.

Reading this *tour d'horizon* of American Indian building projects across the United States and Canada is to eavesdrop on the riskiest of adventures—the search for a rapprochement between what has emerged as currently recognized "traditional" American Indian ways of doing and making things and contemporary building materials and corporate decision-making processes and aesthetics. There is a serendipitous quality to the reader's journey through the book's ten sections and its architectural case studies. Some seem to have come word of mouth to the authors' attention; other constructions were better known throughout the Indian world but awaited wider appreciation through this volume. A final massaging apparently brought them all in equal splendor for the classes we teach, the buildings we make, and the more indigenous future of which we dream.

AUTHOR BIOGRAPHY

Peter Nabokov is professor in the Department of World Arts and Cultures at the University of California–Los Angeles. His most recent book is *How the World Moves: The Odyssey of an American Indian Family* (2015).

William Wyckoff
*How to Read the American West:
A Field Guide*

Seattle: University of Washington Press, 2014.
xvi + 422 pages; 416 color illustrations, 27 maps.
ISBN: 978-029-599351-5, $44.95 PB
Kindle, $31.69

Review by Cathleen D. Cahill

During two long road trips across the American West this summer, I found myself in good company with geographer William Wyckoff through his book *How to Read the American West: A Field Guide.* Wyckoff has a keen eye and an infectious curiosity that encourages readers to look and see not only the landscape but also the story it tells about the history of place. His book is like a chronicle of that road trip we all wish we had time to take—one where we could take our time getting to our destination, enjoying the leisure to pause, contemplate, and photograph the striking, sublime, and sometimes silly landscapes through which we more commonly find ourselves racing at seventy-five miles per hour. Wyckoff has taken both the time and the photos—hundreds of them—to beautifully illustrate this field guide.

Using the classic *Peterson Field Guide to the Birds* as his model, Wyckoff has organized his book around four main principles: (1) defining the key features of landscapes, (2) describing differences among them, (3) providing maps and explaining geological ranges, and (4) situating landscapes within their wider settings such as ecosystems, cultural connections, or economic webs. Like Peterson, he hopes the guide will be less a linear read and more an oft-returned-to reference book readers will make their own.

Wyckoff also draws on Peterson's advice to birders as applicable to landscape observers: don't be afraid to wander and use all of your senses to explore the places in which you find yourselves. And indeed, it is chock-full of questions to ask of the landscape, to encourage readers to see and teach them how to look.

For many readers of *Buildings & Landscapes,* much of the information in the book will not be new. His focus is primarily on landscapes rather than architecture, though he adeptly situates building types within their broader context. Nevertheless, Wyckoff has created a delightful package that would be especially useful in a classroom or, for that matter, as a gift to someone outside the field of cultural landscape studies but curious about it. Indeed, the volume's beauty and usefulness in everyday life make it precisely the kind of book that even today's financially strapped students might choose to keep rather than sell back at the end of the semester.

How to Read the American West is a very clear primer on the kinds of definitions and concepts we use to read cultural landscapes. In his introduction, "Navigating Western Landscapes," Wyckoff explains how to identify key features and offers a series of tips for contextualizing what one sees. Often, these tips are in the form of questions such as "ask who controls the landscape" or advice about what to focus on, including "follow the path of water" or "pay attention to the edges in the landscape" (6–9).

Following the introduction, Wyckoff has divided the book into eight broad western landscape categories: "Nature's Fundament," "Farms and Ranches," "Landscapes of Extraction," "Places of Special Cultural Identity," "Connections," "Landscapes of Federal Largess," "Cities and Suburbs," and "Playgrounds." Each section opens with a general overview of the category followed by a number of carefully described types that suggest "characteristic landscape features in the West" (4), which Wyckoff defines as the eleven westernmost states in the United States, excluding Alaska and Hawaii. There are one hundred types in all, though the book is not, as he cautions, an encyclopedic guide. Some of these types are obvious choices, such as "Rivers and Riparian Corridors," "California

Bungalows," and "Ghost Towns." Others are pleasantly surprising, such as "Cloudscapes," a section in which he emphasizes the protean and fleeting "dynamic geometry of shapes" created by the "atmosphere and terrain" of the West (62–64). Likewise, he notes the Hillside Letters or "mountain monograms" that become "visible symbols of urban and community identity" (334). Each of Wyckoff's types includes a description, often with key identifying features, maps, and examples from across the region. The book is lavishly illustrated with hundreds of Wyckoff's striking photographs from across the West, from isolated abandoned homesteads to sprawling metropolises. Along the way are many maps, a few historical photographs, and some excerpts from historical publications such as guidebooks. Although he encourages his readers to sketch or photograph as they observe, his preferred medium is clearly photography, and on the basis of its sheer good looks, the book could double as a coffee table book about the modern West.

While the text for each of the one hundred landscapes is limited to a few paragraphs each, Wyckoff displays an ability to succinctly summarize a wide range of recent scholarship in physical and cultural geography, sociology, and history of the American West. The book shares strong ties to environmental history, as is clear from Wyckoff's emphasis on connections across space; he asks where commodities come from, where they end up, and how they are transformed along the way (this guide is right at home in the University of Washington Press's excellent Weyerhaeuser Environmental Books series edited by eminent environmental historian William Cronon).

This is an ideal book for students new to the subject, thanks to Wyckoff's clear descriptions and definitions along with his regular reference to specific places as examples. Indeed, while reading the book one wonders whether he might have developed it for a college class: his gentle and useful advice on how to ask questions about what one sees and the numerous textual and visual examples all harken back to a memorable introductory course.

Also useful for students or westerners new to the art of reading the landscape is that they will see themselves and their places in this book; even my small and generally unknown hometown is mentioned twice. And Wyckoff's examples are broad, recognizing a modern and highly diverse West while remaining cognizant of the deep historical roots visible in the landscapes and the way they affect the people who inhabit them. His readings and many of his examples effortlessly recognize the global influences on the American West, especially those from Latin America and Asia, but also the long and abiding presence of indigenous people and the landscapes they have created or remade to suit their purposes. It was refreshing to see Native people acknowledged in discussions of landscapes as various as irrigation, the New Deal, and agriculture in addition to the section "Indian Country." While racial identity does not necessarily form a key category of analysis within the book, Wyckoff does show his awareness of the ways in which race and class as historical legacies and contemporary realities are revealed in and shaped by the cultural landscape. Gender as a category is less visible, though it receives periodic mention, as in the author's discussions of the nuclear family ideal of the ranch house, today's "man camps" of temporary worker housing serving the extractive economy, and the inclusion of "Sexual Commerce" as one of the "Playground" landscapes in the West. One of the strengths of the book is that Wyckoff incorporates rather than shies away from the complicated interconnections of his categories; in fact, he encourages cross-referencing, including through the inclusion of boldface numbers that indicate related landscapes within his discussions. The book also includes a strong set of suggestions for further reading at the end.

In the end, *How to Read the American West* succeeds admirably in the way it "charts a course through western terrain with fresh ideas that render landscapes more tangible and accessible, that show us a view both larger and more intimate, and that foster a way of seeing and thinking that allows us to be better stewards of the West" (21).

AUTHOR BIOGRAPHY

Cathleen D. Cahill is associate professor of history at the University of New Mexico. She is author of *Federal Fathers and Mothers* (2013).

List of Editors: *Buildings & Landscapes*

Perspectives in Vernacular Architecture 1 (1982), 2 (1986)
EDITOR: Camille Wells

Perspectives in Vernacular Architecture 3 (1989), 4 (1991)
EDITORS: Thomas Carter and Bernard L. Herman

Gender, Class, and Shelter: Perspectives in Vernacular Architecture 5 (1995)
Shaping Communities: Perspectives in Vernacular Architecture 6 (1997)
EDITORS: Elizabeth Collins Cromley and Carter L. Hudgins

Exploring Everyday Landscapes: Perspectives in Vernacular Architecture 7 (1997)
People, Power, Places: Perspectives in Vernacular Architecture 8 (2000)
EDITORS: Annmarie Adams and Sally McMurry

Constructing Image, Identity, and Place: Perspectives in Vernacular Architecture 9 (2003)
Building Environments: Perspectives in Vernacular Architecture 10 (2005)
EDITORS: Alison K. Hoagland and Kenneth A. Breisch

Perspectives in Vernacular Architecture: The Journal of the Vernacular Architecture Forum 11 (2004), 12 (2005), 13.1 (2006)
EDITORS: Jan Jennings and Pamela Simpson

Perspectives in Vernacular Architecture: The Journal of the Vernacular Architecture Forum 13.2 (2006/2007), Special 25th Anniversary Issue
EDITORS: Warren Hofstra and Camille Wells

Buildings & Landscapes: Journal of the Vernacular Architecture Forum 14 (Fall 2007), 15 (Fall 2008), 16.1 (Spring 2009), 16.2 (Fall 2009)
EDITORS: Howard Davis and Louis P. Nelson
BOOK REVIEW EDITOR: Marilyn Castro

Buildings & Landscapes: Journal of the Vernacular Architecture Forum 17.1 (Spring 2010), 17.2 (Fall 2010), 18.1 (Spring 2011), 18.2 (Fall 2011), 19.1 (Spring 2012), 19.2 (Fall 2012)
EDITORS: Marta Gutman and Louis P. Nelson
REVIEW EDITOR: Andrew K. Sandoval-Strausz

Buildings & Landscapes: Journal of the Vernacular Architecture Forum 20.1 (Spring 2013), 20.2 (Fall 2013), 21.1 (Spring 2014), 21.2 (Fall 2014), 22.1 (Spring 2015), 22.2 (Fall 2015)
EDITORS: Marta Gutman and Cynthia G. Falk
REVIEW EDITOR: Andrew K. Sandoval-Strausz

Buildings & Landscapes: Journal of the Vernacular Architecture Forum 23.1 (Spring 2016)
EDITORS: Anna Vemer Andrzejewski and Cynthia G. Falk
REVIEW EDITOR: Matthew Lasner

Join the Vernacular Architecture Forum

Please enroll me as a member of the Vernacular Architecture Forum. I understand that membership entitles me to the next two issues of the biannual journal *Buildings & Landscapes: Journal of the Vernacular Architecture Forum* and electronic receipt of the quarterly *Vernacular Architecture Newsletter (VAN)*, and that my subscription will begin with the next issue of the newsletter after the receipt of my dues. Membership also includes registration discounts for the VAF annual conference and other sponsored events as well as access to the VAF member forums.

Membership Categories

☐ Active, $60*   ☐ Multiyear Active, _______ x $60*

☐ Household, $80* (includes one copy of publications per household)

☐ Student, $30* (Name of School: ____)

☐ Institution, $90*   ☐ Contributing, $90**

☐ Patron, $165**   ☐ Lifetime, $2,000** (Payable in four $500 installments over a four-year period)

Membership Outside North America

☐ Add $5 to above categories, other than Lifetime, for postage

Enrollment Information

____
NAME(S)

____
ADDRESS

____
CITY   STATE/PROVINCE   ZIP

____
COUNTRY

____
EMAIL (IF YOU WISH TO JOIN OUR MEMBERS E-MAIL LIST)   TELEPHONE

Go to http://www.vernaculararchitectureforum.org/join for further information, mailing address, and online payment options.

*Active, Household, Institution, and Student Members: Please consider an additional gift in support of VAF programs.

$ _____________ Student and Professional Support Fund (including grants, fellowships, and awards)

$ _____________ Publications Fund (including *Buildings & Landscapes, VAN,* and special publications)

$ _____________ VAF Endowment Fund

**Contributing, Patron, and Lifetime Members: All receipts above the basic $60 active membership category will be applied toward the giving category or categories of your choice (please check one or more):

☐ Student and Professional Support Fund

☐ Publications Fund

☐ VAF Endowment Fund

UNIVERSITY OF MINNESOTA PRESS

WWW.UPRESS.UMN.EDU | 800-621-2736

Airport Urbanism
Infrastructure and Mobility in Asia
Max Hirsh

The first book on infrastructure and migration to focus on the Asian transportation boom

$25.00 paper | $87.50 cloth | 216 pages | 80 b&w photos | 20 color photos

Designing Our Way to a Better World
Thomas Fisher

How design thinking can help create a sustainable, equitable future

$29.95 paper | $105.00 cloth | 248 pages

John Vassos
Industrial Design for Modern Life
Danielle Shapiro

The first biography of a renowned industrial designer and illustrator who shaped the look of modern technology

$35.00 paper | $122.50 cloth | 296 pages | 121 b&w photos

DIY Detroit
Making Do in a City without Services
Kimberley Kinder

When public services fail, neighbors step in to keep a city alive

$24.95 paper | $87.50 cloth | 248 pages | 12 b&w photos | 2 tables | 3 maps

The Rule of Logistics
Walmart and the Architecture of Fulfillment
Jesse LeCavalier

How the world's largest retailer is redefining architecture by organizing flows of merchandise and information across space and time

$30.00 paper | $105 cloth | 264 pages | 101 b&w photos | 11 color photos

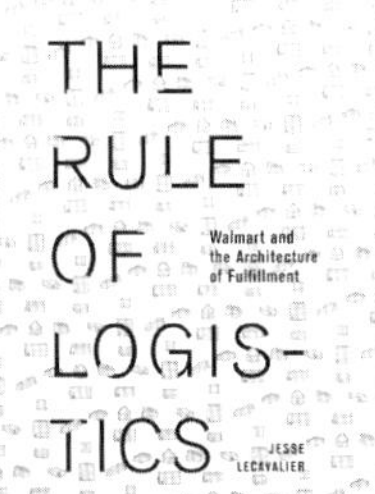